THE
BORDERS BOOK

Books edited and written by Donald Omand

The Caithness Book, Inverness 1972

The Moray Book, Edinburgh 1976

Red Deer Management, Edinburgh 1981

The Sutherland Book, Golspie 1982

The Ross & Cromarty Book, Golspie 1984

A Kaitness Kist (with J.P. Campbell), Thurso 1984

The Grampian Book, Golspie 1987

The New Caithness Book, Wick 1989

A Northern Outlook: 100 Essays on Northern Scotland, Wick 1991

The Perthshire Book (forthcoming)

Caithness: Lore & Legend (forthcoming)

Monograph

The Caithness Flagstone Industry, University of Aberdeen 1981

THE BORDERS BOOK

Edited by
Donald Omand

Birlinn

First published in Great Britain, 1995,
by Birlinn Limited,
14 High Street,
Edinburgh, EH1 1TE

The publisher acknowledges subsidy from
the Scottish Arts Council
towards the publication of this volume.

British Library Cataloguing-in-Publication Data
A Catalogue record for this book is available
from the British Library.

ISBN 1 874744 50 5 (hardback)

ISBN 1 874744 73 4 (paperback)

Printed and bound in Finland by W.S.O.Y.

CONTENTS

* Following the tragic death of Dr Ian Smith, Professor Christopher Morris kindly agreed to edit this chapter from a number of Ian Smith's papers.

Section Two

LIST OF PLATES

LIST OF FIGURES

ACKNOWLEDGEMENTS

We thank the President and Committee of the Scottish Rugby Union for permission to publish material and to the authors of histories of the Border Clubs, especially Walter Bell of Langholm and Dr John Gilbert of Melrose.

Sincere thanks to John Dent, Borders Region Planning and Development Department, for the provision of statistical material.

Plates 7 and 8 along with Figure 8 are Crown Copyright: Royal Commission on the Ancient and Historical Monuments of Scotland. They are reproduced with permission.

Figures 10, 11 and 12 first appeared in Whyte I, 1990. *Edinburgh and The Borders: Landscape Heritage*, David & Charles. They are redrawn and reproduced by kind permission of Ian Whyte.

The index was complied by Frank Dougherty.

The plate for the dustjacket was supplied by Gordon Lockie and the *Southern Reporter*.

Thanks to Donald Paterson for drawing the figures and to Mrs Janet Mowat for secretarial assistance.

D. O.

INTRODUCTION

The Borders Region, comprising the districts of Berwick, Roxburgh, Ettrick and Lauderdale and Tweeddale, was the creation of local government re-organisation in 1974. Yet 'The Borders' is a long-established entity rather than an area defined by political decision.

It is a lovely and much loved area engendering a fierce loyalty and passion amongst its people. 'A day oot o Selkirk is a day wastet' could apply to anywhere within the Borders while the boast that 'Hawick's forever independent' gives an indication of the Borderer's pride in his homeland.

No region of Scotland has so many threads so intricately woven into such a rich and satisfying tapestry. The rolling hills of the Southern Uplands drop imperceptibly into the rich arable fields and parklands of eastern Berwickshire during the 90 mile (145 km)* journey of the river Tweed to the sea. This wide variation of natural landscape provides a habitat for an astonishing number of birds and animals and is a source of delight to human native and visitor alike.

What is the best way to approach the Borders? Some would argue that it is best to study the writings of Sir Walter Scott, James Hogg (the Ettrick Shepherd) and John Buchan (Lord Tweedsmuir). All provide literary keys to unlock pathways to the essence of the Borders.

However, these writers were building on the earlier folk memories encapsulated in the Border Ballads. These were collected by a young Walter Scott who rode the lonely Border hills and valleys, noting each scrap of the declining oral traditions of the time. Even although Scott was taken to task by James Hogg's mother that they were 'naither richt prentit nor richt sett doun', his work has ensured the survival of what has been described as 'the finest oral folk-lore in the world'.

There is a rich seam of legend and history in the ballads – tales of the supernatural, of bloody encounter and of treachery. It was on the Eildon hills, the Trimontium of the Romans, that Thomas the Rhymer met the Queen of Elfland and under the same triple peak King Arthur and his knights lie asleep awaiting the bugle which will call them to the country's aid.

* Please note that there is an imperial/metric conversion table on page 15.

The ballads of *The Border Widow's Lament* and *Johnie Armstrong* tell of the folly of trusting a king's word; in truth, Borderers have never taken kindly to domination of any kind.

Walk through the streets and wynds of the old Border burghs of Lauder, Selkirk, Duns or Jedburgh and there is a sense of history all around you which generates the feeling of belonging.

The Common Riding of each burgh is a survival of the ancient practice of riding the boundaries of commonly-held lands to ensure that no neighbouring laird had usurped some of the burgh's acres. The Common Riding turnouts show that this is Scotland's horse country and the Selkirk procession of around six hundred riders is ample proof that the reiver spirit of their ancestors lives in the horsemen and horsewomen of the present day.

This is not to say the Border towns and burghs live solely on their past glories. Galashiels had an early start in tweed making thanks to the fast flowing lower Gala Water and still retains a notable tweed manufactory. Selkirk was also a tweed town but has recently switched to electronics. Hawick had a large number of stocking makers in the eighteenth century and developed into the knitwear and hosiery centre. Jedburgh was an early market/abbey town and had a thriving rayon factory during the Second World War but now has a plastic industry as its biggest employer.

The Borders has a vast number of towers, usually in ruins. The evil, brooding bulk of Hermitage reminds us that there was a bloody Three Hundred Years War between Scotland and England in the period from the Wars of Independence to the Union of the Crowns. This was the time of the reiver, the Border ruffian who survived by plundering neighbour and English alike; a rough time which produced a turbulent race of survivors.

The lesser but still impressive towers of Neidpath, Smailholm and Ferniehirst (which was demolished and rebuilt thrice between 1490 and 1540) had their own important parts to play in warfare, politics, family history and the evolution of rural settlement.

The four Border abbeys were founded in the early twelfth century. They were destroyed by English invaders on many occasions but rebuilt by the monastic masons. Even although many of the Georgian and Victorian houses in Melrose, Kelso and Jedburgh have carved abbey stones inbuilt, there are still architectural gems such as the carved tracery of Melrose Abbey. As well as providing religious needs, the monks gave a legal and education basis to the area and introduced agricultural and manufacturing innovations. Thus, in the four centuries of their existence the abbeys had a crucial role in the development of the Borders. The monks established sheep farming for the wool crop which initially was the principal Scottish export to the Low Countries but this developed into the Tweed/Woollen industry which was to become such a key element in the Borders economy.

After the Union of the Crowns and then of the Parliaments, 'big hooses' started to dominate the Borders' landscape. These great mansions were usually the homes of the lairds who had risen in importance and wealth and reflect the style and taste of the 18th and 19th centuries; many are still inhabited by their original families.

Near Kelso stands the exuberant Floors Castle looking over the old town of Roxburgh and the much fought over Roxburgh Castle. There are many other mansions which charm and appeal through structure, content or both. Manderston has its sumptuous staterooms and gardens; Mellerstain is a fine example of Georgian architecture; Bowhill is famous for its art treasures; Traquair claims to be the oldest inhabited house in Scotland and has welcomed twenty seven monarchs within its ancient walls; the much visited Abbotsford was the home of Sir Walter Scott and houses many relics associated with him.

For many people Scott's viewpoint, looking towards the Eildon Hills, encapsulates the ethos of the Borders.

Conversion: Metric/Non Metric

1 metre = 3.28 ft	1 foot = 0.30 m
1 kilometre = 0.62 miles	1 mile = 1.61 km
1 hectare = 2.47 acres	1 acre = 0.40 ha

Figure 1

Borders Map

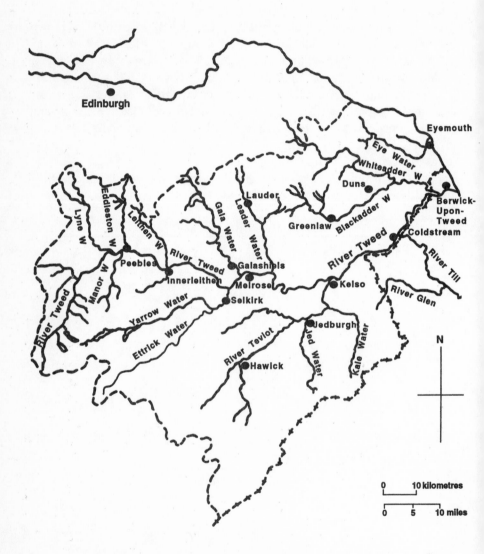

SECTION ONE

ONE
ROCKS

Geologically, the Borders Region forms part of the Southern Uplands of Scotland, a belt of high ground running north east to south west from the North Sea to the Irish Channel. The rocks are relatively old (400–450 million years) folded sediments, forming a geological unit that is distinct from the younger rocks in the central belt or Midland Valley of Scotland to the north west. Separating these two very different areas is the Southern Upland Fault, which runs from south of Dunbar to Ballantrae near Girvan in Ayrshire. The north eastern portion of the fault line is marked by the Lammermuir and Moorfoot hills which form a natural border to the Region, the other natural border being the Cheviot Hills. Figure 2 (overleaf) shows the geology of the Region as it would appear if the soils, trees and vegetation were removed and Table 1 outlines the geological history of the Region.

The oldest rocks in the region are a thick series of sediments which were laid down in the centre of a deep, wide ocean that once separated Scotland and Greenland from England and Europe. These sedimentary rocks are greywacke, a hard compact type of gritty sandstone containing tiny pieces of rock, broken crystals and sand grains cemented together by a fine greenish mud; siltstone, a very fine sand rock with closely spaced sedimentary layers; and shale, an extremely fine grained rock rich in clay minerals, which splits easily along bedding planes. Due to the folding and heating of these rocks during earth movements, the shales in some places have been converted into rough, poor quality blue grey slates. In terms of their age, these sediments formed in Ordovician and Silurian periods of Earth history which spanned the interval from about 500 million to 400 million years ago (Table 1, page 5).

By examining the structures in the rocks, we know that the greywacke, siltstone and shale rocks were repeatedly laid down in cycles by fast flowing muddy currents that swept down the slopes of the ancient ocean and spread out blankets of sediment on the sea floor. Currents of mud, water and pebbles may have been triggered off by earthquake movements. The sediments are usually coarse at the base, grading up into finer material, since the larger heavy particles were deposited first, then fine grains settled on top. Scouring of the sea floor by currents and by pebbles being dragged along or falling down frequently caused long lines or grooves

3

Figure 2
Borders Geology

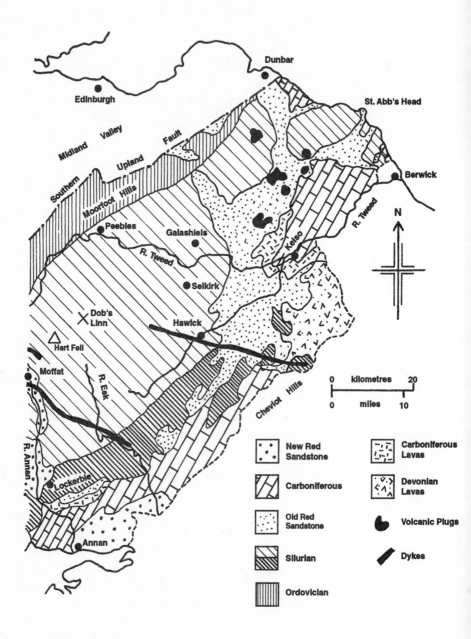

to form. These are still preserved and can be seen on many bedding planes, for example at Cowpeel Bridge and in the old roadside quarry at Innerleithen. These groove marks are often aligned NE SW, parallel to the rock trend, and indicate current flow direction. Black shales were deposited in quiet periods between the muddy currents and these shales sometimes contain graptolite fossils. Graptolites are now extinct, but were once abundant as floating colonies in the ancient ocean. When they died, their fragile remains sank into the soft, fine black mud on the still bottom and were preserved as thin, black, shiny pencil like marks which resemble little bits of hacksaw blade. Many graptolites can be found at Greiston Quarry, near Innerleithen, but the best localities are at Dob's Linn and Hartfell Scar near Moffat, just outside the western boundary of the region. These localities became famous in 1878 due to the pioneering work of Charles Lapworth, a local school teacher, and Dob's Linn is now an internationally important site for the Ordovician-Silurian boundary. Graptolites evolved rapidly, and the many different, highly distinctive species were used by geologists to work out the age, rock sequence and overall structure of the complexly folded and faulted rocks in the Southern Uplands long before laboratories were able to give exact rock ages using analyses of radioactive decay in minerals.

Table 1
Geological History of the Borders

Period	Age	Main Rock Types
Quaternary	1–2 million years	Glacial erosion and deposition.
Tertiary	2–65 million years	Erosion and formation of river system; intrusion of a few NW igneous dykes.
Triassic	248–213 million years}	Red sandstone desert deposits in
Permian	286–248 million years}	Dumfries and Galloway.
Carboniferous	360–286 million years	Sandstone, limestone, coal; lava at Kelso; intrusion of plugs and volcanic necks, eg Eildon Hills.
Devonian	408–360 million years	Old Red Sandstone conglomerate and sandstone river deposits; lava at St Abb's Head, Cheviot Hills.
Silurian	438–408 million years	Greywackes, shales, mudstones; closure of Iapetus Ocean, folding, faulting, thrusting, uplift, formation of Caledonian mountain Belt, Southern Upland Fault.
Ordovician	505–438 million years	Greywackes etc in Iapetus Ocean.

Further evidence for the existence of an ocean (named 'Iapetus' by geologists) in the area of the present Southern Uplands is to be found at Romanno Bridge, Lamancha, in the form of pillow lavas that were erupted from an underwater volcano onto the sea floor. Associated with the lavas is a hard, red, iron rich silica rock known as chert (rather like flint), together with black shales and very coarse greywacke or 'haggis rock'. The lavas and cherts probably represent the remains of the oceanic crust on which the greywackes of the Southern Uplands were deposited.

Almost everywhere in the region, the greywackes are strongly folded and steeply dipping. Some of the most spectacular examples of this complex structure can be seen on the coast, especially at Pettico Wick, St. Abb's Head (Plate 1) and at Fast Castle. Soon after the sediments were deposited, the area was subjected to tremendous upheavals in the Caledonian mountain building event that led to a collision of continents. As the two earth plates containing Scotland, Greenland and Canada in the north west and England, Scandinavia and Europe in the south east drifted towards each other, the Iapetus Ocean separating the two became narrower. Sediments on the ocean floor were then compressed and folded and eventually the ocean closed completely and new rocks formed in a fold belt that marks the welded join between the two great land masses. As the ocean slowly closed, wedges of sediment were sliced off the floor and stacked up in great piles. Continued movements caused many of the sediments to be cut into fault blocks that were rotated, steepened and pushed or thrust upwards in reverse fashion one above the other. Heating and compression led to some of the shaly rocks being altered to slates. Virtually nothing remains of this ocean, save possibly for the lavas and cherts at Romano Bridge, and a few rock slices at Ballantrae far to the south west. One of the latest features to form during this event was the Southern Upland Fault.

The Southern Uplands belong to the Caledonian mountain chain, and once the mountains had formed by 400 million years ago, they were immediately subjected to massive erosion by rivers and landslides during the Devonian Period (400–360 million years ago). Sediments formed then make up the Old Red Sandstone – river deposits of boulders, sand and gravel washed off the young bare mountains down into low lying depressions or basins in Lauderdale and north of Duns. These valleys were rapidly filled with conglomerate (coarse pebbly rock) at the base, followed upwards by finer red sandstone. Volcanoes were active at the same time, producing the lavas seen at St. Abb's Head and in the Cheviot Hills. The Cheviot itself is a granite intrusion that forced its way into the base of the lavas and caused the land surface to be domed upwards. Tilting of the land and further erosion led to more deposition of sandstones in the Upper

Devonian by rivers that flowed across a semi-arid landscape.

The best place in the region, if not in Britain, where the Old Red Sandstone can be seen piled up on top of the older, folded, vertical greywackes is at Siccar Point near Cockburnspath on the Berwickshire coast (Plate 2). This locality was made famous in the annals of geology world wide by the Edinburgh naturalist James Hutton who visited the site by boat in 1788 and described the relationship as an unconformity caused by the tilting of the older rocks by earth movements before the later rocks – the scree deposits of the Old Red Sandstone – were laid down in flat sheets directly on top of the eroded base of Silurian greywacke. Hutton concluded from his observations here and at Jedburgh and Arran that the earth was "immeasurably old" and that natural processes in the past acted very slowly in ways that are similar to modern processes, thus disproving the catastrophe theory in vogue at the time, that sought to explain natural phenomena in terms of the biblical flood.

There was a gradual transition into the next great geological period, the Carboniferous (360–286 million years ago) when red desert sandstones eventually gave way to tropical swamps, river deltas and coastal lagoons that were frequently flooded by the sea, producing marine limestone bands. In the south of the Borders Region the start of the Carboniferous Period was marked by volcanic activity. Volcanic vents forced their way up through the older folded rocks and their eroded remnants can now be seen in the Eildon Hills (Plate 3), Peniel Heugh Hill, Black Hill, Redpath Hill, Smailholm (Plate 4), Dirrington Laws, Dunion Hill, Rubers Law and Minto Hills. All these volcanic plugs can be seen from the Wellington Monument on Peniel Heugh Hill (Plate 5), as can the older volcanic hills of the Cheviots. Most of the Carboniferous volcanic vents are made of black to dark bluish grey dolerite ('whinstone') and sometimes agglomerate – fragments of rock caught up with lava during eruptions and filling the pipes that brought lava to the surface. One such vent can be seen in Chiefswood Quarries at Melrose. The Eildon Hills (Plate 3) were formed when sheets of greyish trachyte and pink felsite lavas forced their way into the Old Red Sandstone beds and caused slight upward bulges to form, rather like mushrooms. Trachyte and felsite in North, Mid and Wester Eildon are rich in pink and white feldspar and quartz minerals. Little Hill formed slightly later in the Carboniferous, a small black basaltic plug which now stands proudly above Bowdenmoor Reservoir. These rocks are similar to those of the Bass Rock and Traprain Law, Haddington. Around Kelso is a horseshoe-shaped outcrop of stepped hills known as the Kelso Traps. These are Carboniferous basalt lavas that were erupted onto the surface as lava flows from any of the volcanic plugs mentioned above. The step-like feature of the local landscape is a result of the lava being more resistant to erosion than the surrounding shaly sediments along the river bank at Kelso.

Carboniferous sediments underlie the Merse, a low-lying valley of fertile agricultural land between Berwick and Duns. The Merse formed as a slowly subsiding basin connected to the much more extensive Northumbrian basin. An important characteristic of Carboniferous rocks is that they were deposited in cycles which were repeated many times over, due to rising and falling sea levels. At the time, Scotland lay in the tropics and bands of cementstone and salt beds which show sun cracks and rain pits indicate periodic drying up of shallow lagoons. Fossils are few because of the highly saline conditions. When the sea flooded the dried-up lagoons, limestone beds made of shelly marine animals such as corals formed. Other fossils include fish and brachiopods. Then, during periods when the sea retreated, coastal swamps became established with dense tropical forest which later produced root-beds and coal seams once the vegetation was buried and compressed under the weight of overlying sediments. Earth movements caused the Carboniferous rocks to be folded, sometimes into spectacular shapes that are well seen on the coast around Burnmouth and Berwick, or into more gentle structures such as the downfold or syncline around Kelso.

From the end of the Carboniferous Period until the last Ice Age of one to two million years ago, the Borders region has no geological record of rock-forming events, apart from a few large North West trending vertical igneous dykes (walls of basaltic lava) belonging to the Tertiary Period and originating from the volcanic centres of the Inner Hebrides – Mull, Skye, Ardnamurchan, Rum and Arran which were active 55 million years ago. A vast amount of erosion took place during the Tertiary, and the river system of the region became established then. To the west of the region there are deposits of bright red desert sandstones around Moffat, Annan, Dumfries and Thornhill – the 'New Red Sandstone' of Permian and Triassic age (286–213 million years ago).

During the Ice Age, Scotland was completely covered by ice-caps on many occasions, and the last of these finally melted about 15,000 years ago in the Borders. One of the main centres of glaciation in the Southern Uplands was at Moffat. Generally, the ice flowed in a north easterly direction away from the high ground in the centre of the Southern Uplands towards the North Sea and interfered with southerly moving ice coming out of the Midland Valley. The weight of moving ice helped to sculpt the landscape into various features; these form the subject of the next chapter. Melt waters from the retreating glaciers transported and deposited vast quantities of sediment in the lower ground, particularly in the Merse, and again produced characteristic land forms.

PHYSICAL RESOURCES

The main economically useful geological material in the Borders is stone for construction purposes. Mineral deposits are very rare and small in scale. Previously worked localities include iron ore (hematite) in red shales and cherts (silica-rock) associated with pillow lavas as Lamancha, which was mined in the mid-1880s; a band of manganese ore is also present above the iron rich beds. Copper and barytes were once mined in the Priestlaw granite just on the northern border, and there are old trial mines near Lauder and Abbey St. Bathans. Lead and zinc were previously worked near Traquair, and sedimentary or alluvial ('placer') gold was obtained in the 16th century from Glengaber Burn near St. Mary's Loch. All these metal ore deposits occur in veins within the greywacke rocks, except for the Priestlaw granite. But the largest concentrations of ores lie just beyond the western boundary of the Region, around Moffat, Leadhills and Wanlockhead, where the greywackes have vein deposits of lead, zinc, copper, silver, gold, antimony and arsenic.

Fuel resources are also scarce, although wood and peat were cut extensively in the past. Coal occurs only in the Carboniferous rocks, and in the Borders there are old coal mines at Burnmouth. More extensive deposits occur to the west, in the Sanquhar basin, and coal was formerly worked in Liddesdale for local use as a fuel. No oil or gas exists in the Southern Uplands, since the Ordovician and Silurian rocks are too old.

All the main rock types in the Borders – greywacke, slate and sandstone with minor amounts of limestone, cementstone, basalt and granite – have been exploited extensively for use as building materials and road stones. The greywackes are rough and compact rocks that lack good bedding plane partings and they are rather difficult to shape for building stones ('freestone'). That has not prevented their use in the past, though, for construction, but they are mainly employed for dry stone dykes. Old Red Sandstone is more readily quarried and shaped and has been used for centuries in buildings, notably the Border Abbeys (Plates 10–13) and Thirlestane Castle (Plate 21) although even here you will find rough greywacke and whinstone blocks forming rubbly cores that were then faced with red sandstone. Dryburgh Abbey is located in the vicinity of Devonian (Old Red Sandstone) and Carboniferous sandstone, while Melrose Abbey is situated on top of Silurian greywacke but is close to the Old Red Sandstone outcrops around the Eildon Hills volcanic rocks. Ploughlands Quarry provided most of the facing stone for these Abbeys, but it is now almost totally overgrown. Chiefswood volcanic vent supplied much of the earlier building stone for Melrose Abbey. It lies close to the Melrose bypass, but it too is infilled and overgrown.

Yellow and creamy white Carboniferous sandstone has also been much used, especially at Kelso, Swinton and Langholm. At Kelso the dolomitic Carham Stone (with a calcium magnesium limey cement) was used both for buildings and was once burnt as a source of agricultural lime. Greywacke is still much in use for road stone and concrete aggregate, although it is not always ideal in terms of its strength and the presence of harmful impurities in the volcanic fragments within the rock. Near Innerleithen the slates were once quarried for roofing materials, but they are poor in quality as they tend to split into sheets that are too thick, heavy and irregular. Sand and gravel deposits are abundant in the Region, being the products of an extensive river system that washed out sediment from the melting glaciers. Often the sand is clean and well sorted and hence there are many old extraction pits, especially around Peebles.

Water is another obviously important natural resource, and the Southern Uplands provide ample supplies of high quality surface water. Reservoirs in the Upper Tweed valley are important constituents of Edinburgh's water supply system. Interesting underground waters include sulphur and iron rich minerals waters, such as St. Ronan's Well at Innerleithen.

Two

LANDSCAPES

The overall landscape of the Borders Region is made up of land forms such as the rounded, rolling hills and ridges of the Southern Uplands, lochs and reservoirs, rivers, streams and waterfalls, coastal cliffs, beaches and sand dunes. All landscapes – the physical features we see out of doors – are made up from different combinations of land forms. This chapter considers the shape of land forms in the Borders, and how they have evolved over time to create the present day scenery. Processes which have shaped the land are ice, wind, running water, the sea and more recently human activity. These processes, or series of events have acted on the various rock types described in the previous chapter.

Rocks are broken down by weathering and erosion, then removed by rivers, glaciers, the sea and the wind, and by gravity. Materials which are transported can be of any size, from large boulders of rock down to fine sand and mud, or tiny particles dissolved in water. Eventually, these fragments and particles settle out by a process called deposition. Rivers deposit sand, silt and mud in the sea, rocks once trapped in glaciers were dumped when the ice sheets melted, scree piles up at the foot of mountain sides, the sea breaks up cliffs; then this broken material is carried away by currents to be deposited as sediment elsewhere.

The land forms of the Borders can be classified as a dissected plateau in the west, followed by moderate to low rolling hills, basins in the east (mainly the Merse) and finally high, rugged coastal cliffs of tough greywacke and volcanic rocks giving way to a flat featureless coastline where soft Carboniferous sedimentary rocks reach the sea south of Eyemouth. Figure 3 (overleaf) is a sketch map of the major physical features of the Region. Note that the boundaries are to a great extent controlled by the hill ridges that form water divides: the rivers in the Borders largely flow to the east and north east as they run off the Moffat and Tweedsmuir hills, the Pentlands, Moorfoots and Lammermuirs, and the Cheviot Hills. Another distinguishing feature between the Borders and western Scotland is the predominance of undulating hills and broad basins in the east, contrasting with many more deeply incised and closely spaced, relatively short river valleys on the west coast. One explanation is that much of Scotland's present landscape in fact derives from weathering in Tertiary times (55–2 million years ago), when the country was located much farther south and experienced wet, warm, sub-tropical climatic conditions. The land surface was tilted to the east in response to the intrusion of volcanic centres in the Inner Hebrides and the surface was deeply eroded and planed off. Scotland's river system then became established and the line of the major north-south water divide (Figure 4) dates from that time. This same divide was utilised by the great ice sheet that formed some two million years ago, so that valley glaciers flowed towards the Minch on the west and towards the North Sea on the east. Our present rivers now occupy more or less the same valleys with large, widely spaced rivers like the Tweed on the east and smaller rivers on the west.

Figure 3
Major Physical Features of the Borders Region

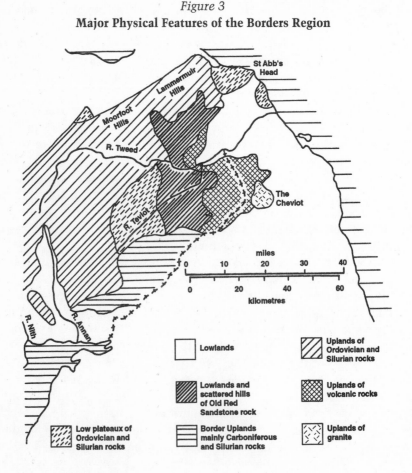

Land form types related to geology in the Southern Uplands.
Adapted from Sissons (1976).

During the warm humid conditions that existed during Tertiary times, the rocks were affected predominantly by deep chemical weathering. Landscape development then would have been more rapid than during the Quaternary Ice Age. Physical shattering of the rocks must have predominated in the intensely cold glacial episodes when continental ice sheets were developing. Glacial erosion is very effective at removing large quantities of hard rock and the deep mantle of chemically weathered material dating from old periods.

Figure 4
River Systems of the Borders Region

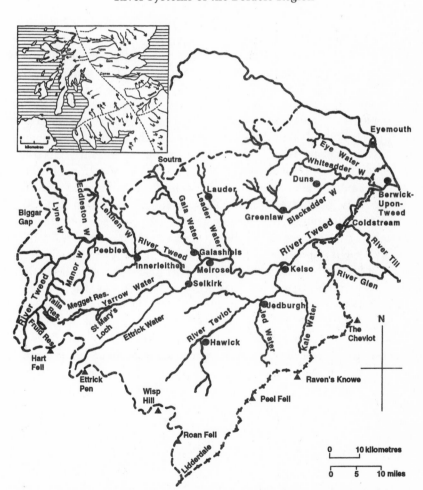

River system of the Borders Region and hill summits marking regional boundary.
Inset: Initial drainage and main water divides of southern Scotland.
Adapted from Sissons (1976).

A notable feature of the Borders landscape is the existence of plateau surfaces and hill summits at fairly constant levels and at several different altitudes, mainly 400 m and 650 m. This is well seen for example around Carrifran Glen. Such surfaces are believed to result from prolonged denudation, so that the landscape was reduced to peneplains of low relief with gentle rounded hills and rather wide valley floors. Thus, the landscape can generally be considered to have formed by 55–2 million years ago and was modified by glaciation which started 2 million years ago. Fragments of an older landscape may exist in the form of Lauderdale, where Old Red Sandstone sediments rest on a harder bedrock of Silurian greywacke. Erosion has removed most of the soft rocks and an ancient buried valley has now been 'exhumed' or uncovered, and once again is a valley at the surface.

Glaciation affected Scotland several times in the last two million years. Evidence for the earliest glacial episodes was destroyed by later events, and in the Borders the landscape we now see results from low modification of the Tertiary landscape by ice sheets and mountain glaciers. The maximum build up of the last ice sheet was 18,000 years ago, when the whole country was buried under a 2000 m thick sheet. As far as the Borders are concerned, the thickest local ice dome was located on the Moffat and Tweedsmuir hills. The ice moved generally eastwards, eroding large amounts of bedrock. Since the eastern side of the country has relatively fewer valleys, there are fewer corries (which were cut by small independent mountain glaciers) and most of the erosion in the Borders resulted from ice sheet glaciation. Although relatively few in number, corries do of course exist in the Tweedsmuir Hills, together with other steep, glacially eroded slopes. The climate on the east was probably colder and drier, so that large areas of the ice sheets in the Borders may have been frozen to the bedrock, thus preventing the widespread, deep scouring effects that are so spectacularly seen in north west Scotland. Hence the landscape in upland regions of the Borders is mainly one of high rolling hills with deeply dissected river valleys.

An important feature of the moving ice was extensive streamlining of bare rock surfaces and of glacial 'drift' (the name given to deposits from the melting ice). On the plateau between the Ettrick, Yarrow and Teviot valleys there are linear rock ridges on well scoured, ice-scratched Silurian greywacke, creating a pronounced south west to north east grain, parallel to the strike of the Silurian rocks. Valleys which lie across the direction of ice movement have drift covering the NE-facing slopes, while the SW-facing slopes are frequently bare, with rock exposures at the surface. Near Melrose and St. Boswells there are crag and tail features on the hard, resistant Carboniferous volcanic rocks, the crag having been plucked by passing ice and the tail formed by deposition on the leeward side, usually the north east. Hills such as Peniel Heugh and Smailholm show this rather well (Plate 4). In the central Tweed Valley, and eastward from Kelso on the lower ground which is covered by extensive sheets of thick drift, the glacial deposits themselves have been shaped and streamlined by the ice to form clusters of rounded elongate hills known as drumlins, with their long axes pointing north east, then more nearly east as the coast is approached (Figure 5).

Figure 5
Glacial Deposits and Glacial Landforms of Southern Scotland

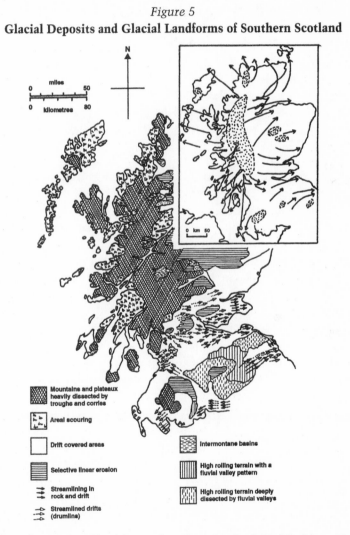

Glacial deposits and glacial land forms of southern Scotland. *Modified from Haynes in Clapperton (1983).*
Inset: Main ice domes in Scotland and principal directions of ice sheet movement; all map area was totally covered by ice. *Modified from Sissons (1976).*

A very large drumlin field occurs in the Merse, where some of the hills merge with each other to form a rolling terrain. In general, the glacial drift tends to be thickest in the valleys and to thin out against higher ground, which is more evidence in favour of the argument that the topography prior to the Ice Age was very similar to the present form of the ground.

Some impression of the erosive power of the moving ice can be gauged from such features as rock basins or hollows scoured out of solid rock and then over deepened. St. Mary's Loch occupies just such a rock basin and neighbouring Loch of the Lowes which was once connected to St. Mary's Loch but is now separated by a small delta at Tibbie Shiel's Inn. The Talla reservoir is situated in a rock basin on the floor of a short, deep glacial trough which leads to the Tweed. This basin was once occupied by a loch. The Megget Water flows in a more open rock trough in the opposite direction to St. Mary's Loch. Just outside the Region is another spectacular and famous example of glacial erosion – the Grey Mare's Tail which is a waterfall in a stream emerging from the corrie occupied by Loch Skene and cascading from a hanging valley into the main Moffat Water valley 100 m below. Hanging valleys are tributaries joining a main valley but at discordant heights due to the strong downward erosion by the ice which in the Southern Uplands was thickest in the Moffat and Tweedsmuir hills. The Moffat Water itself follows a shatter belt where rocks were faulted, and the straight deep U-shaped valley is a trench deepened by the ice.

Glacial breaches in the Southern Uplands – where ice broke through to create new escape routes – include the gap between the Talla reservoir and the Megget valley in the heart of the Tweedsmuir Hills. To the north west is another breach, the Biggar Gap (Figure 4). Separated from the Tweedsmuir Hills by the Tweed are the Culter Hills, forming the water divide between the Clyde and the Tweed. The northern boundary to the Culter Hills is formed by the Biggar Water and the Biggar Gap. This glacial breach and the water divide that it marks is another physical feature that forms part of the Regional boundary. The Biggar Gap is a deep, flat hollow, some 11 km long, linking the Clyde and Tweed Valleys. In periods of exceptional flood, water from the Clyde can find its way to the Tweed due to the fact that the Bigger Gap is so flat and just about at the level of the Clyde. It is a glacial breach probably formed by ice moving eastwards in the Southern Uplands, which was unable to spread freely into central Scotland since the Midland Valley was occupied by ice that had moved down from the Highlands.

A sudden warming of the climate occurred just over 10,000 years ago and in a relatively short period (a few hundred years) the ice had melted completely. During the Ice Age, sea level fell by about 100 m due to water being locked up as continental ice. Now all this water was being poured back out as glacial melt water streams, which were transporting huge quantities of boulders, pebbles, sand and gravel. These sand and gravel deposits are common in all the main rivers of the Region, particularly the Tweed. The sand and gravel ridge known as the Kaims at Bedshiel near Greenlaw, south of the Dirrington Law hills, is a well defined depositional feature formed by glacial streams at the edge of the ice sheet where the ice margin temporarily halted during the retreat phase. This feature is known as a kame-moraine. Irregular mounds of sediment were frequently laid down around detached blocks of ice which then melted, leaving hollows or 'kettle holes' where the ice was, and mounds or 'kames' where the loose deposits were dumped. This type of land form is characteristic of the area around Eddleston, north of Peebles. At the edge of the Merse, between Duns and Greenlaw there are gravel deposits that mark the former positions of the lateral edges of the ice, and of melt water streams that flowed under the ice. Glacial sands and gravels make excellent building materials, since they are clean and well sorted. And the finer outwash from melt water streams has found a ready use in rugby pitches!

The enormous weight of the ice sheet depressed the land surface by up to 100 m during the Ice Age and once this load was removed, relatively suddenly, the land level gradually rebounded, but at the same time the melt waters caused a rapid rise in sea level, and adjustments have been taking place over the last 10,000 years. The land is still rising at around 52 mm per century at Dunbar. South of Cockburnspath the coastline is predominantly rocky and it is difficult to see any evidence for sea level changes, although marine terraces at Eyemouth may have been formed by the action of the sea immediately after the end of the Ice Age. North of Cockburnspath, all the way to Dunbar and North Berwick in East Lothian, there are remnants of rock platforms and raised beaches lying at 18 m and 25 m above present sea level. There is also a marine abrasion platform several hundred metres wide between present high and low water marks. Its width suggests that it may have formed by marine erosion in post glacial times. Sandy beaches, dunes and cliffs are the results of recent activity along the coast, and demonstrate that these physical processes are still continuing. During the last 500 years there has been a major change in the rate of river activity and periglacial activity (ie, frost action and mass wasting) on high tops, possibly due to increased grazing pressure in upland areas.

Soon after the melting of the great ice sheets 10,000 years ago, the next event to alter the bare landscape was colonisation by trees, shrubs, mosses, lichens and grasses. Conditions would have been similar to the Arctic and sub-Arctic Tundra found in northern Canada. The period around 5500–3000 BC was one of climatic optimum for tree growth throughout Europe.

Conifers were the first migrants to arrive, followed by broad leafed woodlands with birch and hazel, giving way eventually to oak and elm, and areas of scrub which gradually replaced and reduced the areas of coniferous forest. From about 3000 BC onwards, the decline of elm and the rapid spread of blanket peat, heath and grassland over previously forested areas can be connected with a climatic deterioration to cooler, wetter conditions.

Early humans may have played a part in deforestation and once the tree cover was reduced, there was infiltration of peat and ground covering plants. During wetter periods, alder would have flourished at the expense of other species such as Scots pine.

In addition to the changes made by humans in deforestation and by agricultural methods, the landscape of the Borders has been utilised and modified in several other ways. Examples include the cultivation terraces at Romanno and Knowe and the numerous small quarries throughout the Region as well as the prominent buildings constructed from these quarried rocks, which now form major landscape features themselves owing to their geographical sites – Floors Castle, Smailholm Tower, the Waterloo Monument on Peniel Heugh (Plate 5), the Border Abbeys. The Abbeys occupied a strategically important site in the landscape of the Middle Ages at a time when the Merse would still have been poorly drained. Many of the higher isolated hills, especially in the east, were important sites in antiquity for communications, signals, defence and settlement, such as the Eildon Hills (Plate 3). Transport was predominantly along the coast and up the river valleys initially, which is where most of the main settlements occur. Routes on dry land include the old cattle drove roads from Northern Scotland, such as at Kailzie Hill, south of Peebles. The drove roads went along the high ground, just below summit height, to avoid boggy valley floors. Another important use for the rivers has been their water flow to drive the mills for the woollen industry. Most of the mill towns are clustered around the mouths of the main tributaries of the Tweed. Transport routes in earlier times were dictated by the natural landscape features, but engineering developments in the Industrial Revolution allowed natural obstacles to be overcome. Thus we see some remarkable bridges, viaducts and embankments related to road and railway construction (Plate 6).

The effect of buildings on the landscape, in terms of the natural geological materials employed, has been referred to in the previous chapter. Dark greywacke is commonest in most of the Region, with some pale yellow, creamy, grey and reddish sandstone used in Lauderdale, Roxburghshire and in the Border Abbeys and Abbey towns. Locally derived clay bricks were once common as a building material on Coldingham Moor, and roofing slates were quarried for some time in Tweeddale. These natural materials blend in with the landscape and to quite an extent reflect the underlying geology.

A number of valleys have been dammed in reservoir construction to feed Edinburgh and the Border towns. This has had a double effect on the landscape in the creation of artificial lakes and the diversion and drying up of otherwise active rivers. Human activity still continues to exert an influence on the landscape, mainly in changed agricultural methods and grazing patterns and resulting erosion, the growth of towns, and reforestation of previously cleared areas.

THREE

THE BORDERS IN PREHISTORY

INTRODUCTION

The history of settlement in the Border counties extends back in excess of 8000 years. Following a brief period of glaciation in the Scottish highlands between 9000 and 8300 BC (the Loch Lomond stadial), birch forest had spread rapidly across the Southern Uplands, hazel making its appearance at around 7200 BC, and elm and oak between 6500 and 6000 BC. From the unique record of these forests provided by pollen grains preserved in peat deposits, man's presence can be detected across wide areas of the Borders by 6500 BC.

In many respects, the environmental evidence derived from peat deposits provides the storyline for prehistory, revealing far more than the pattern of natural vegetation across the landscape. A picture of dynamic change emerges, in which the shadowy hand of man can be detected against the backdrop of natural developments in the environment. Telltale plant species signifying open ground, often accompanied by the increased incidence of microscopic fragments of charcoal, reveal clearings opening up in the forest, while the appearance of cereals and weed species associated with cultivation mark the arrival of the first farmers by 4000 BC. Thereafter, the fortunes of farming communities across the Borders are charted in the balance between clearance and regeneration that can be detected, eventually culminating in a wholesale assault on the forest in the second half of the first millennium BC.

THE CHARACTER OF THE ARCHAEOLOGY

The archaeological evidence is often more sketchy, lacking both the dynamic continuity of pollen diagrams and the general overview across wide areas. By comparison, the archaeologist is confronted with only the briefest of glimpses of the past, often snatched from obscure angles: a single artefact turned up by the plough here; a burial-cist there; and the earthworks of an enclosure somewhere else. Nevertheless, archaeology is the study of the past through its *surviving* remains, and it is from these unyielding and unlikely sources of evidence that the history of Border settlement must be wrung. The emphasis must be firmly placed on the word *surviving*, for the character of the available archaeological material is not uniform throughout prehistory, but changes from period to period: from 6500 to 2500 BC, the weight of evidence falls on stone artefacts; from 2500 to 1000 BC, the emphasis shifts to funerary sites and to the discovery of bronze artefacts; after 1000 BC, funerary sites all but disappear from the record, and it is the settlement sites themselves that form the bulk of the evidence.

Three important factors emerge from this crude caricature of the surviving archaeology. Firstly, the categories of evidence that may survive from any period of the past have been conditioned by contemporary patterns of activity; thus, the way some groups of people lived in the past may have left no physical traces that can be identified today. Secondly, subsequent patterns of activity, principally cultivation, have selectively obliterated some categories of evidence and modified others. And thirdly, modern land use regimes strictly control our ability to identify and record the evidence that has managed to survive to the present day. Indeed, the pattern of land use over the last two centuries has effectively dictated the extent of the geographical distribution of every category of surviving evidence. On the one hand most of the upstanding remains have been removed from the cultivated areas, while on the other, the majority of artefacts and subterranean burial-cists only come to light where the ground has been laid bare by cultivation. Thus the distribution of evidence in the earlier periods, where it is skewed to artefacts and burials, broadly mirrors the pattern of modern cultivation, although round burial cairns, often of considerable size, are also a familiar feature across a wider area of the Border hills. Conversely, the settlements dated from after 1000 BC tend to survive on the hills, beyond the areas of intensive cultivation, although to a certain extent that pattern has been tempered by the cropmarkings (discolourations in the foliage of crops, mainly cereals, above buried pits and ditches) revealed by aerial photography in the lowlands. In effect, archaeological distribution maps tend to present the extent of the modern activities that lie behind the collection of the archaeological material, not the extent of the activities that led to the deposition of the material itself.

HUNTER-GATHERER COMMUNITIES

Despite the inherent difficulties of interpreting archaeological material, the surviving remains reveal a rich and varied history of settlement across the Borders. Whether the disturbance identified in the environmental record at 6500 BC marks the first arrival of small hunting communities is far from certain, and it is not clear how large the population would have been to make the impact recorded in the pollen diagrams. In other areas of Europe, such a late date for colonisation after the retreat of the ice sheets would be anomalous, and there is circumstantial evidence for man's presence in northern Scotland before the end of the Loch Lomond stadial.

Apart from the clearings that appear to have opened up in the natural forest at this time, the majority of the evidence for these communities is provided by scatters of flint tools and flakes. Over much of Scotland, such sites tend to be concentrated in coastal areas, presumably indicating that these people were equally adept at exploiting both the forest and the sea for food, but in the Borders they are found well inland, and no less than 100 examples have been identified along the middle reaches of the River Tweed and its tributaries. Major concentrations of material occur at nine locations.

Much of the flint that has been recovered is debris from the manufacture of various types of tools, but even waste flakes and blades are often razor-sharp and would have been suitable for immediate use; some flakes have been retouched to modify the edges for more specialised tools. These include scrapers, awls and burins, modern names derived from the assumed uses of the various types of tool. One of the most distinctive components in these assemblages are small flints fashioned from both broad and narrow blades and deliberately blunted along the edges. Known as microliths, these were probably mounted in wooden hafts and arrow shafts, and there are also leaf-shaped points which probably formed the tips of arrows.

The precise character of the scatters of these flint tools is uncertain, and trial excavations at Springwood and Kalemouth near Kelso, and at Rink Farm between Selkirk and Galashiels, have provided little information beyond the flints themselves. Typically, they occur on sloping ground near a river or burn at heights of between 50 m and 300 m OD, and it is reasonable to assume that the majority mark the positions of hunting camps. Some were perhaps only occupied briefly, but others would have been used on numerous separate occasions, and there is evidence from some coastal sites elsewhere in Scotland for seasonal occupation. There is little reason to suppose that hunting was restricted to the areas of cultivated fields from which the flints have been recovered, and there can be little doubt that these people ranged far and wide across the Borders.

The role of the forest clearance and fire recorded in the palaeo-environmental record is not fully understood in relationship to these early settlers. It is hardly credible that clearance for campsites would be detectable in pollen diagrams, and we must assume that the recorded disturbances in the tree cover reflect widespread activity on quite a large scale. It has been suggested that fire was used to drive game for the hunt, but there is also the possibility that it was to improve the browse for grazing animals. The latter is an attractive idea, which implies that the clearings recorded in the natural forest cover at about 6500 BC do not so much signal the arrival of the first settlers, as the first attempts of an existing population of hunters to manage the landscape and its resources. In this sense, they herald the arrival of the first farming communities some two millennia later, and set the framework of the landscape into which the new subsistence strategies were introduced.

THE FIRST FARMERS

Traditionally, the arrival of the first farmers is signalled in the pollen diagrams by a marked decline in the values of elm, usually at a date of about 4000 BC. At about the same date, large burial monuments were constructed in the landscape for the first time, and contemporary artefact assemblages include both pottery and polished stone tools, the latter mainly in the form of axes. The explanation of the Elm Decline was sought in the use of elm boughs for winter fodder. More recent work has tended to question this interpretation, pointing out the impact of disease on the modern elm population. Nevertheless, several pollen diagrams reveal the coincidence of an Elm Decline with an episode of clearance and cereal cultivation, and in these cases elm may well have fallen victim to selective lopping and felling by early farmers. Clearly of much greater significance is the appearance of cereal pollen, and there are now several records in Scotland of cereals occurring before the Elm Decline, although no examples of this phenomenon have been discovered in the Borders yet.

The most distinctive types of artefact belonging to this period are leaf shaped flint arrowheads and polished stone axes, and these have a widespread distribution across the Borders. Inevitably, this distribution mirrors the pattern of modern cultivation in the heart of the Tweed basin, while the thin scatter of long burial mounds is restricted almost entirely to the periphery. The most spectacular of the burial mounds is the long cairn known as the Mutiny Stones, Berwickshire, which is situated in a remote area of heather moorland at about 375 m OD in the Lammermuir Hills. A classic example of this type of monument, it measures about 80 m in length and still stands over 2 m high at the broad east end. Although nominally classified as a burial mound, excavations in 1871, and again in 1924, failed to recover any evidence of funerary activity, and it should be emphasised that such cairns probably played a variety of roles in the rituals of the communities that built them. Not all long cairns need have been built on the scale of the Mutiny Stones and the most recent example to come to light, on Broughton Knowe in Peeblesshire, only measures about 20 m in length.

At least one long mound is known to have been destroyed in the lowland parish of Eckford at the end of the eighteenth century, but there is little reason to believe that such monuments ever existed in any numbers in the areas that are under cultivation today. In any case, the combined distributions of polished stone axes across the core of the Tweed basin, and long cairns around the periphery, clearly show that the early farming communities were exploiting a variety of environments the length and breadth of the Borders. The palaeo-environmental record reveals a similar picture, suggesting that small clearances and cereal cultivation were widespread throughout the district.

Precisely where these cereals were being cultivated is unknown, but it is reasonable to anticipate that the main focus of cereal production would have concentrated on the better lowland soils, and, by and large, the first records of cereal pollen in the uplands are considerably later than those for the lowlands. Physical evidence of the contemporary settlements is more fleeting, and none can be identified with any confidence. Scatters of pits and pottery have been recovered from three locations, while typological study of stone tools has shown that some of the material recovered from flint scatters is probably of this date too. It has also been suggested that a rectangular structure recorded as a cropmark at Sprouston in Roxburghshire may be a building of this period, and it is worth noting that a nearby enclosure, also revealed by cropmarks, coincides with the main concentrations of flintwork recorded in the vicinity.

Some of the clearances recorded in the palaeo-environmental record do not appear to have been associated with cultivation, and these were almost certainly created for pasture and maintained by browsing. Thus, two strands of a mixed farming economy can be recognised in the pollen data. In the absence of any evidence of stockproof enclosures of this date anywhere in Scotland, it seems likely that areas given over to pasture would have been kept separate from the areas of cultivation, and it may be permissible to speculate that the origins of agriculture lie in semi-nomadic pastoral farming regimes at a considerably earlier date than is usually allowed in this country.

The Third Millennium BC

From about 3100 BC the intensity of agricultural activity appears to fall off and evidence for a period of forest regeneration can be detected in many of the pollen diagrams. The significance of this period of regeneration, which has also been identified in northern England and Scandinavia, is not fully understood, but its appearance over such a wide area may well indicate that climatic factors were in play. Clearings were still being created but no recurrent pattern can be detected in either the lowlands or the uplands until 2400 BC, when there is consistent evidence that farmers were moving into the uplands. The majority of these upland clearances appear to have been quite short lived, but in the lowlands this was the prelude to a period of sustained assault on the forest which was to last well on into the 2nd millennium BC.

The character of settlement at the beginning of the episode of regeneration is no less sketchy than before, although it is possible to point to at least one major enclosure in Peeblesshire that was in use at this time. This lies at Meldon Bridge to the west of Peebles, on a gravel terrace at the mouth of the Meldon valley, and was first recorded as a cropmark. Its perimeter is marked by a line of large pits, and there are also two rows of pits forming an avenue aligned on the summit of Hamildean Hill to the north- west. Excavation of several stretches of the perimeter has shown that the pits held massive upright timbers, and in some sectors there were intervening pairs of smaller posts. Whether the perimeter was originally a solid barrier, as interpreted by the excavator, or a symbolic boundary marked out by spaced timbers is not known. When it was originally discovered, the Meldon Bridge enclosure was unique, but it is now becoming clear that structures of this type were constructed throughout eastern and southern Scotland. At Blackshouse Burn in neighbouring Clydesdale, evidence of a row of spaced posts was recovered from beneath the massive stone built perimeter of another large enclosure, while in Lauderdale, cropmarks have revealed a small enclosure about 100 m across, defined by close set pits.

The balance of evidence recovered from Meldon Bridge suggests that the enclosure was probably a ritual or ceremonial centre rather than a settlement, and it should perhaps be seen alongside the rather smaller circles of spaced stones which are thinly scattered across the Border counties. The majority of these are small rings comprising no more than ten stones, but at Borrowstoun Rig, a hill on the east side of Lauderdale, there is an oval setting of about thirty small stones, measuring about 48 m by 41 m. Other ceremonial structures broadly dating from this period are the ditched enclosures known as henges, but only one certain example, ploughed-out at Overhowden in Berwickshire, has been identified in the Borders. Roughly circular, with either one or two entrances and the bank on the outside of the ditch, henges often contain a ring of large timber uprights; at a number of sites the timber rings were eventually replaced in stone.

THE ARRIVAL OF BRONZE TECHNOLOGY

Despite the difficulties of identifying many structures and monuments dating to the period of regeneration in the pollen record, the succeeding period of expansion from 2400 BC onwards is well attested. This date coincides approximately with the development of the first metal technologies, and can be seen in the appearance of several new styles of pottery interred with inhumations in burial-cists. Apart from the burials and grave-goods, the major source of information for the period until 1000 BC and indeed for several centuries thereafter, is derived from the chance discovery of bronze implements, both singly and in hoards. This is the period known as the Bronze Age, its chronology traditionally mapped out by the typological study of the various types of tool.

Unfortunately, there are very few links between the typological studies of the bronzework and the other classes of evidence surviving from this time: the first appearance of bronze metallurgy cannot in itself be recognised in the environmental record; relatively few bronze tools were ever deposited as grave-goods with burials; and, even where it is possible to identify settlements of this period, bronze tools have rarely been found at them. Nevertheless, the development of the bronzework is an important aspect of this period. At first, the bronzesmiths' repertoire was strictly limited, and it is likely that ownership of a bronze object carried considerable social significance. The bronze was cast in simple moulds cut into the surface of a flat stone, and the range of tools was restricted largely to flat axes, tanged and riveted knives and daggers, pins, and awls. By the middle of the 2nd millennium BC, clay was being used for some of the moulds, and shortly afterwards closed moulds made up of two or more pieces were to come into universal use. The smiths developed more complex shapes in their castings and a much wider range of personal ornaments and small tools was manufactured. The earlier flat axes acquired flanges along their sides and ultimately developed into the forms known as palstaves, which were to remain in use until the introduction of socketed axes at the turn of the millennium. In the palstave, the flanges and a raised stop-ridge between them form a pocket on either face of the blade to receive the split end of the wooden haft. Alongside the palstaves, socketed spearheads developed from earlier tanged spearheads, and there is also a series of short dirks and rapiers. After about 1000 BC there is a major change in the industry; the bronze was adulterated with small quantities of lead to improve its casting properties and a mass of different tools make their appearance. Swords designed for slashing, as opposed to the thrusting actions implied by the earlier rapiers, are found and there are also exotic items of sheet bronze such as bowls and shields. By this time it is likely that bronze tools had become available to craftsmen and artisans across the entire spectrum of society.

While finds made across the whole of the British Isles allow the development of the bronze industry to be traced in some detail, discoveries in the Border counties represent little more than a thin scatter of single items. Of the early bronzework there is little more than a scatter of flat axes, other surviving material only extending to a knife from Peeblesshire, another type of blade known as a halberd from Lyne Farm, also in Peeblesshire, and an armlet from Cappuck in Roxburghshire. Also of this date are the two gold neck ornaments known as lunulae which were found on Southside Farm in Peeblesshire. Later flanged axes and palstaves, and the contemporary spearheads, are also scattered across the area, and there are records of five dirks or rapiers. A similar pattern of socketed axes, dirks and spearheads dating from after 1000 BC has been recovered, together with a few swords with their characteristic leaf-shaped blades, but for the first time there are a few hoards. The largest of the hoards contained fourteen socketed axes and was found tucked into the edge of an earlier burial cairn at Kalemouth in Roxburghshire; another of seven axes has been discovered more recently on Eildon Mid Hill near Melrose. The significance of these deposits is uncertain but in some instances it appears that they are personal possessions, perhaps buried for safekeeping or as ritual offerings; one of these comes from Corsbie Moss in Berwickshire, and comprised a sword, the chape from the bottom of a sheath or scabbard, and a spearhead. More unusual finds include three bronze shields found near Yetholm in Roxburghshire, and the hoard of harness rings and miniature cart trappings from the scree at Horsehope in Peeblesshire.

THE FUNERARY RECORD

Although there is very little evidence to link the bronzework to the funerary record in the Borders, most of the burials that have been found may be safely attributed to a period of about one thousand years from 2500 to 1500 BC. The majority are inhumations, interred in slab-built cists set in a pit in the ground. More often than not, it is the coverstone that has caught the tip of the plough, thus leading to its discovery. As a result, cists tend to be recorded singly, but several well-documented cemeteries were found in the nineteenth century and it is probable that these were far more common than is usually recognised. Furthermore, other forms of burial, such as in-urned cremations, are more likely to have passed unnoticed. Other cemeteries may be indicated by the burial cairns, most of which appear to have provided the focus for a series of separate burials, often spread over a considerable period of time. One excavated recently at Harehope in Peeblesshire provided evidence of two phases of construction and at least eleven burials, both inhumations and cremations, some in cists and others in pits. While this cairn clearly acted as a marker for the cluster of burials, other cemeteries, such as the group of nine cists recently discovered on the shore of the Westwater Reservoir near West Linton in Peeblesshire, were apparently anonymous in the landscape, although there is a possibility that the positions of two of the graves were marked with stones. Some of the cairns that survive on the Border hills, such as the two on North Muir near West Linton in Peeblesshire, or the row of three on the summit of Dirrington Great Law in Berwickshire, are such imposing monuments that there can be little doubt that they were far more than simple markers; they were intended to dominate the surrounding landscape in ways that they still achieve today.

In the absence of radiocarbon dating, the burials can only be approximately dated if they are accompanied by grave-goods. In the Borders, the grave-goods are largely restricted to pottery vessels, occasionally with a few other stone artefacts. These vessels can essentially be divided into three types – Beakers, Food Vessels and various forms of Cinerary Urn, the last usually found inverted over a cremation in a pit. Of the Beakers, a distinctive type of pottery that swept across northern Europe and the British Isles in the middle of the third millennium BC, a total of twenty seven are known from the Borders, including two of the earliest form, decorated with cord impressions all over the body of the vessel. Other grave-goods associated with these burials are restricted to a handful of flint flakes and blades from three, and five barbed-and-tanged flint arrowheads and a bronze awl which accompanied a burial in Springwood Park, near Kelso in Roxburghshire. The appearance of the Beakers in British graves used to be seen as evidence of extensive immigration from Europe, but today they are usually considered as a result of some ritual or cult package, which was rapidly disseminated throughout Europe along trade routes and by cultural exchange. Other elements of the package found elsewhere include archers' wristguards and the first metal artefacts, usually of pure copper rather than bronze (90% copper, 10% tin). It has been suggested that this was the route by which knowledge of copper metallurgy and the manufacture of bronze was carried across Europe.

Other inhumations were accompanied by Food Vessels of which at least thirty have been discovered in the Border counties. Food Vessels owe their name to the perceptions of antiquarians; if, as they supposed, the Beakers were drinking cups, and the much larger and coarser vessels containing cremations were urns, then these vessels, with their open mouths and broad bevelled rims, must have been food containers. Many are highly ornate and attractive artefacts. As with the Beakers, associated grave-goods are few and far between, although in other parts of Britain flint knives and jet necklaces are familiar finds in Food Vessel graves. The most recent discoveries at the Westwater Reservoir include four burials with Food Vessels, two of which were accompanied by a flint tool and the third with a copper alloy awl. Another of the cists here contained an inhumation which had been interred with two strands of beads around its neck; one strand comprised 180 disc beads of Cannel Coal, and the other both organic and lead beads, the latter an unique discovery in the British Isles. Another

necklace of disc beads, probably with an inhumation, was found in one of
the cists beneath the Harehope cairn, while a pit which had contained
another inhumation also held a deposit of thirty two jet buttons and a belt
fastener. Oval fusiform jet beads and spacer-plates from more complex
patterns of necklace have been discovered with burials at three other
locations in the Borders.

Urns of various types are also scattered across the Borders, occurring in
both flat graves and inserted into cairns. Most of them were inverted over
cremations and those that survive tend to have been heavily damaged by
ploughing and the very act of their discovery; many others must have
crumbled to dust when they were removed from the ground. While the
Beakers and Food Vessels are broadly contemporary, it is possible that the
series of recorded urn-burials spans much of the second millennium BC. A
relatively late radiocarbon date has been returned for a cremation from a
Collared Urn found in the Harehope cairn, a burial which was also
accompanied by a small Accessory Vessel, and the pottery recovered from
an adjacent settlement of house platforms (see below) is clearly in the
same ceramic tradition. A similar case might be made for a sherd of a Food
Vessel Urn and a palstave said to have been found together at Lilliesleaf in
Roxburghshire, but the association between the two objects is by no means
certain. The three scraps of bronze from a blade or razor in a Cordoned Urn
found near Horsburgh Castle in Peeblesshire, are of little assistance for
dating.

SETTLEMENT IN THE SECOND MILLENNIUM BC

While the distribution of burials and bronzework gives a clear view of the
general extent of settlement across the Borders from the middle of the
third millennium BC to the end of the second millennium BC, the actual
settlements themselves remain elusive. Even the environmental evidence
becomes increasingly difficult to come by, although the little pollen data
available suggests that the proportions of forest to open country stabilised
after about 1800 BC, with limited clearings and a substantial amount of
surrounding woodland. Nevertheless, excavation has shown that some of
the groups of unenclosed house-platforms recorded in the Peeblesshire
hills date from at least the second half of the second millennium BC, and
others may be even earlier. These settlements comprise anything from two
to twelve individual platforms, each providing a level stance for a circular
timber house. The only excavated example in Peeblesshire lies close to the
Harehope cairn, on a low hill called Green Knowe, and comprises nine
platforms, seven of them strung out along the slope to the rear of a natural
terrace. Although most of the terrace has been cultivated relatively
recently, traces of a few field-banks and clearance heaps survive immediately

downslope of the platforms and the excavations recovered pottery interleaved with field-gathered stones immediately outside the door to one of the timber houses. There can be little doubt that this was a farming settlement, with its fields extending across the terrace below. How long the settlement was occupied, and how many of the platforms were in use at one time, is impossible to determine, but the largest platform produced evidence of three successive timber round-houses about 10 m in diameter, and the radiocarbon dates span the period from the middle of the second millennium into the early centuries of the first millennium BC.

Unfortunately such settlements have not survived throughout the Borders, and, in any case, there is no reason why the strings of platforms that are found in Peeblesshire and neighbouring Lanarkshire should ever have characterised the settlements to the south and east. Contemporary house-sites in Northumberland are often marked by stony ring-banks, and the handful of ring-banks recorded at Dryhope in Selkirkshire, together with the clusters of stone clearance heaps that turn up at the mouths of most of the side valleys along the upper reaches of the Yarrow, may well reflect this period of settlement.

The evidence for contemporary fields around the platform settlements is very limited, and there is a strong possibility that they originate as pastoral settlements, perhaps occupied by a transhuming population from lower down the Tweed. This might well explain their clustering high up in the headwaters of the Tweed and the Clyde, in locations that are better suited to high summer pastures than permanent arable farms. That sites such as Green Knowe have contemporary fields may simply indicate that an expanding population in the lowlands was pushing permanent settlement on to the summer pastures, a process reflected at a much later date by the Border farms with *shiel* placenames (see Chapter 15).

There is some circumstantial evidence to support this case, albeit drawn from an unlikely source. In the course of fieldwork, it has emerged that the crests of many hills in the Borders are scarred with shallow pits. Similar features have formed where trees have blown over in old forestry plantations, but in this case the trees appear to be of a prehistoric date, since none disfigures any fort or settlement. That trees should blow over is unremarkable in itself, but, in the normal course of events, the gaps in the forest canopy would be quickly filled by young saplings. This does not appear to have happened, and the most likely cause is concentrated and prolonged browsing by sheep and cattle. Extensive woodland continued to grow on the hills and provided the timber for forts and settlements until the end of the first millennium BC, but the crests of the ridges, which have always provided the traditional routeways, must have been turned over to grazings by the end of the second millennium BC, if not long before.

SETTLEMENT AND SOCIETY IN THE FIRST MILLENNIUM BC

The question of where this transhuming population was coming from may have been answered in part by the recent excavations on Eildon Hill North, the 39 acre fort set in the heart of the Tweed basin overlooking Melrose. Only a tiny fraction of the site has been examined, but the results point to two major periods of occupation, one in the first quarter of the first millennium BC, and the other in the Roman period. Even though the lower circuits of rampart can only be dated on very slender evidence, there can be no doubt that Eildon Hill North, which has room for as many as 500 house-platforms within its interior, was a major centre of population by the beginning of the first millennium BC. The same may be true of some of the other large forts whose interiors are dimpled with numerous house-platforms, such as Hownam Law in Roxburghshire (22 acres), and perhaps even Cademuir in Peeblesshire (5 acres).

Of the smaller forts, there are several which may be equally early in date. One of these is on Penchrise Pen in Roxburghshire, within sight of Eildon Hill North, where the defences enclosing the summit of the hill are overlain by an annexe containing traces of houses belonging to the next identifiable horizon of settlement on the Border hills. These larger timber round-houses have an annular depression or ring-ditch lying within the line of the wall and are known as ring-ditch houses. The details of their plans, together with the shallow grooves that mark the positions of timber palisades, can still be seen in the turf on the Border hills. It has been speculated that the ring-ditch was created by the stalling of cattle. Radiocarbon dates available from outside the district indicate that they were probably in use in the period 800–500 BC, during which time the manufacture of cast bronze tools was also being supplanted by the new and very different technology of forged iron.

The size and character of the settlements belonging to this period cover a much wider range than at any time before or after. The small ring-ditch houses within the annexe on Penchrise Pen have already been mentioned, and numerous other example could be cited. They are found tightly packed in the interiors of forts (Sundhope Kipp, Roxburghshire; Waddenshope, Peeblesshire) and lesser enclosures (Todshaw Hill, Roxburghshire). Looser groups of houses are found too, some of then unenclosed (fourteen on Huskie Rig, Peeblesshire) and others within the interiors of forts and earthworks (Wester Essenside, Selkirkshire). Single houses and pairs turn up in palisades and small enclosures throughout Roxburghshire (Gray Coat, Scowther Knowe) and Peeblesshire (Orchard Rig, South Hill Head), and the narrow ridged cultivation known as cord rig is often found in the vicinity, together with extensive evidence of tree-holes. Settlements of this type of building survive in sufficient numbers to demonstrate that they represent a major period of expansion out of the lowlands and on to the hills. Equally, the fact that they are still visible, unencumbered by any later settlement remains, shows that the expansion was followed by a period of abandonment. Once again, the most convincing explanation of the choice of the exposed locations where these settlements survive lies in an attempt to adapt the high summer pastures to arable farms.

By their very nature, this type of house is vulnerable to ploughing and it is difficult to identify this phase of settlement across the lowlands of the Border counties. A scatter of palisades has been revealed by cropmarkings, but it is very rare that the character of the internal houses can be discerned. The majority of the cropmarks are of ditched enclosures, some of them of considerable size with multiple ditches. These latter are undoubtedly fortifications, which, as we have seen, have been a component of the settlement pattern from the beginning of the first millennium BC. The evidence for their date is fairly scanty, and the only recurrent patterns that can be detected are that, on the one hand, the defences often supersede a palisaded perimeter, while on the other, those surviving on the hills are often overlain by clusters of unenclosed stone-walled houses or lightly-built enclosures dating from the late first millennium BC – early first millennium AD. The same basic sequence has been recovered by excavation at Broxmouth on the East Lothian plain, and hints of it can also be detected amongst the cropmark evidence.

The significance of the palisaded phase has been consistently misunderstood, largely as the result of the uncritical application of the sequence recovered by excavation from Hownam Rings in Roxburghshire across the whole spectrum of settlement evidence from the Borders (and indeed beyond). It is now known that palisading turns up throughout the first millennium BC, and probably the first millennium AD too, and is commonly found beneath the banks and walls of a wide range of settlement types. The majority of the recorded palisades form relatively small enclosures and cannot be usefully compared with those that underlie much larger forts. In a few instances, however, large palisaded enclosures have been detected, such as on Stanshiel Hill in Roxburghshire or White Hill and Hamildean Hill (the latter otherwise recorded as an unfinished fort) in Peeblesshire. These are surely the sites that are the equivalents of the forts. Indeed, at one point along the circuit of Stanshiel Hill, sheep rubbing has revealed that the palisade trench is over 1 m in depth with large packing stones. This is no palisade in the sense of a fence. It is a timber rampart set on the slope in much the same way as a stone rampart. We would anticipate that it may have stood in excess of 3 m in height, probably with a raised fighting platform behind a parapet. The same may be said of the double palisades set about 2 m apart which have been recorded at sites like Hayhope Knowe in Roxburghshire or Castle Hill, Horsburgh, in Peeblesshire. Rather than parallel fences, these are much more likely to be the foundations of timber box ramparts without any solid filling. Such ramparts are usually found by excavation at the core of an earthen or stone rampart.

With so little excavation data to fall back upon, the dating of the bulk of the forts, poses considerable problems. Those containing ring-ditch houses are probably of relatively early date, as are those where the houses are defined by one or two narrow ditches enclosing a shallow central platform. Hayhope Knowe has houses of this type and so does the 9 acre fort on the summit of the White Meldon in Peeblesshire, other examples turn up in a range of other earthworks and palisaded enclosures. In three instances, houses defined by two concentric narrow ditches appear to overlie ring-ditch houses, probably pointing to a date for these structures well after the introduction of iron technology. This would happily accord with the iron spearhead found at Hayhope Knowe (others have sought an earlier continental origin for this).

The majority of the forts, however, do not contain such distinct types of houses. The clue for their date is probably provided by the excavations at Broxmouth in East Lothian, which revealed a series of defensive systems spanning the middle of the first millennium BC, and finally falling into disrepair by about 200 BC. At Broxmouth, as at so many other forts, there is an overlying settlement of stone-walled houses. Such settlements consistently overlie the forts which only contain house-platforms or no traces of any houses at all. Presumably these were the forts which were still in use when the security of defences eventually became redundant. Thus, the defensive sequence from Broxmouth reflects a long period from the middle centuries of the first millennium until the third century BC when communal security was paramount throughout the Borders, a period when the forts were a basic unit of settlement. As such, they must reveal something of the nature of contemporary society, as do the leaf-shaped slashing swords and the spearheads from the final stages of the bronze industry at a rather earlier date. No other weapons survive from the Borders, although sword chapes have been found at Glencotho in Peeblesshire and Houndslow in Berwickshire. While the farmer must have underpinned the economy, later classical sources leave little doubt of the presence of warriors and the importance of personal ornament and display. Although there is very little surviving artefactual material to illustrate this aspect of society, the quality of the objects in circulation may be judged from the gold torc terminal from Cairnmuir in Peeblesshire, and the later bronze collar from Stichill in Roxburghshire. Some of the fort defences may also enshrine elements of display, particularly in the case of the *chevaux de frise* (belts of stones set upright against mounted attack) at Dreva and Cademuir in Peeblesshire.

THE OPENING UP OF THE LANDSCAPE

From the middle of the first millennium BC, the environmental evidence shows that clearance activity in the forest begins to increase, usually culminating in a dramatic event when entire pollen catchments are apparently felled within a space of perhaps fifteen years. The date of this devastating clearance varies from place to place, ranging from the first millennium BC into the Roman period, but it is invariably coupled with the telltale signs of agriculture. Broadly speaking, it would appear that the fort defences falling into disrepair not only signal a period of peace and security, but also a massive expansion of settlement throughout both the lowlands and the hills. Excavation of both stone-walled houses and their timber predecessors in Northumberland has provided enough circumstantial evidence from which to assert that the majority of small earthworks and enclosures found on the flanks of the Border hills arrive with this massive clearance of the landscape, and many were in use during the first two centuries AD. The excavation of an enclosure in Eskdale, Dumfriesshire, has revealed a similar pattern, as has more recent work at The Dod in Roxburghshire.

As a result of later agriculture, relatively few traces of contemporary fields have been located. Nevertheless, occasional field-systems have survived, and there are good grounds for suggesting that some of the cultivation terrace systems that have been subsumed into medieval rig-and-furrow systems, as distinct from those that appear to have formed as integral components of medieval rig-and-furrow systems, are of this date. Of the surviving field-systems, Hut Knowe East in Roxburghshire is perhaps the most impressive, with a trackway leading up to the entrance to the settlement and enclosed fields of cord rig to either side. Similar patterns of enclosures are found at Blakebillend and Tamshiel Rig in Roxburghshire, and at Dreva in Peeblesshire, and it is clear that sophisticated farming systems were in operation. The evidence that is now emerging from aerial photography in the lowlands, however, is more spectacular. Large areas of Berwickshire from Ayton across to Bunkle Edge are divided up by the lines of pits known as pit-alignments, and similar features have been recorded in Roxburghshire and on the Lothian plain; one example on the latter has been radiocarbon dated to the late first millennium BC. Apparently the lowland landscape was being carved up and enclosed by these curious boundaries, a sure sign of the intensification of agricultural production and the expansion of settlement attested by the environmental record. The hills do not appear to have been rigorously divided up in the way of the lowlands but several boundary systems have survived. Generally these comprise banks and ditches, such as on White Hill overlooking The Dod in Roxburghshire, but on Milkieston Hill in Peeblesshire the banks are flanked by lines of pits, a graphic demonstration of the true character of the pit-alignments known from the cropmarks. In many areas, however, the only boundaries are those of the landscape itself, namely the spurs and the burns. These provide the framework for the modern farms, and the pattern of earlier settlements suggests that they were equally appropriate for farms dating from the end of the first millennium BC.

ROMAN INTERVENTION

For some parts of the Borders, the peace and tranquillity that had apparently developed by the beginning of the first millennium AD was to be rudely shattered by the arrival of the Roman army in AD 79. For the first time the archaeology can be supplemented from historical sources, albeit from the perspective of classical authors, and the native peoples can be named. In so far as the political geography is understood, the *Votadini* inhabited a swathe of country in the eastern Borders, from the Lothian plain down into north Northumberland, while the hills to the west were occupied by the *Selgovae*. From the disposition of the Roman garrisons, which are almost entirely absent from the country east of Lauderdale, it is generally surmised that the *Votadini* were a peaceful tribe, whereas the lands of the warlike *Selgovae* had to be held in some strength. To what extent this is true is uncertain. The scanty artefactual evidence from settlements throughout the first millennium BC provides few clues to any differences between the two tribal areas, and, as we have seen, the broad patterns detectable in the settlement record are much the same too. Recent excavations in the Borders have also shown that the occupation of Eildon Hill North, in what is presumably Selgovan territory, matches that of the Votadinian tribal centre on Traprain Law, and the 13.5 acre fort on the Dunion to the east of Jedburgh had also developed into what was essentially a small town in the late first millennium BC.

The question that should really be asked is what was the impact of the Roman invasion on the native tribes, and what happened when they finally withdrew to the Hadrianic frontier on the Tyne Solway line. Life in the territory of the *Votadini* appears to have continued much as before until the Roman withdrawal. Thereafter, it is difficult to detect much evidence of occupation on the handful of sites that have been excavated to date. There is a strong possibility that the withdrawal had a far greater impact on the *Votadini* than the initial invasion. Evidence from Selgovan territory is even more difficult to come by, but there are subtle differences in the settlement record of Peeblesshire that may be of some significance. The stone-walled houses do not overlie the Peeblesshire forts in the same way as in Roxburghshire, and at Helm End and Rachan Hill, for example, they are neatly enclosed by the defences, possibly indicating that they remained in use or were reoccupied at this time.

Even in Votadinian territory we should perhaps expect to encounter a few forts which functioned as minor tribal centres, or perhaps the administrative cores of large estates, and maintained some form of defensive perimeter. Some kind of organisation into estates, which is surely implicit in the pitted land divisions that have emerged from the cropmarks, might then provide a suitable context for the brochs and duns (small massively constructed towers or defended houses) that were built in the Border counties at the beginning of the first millennium AD. These vary considerably in size and location, the best known being Torwoodlee in Selkirkshire and Edinshall in Berwickshire. When compared in detail, few of the lowland brochs would sit happily amongst their northern counterparts, and their exotic architecture is more convincing in terms of an ostentatious affectation of a local aristocracy than the homes of invading warriors coming in from the north. The date of the Roman artefacts recovered by excavation would certainly suggest that none of the brochs and duns survived the Roman withdrawal and it is generally argued that they fell victim to Roman assaults.

Whatever the upheaval that followed in the wake of the Roman withdrawal at the end of the Antonine period, there can be no doubt that a substantial population remained in the Borders. This population must surely have participated in the invasion of the Roman province in the AD 180s and would have belonged to the confederacy identified as the *Maeatae* in classical sources at the end of the 2nd century AD. The *Maeatae* and their neighbours, the *Caledonii*, were to cause considerable trouble, leading to the campaigns of the Emperor Severus and his sons AD 208–11. The course of the Roman intervention in the Borders is dealt with in the next chapter, but the turmoil that is recorded historically must surely provide the clue to the apparent lack of 3rd and 4th century AD occupation on the majority of the earlier settlements. Roman masonry was incorporated into a souterrain or underground passage discovered at Newstead, one of a small number of these structures in the Borders, and also in the wall of the fort that crowns the summit of Rubers Law in Roxburghshire, perhaps providing small clues to the reorganisation of the pattern of settlement that appears to have taken place at this time.

Note

The old counties have been retained throughout this chapter to conform to the inventory system of the Royal Commission on the Ancient and Historical Monuments of Scotland covering Berwickshire (1915), Roxburghshire (1956), Selkirkshire (1957) and Peeblesshire (1967). Aerial photographs and plans of many sites will be found in the National Monuments Record of Scotland, John Sinclair House, 16 Bernard Terrace, Edinburgh EH8 9NX. A synthesis of the environmental evidence by Richard Tipping will appear in the forthcoming RCAHMS volume on the archaeology of Eastern Dumfriesshire.

FOUR

THE ROMANS

With the arrival of the Roman army in Southern Scotland in the spring or
early summer of AD 79, the Borders entered recorded history.

INVASION

A watcher perched high on the southern flank of the Eildon Hills would
have seen one morning, approaching from the south, marching columns of
infantry in colourful cloaks, preceded by widely ranging swarms of cavalry,
their shields and standards glinting in the crisp air as they swept around
the Eildons, with their immediate destination the line of the Tweed. As
the afternoon grew on, infantry, with their standard-bearers at their head,
and centurions regulating their step and directing the route, and the
cavalry returning from sweeping the adjacent valleys, congregated on
gently sloping ground on the south bank of the Tweed, opposite the
junction with Leader Water. Within a couple of hours, a perimeter ditch
was dug to enclose a large squarish encampment, the soil piled to form an
internal rampart with palisade stakes on top, gateways were demarcated,
tents unfolded from the backs of mules and from wagons and arranged in
lines neat from long experience. The groups of soldiers then settled to the
preparation of an evening meal.

This picture is not wholly fanciful. It is based on accounts by Roman
historians of an army on the march. The routine of encamping resulted
from the experience of many generations. The scene is set on the rolling
ground east of Newstead village, beside the Leaderfoot viaduct, in an area
where archaeological excavation and aerial observations have identified
encampments which doubtless had their origins in the circumstances
described above.

The Roman army advanced to the Tweed and beyond in AD 79, not from
sudden whim. The invasion of the island of Britain had been undertaken in
AD 43, and successive generations had witnessed the slow expansion of the
new province, which the Romans called *Britannia* after the name of the
island itself. The advance was punctuated by reverses, most notably the
serious rebellion of Boudica in East Anglia in AD 60–61. After a bout of civil
war in AD 68–69, the new emperor Vespasian, who had himself served in
the invasion force of AD 43 as commander of one of the four legions

committed to the new province, authorised a northwards push in Britain which was maintained over more than a decade, with the aim of incorporating the entire island, or as much as was feasible, inside Roman jurisdiction. This objective was not in the end achieved, but was to carry Roman arms first to the Tyne and then to the Tay (AD 79) and then finally to the Moray Firth by AD 83.

The arrival of Roman forces in the Borders was neither unplanned nor unannounced. Advance parties had doubtless assessed the geographical realities of the ground to be traversed or fought over: the crossing of the Cheviots to the Tweed and the coastal route to the river's mouth and beyond; the line of the Tweed itself and rivers which united with it; the northwards route through Lauderdale to the Forth. At much the same time, it is very likely that a second route was being opened up via Annandale to Crawford in Upper Clydesdale, then along the south flank of the Pentlands, the two routes uniting on the Forth at the mouth of the River Esk. The Romans had long experience and a ready eye for identifying strongpoints and advantageous lines of communication.

HOW DO WE KNOW ABOUT THE ROMANS?

The sources for the study of this Roman phase in Borders history are markedly richer than those available for earlier periods. Or put rather differently, new categories of evidence are available, to be exploited alongside archaeological excavation and aerial survey.

Firstly, we can now bring into play documentary evidence, most usefully for our purpose a Latin biography of the commander of Roman forces which reached the Tweed in AD 79; Gnaeus Julius Agricola, father-in-law of its author, the distinguished historian Cornelius Tacitus. Soon after Agricola's death, Tacitus outlined his career, with valuable, though often infuriatingly vague details of his achievements in Britain, of which Agricola was governor from 77 to 83. It is Tacitus' biography which tells us who led the Roman forces, the precise date-range within which the campaigns took place, and that there were five campaigns which culminated in a victory over the massed Caledonian forces at the unidentified Mons Graupius, somewhere north of the Forth, in AD 83. Agricola's campaigns all but doubled the size of Rome's British province.

The archaeological evidence itself takes on a new sophistication: stone tablets inscribed in Latin record building work at forts; altars were dedicated to various deities, Roman and local, and tombstones recorded those whom death overtook on the far frontier. These memorials provide specific details about named individuals. Moreover, the Romans brought money to northern Britain for the first time; soldiers had their pay to spend, and traders brought cash to pay for local produce. Roman coins are closely dateable to a particular month or year; their presence on a site helps to determine its date of occupation. In addition, the soldiers carried with them a wide range of sophisticated weaponry, tools, jewellery, accessories and specialised types of pottery for the kitchen and the table; widely studied across the Roman world, such pottery often provides a very close dating for the use of the site itself.

THE ROMAN ARMY

The army which advanced northwards into the Borders in AD 79 was drawn from, and comprised the larger part, of *Britannia*'s Roman garrison. There were four legions each of 5000 men: the Second *Augusta* the Ninth *Hispana*, the Twentieth *Valeria Victrix*, all of which had served in Britain since AD 43, and the Second *Adiutrix*, a relatively recent creation, for which Britain was its first posting. Alongside the legions, whose members were all Roman citizens but by this date an amalgam of many nationalities, came non-citizen auxiliaries, infantry and cavalry, organised in regiments usually of 500 or up to 1000 men strong, drawn from less civilised elements and frontier districts of the Roman world; we can specifically identify cohorts of Batavians and Tungrians from the Low Countries, and others from Spain. Also among the auxiliaries, almost certainly, were men recruited from tribes in southern England.

The legions, the backbone of the force, were destined in due course to return to fortresses in England and Wales, though not before playing a major part in the construction of the various forts which the auxiliaries would in due course occupy, in the Borders and beyond, as the army of Britain strained to embrace a much enlarged province.

THE MAIN PHASES OF OCCUPATION

A combination of documentary and archaeological evidence identifies three quite distinct historical periods of invasion and occupation:

1. The Flavian period (called after the Flavian dynasty of emperors at Rome) began with Agricola's campaigns and lasted until about AD 100 when Roman forces withdrew to the Tyne – Solway line and were soon engaged in the construction of a permanent barrier across the island of Britain, Hadrian's Wall, in AD 122–28.

2. The Antonine period (named after the emperor Antoninus Pius) saw the reversal of Hadrian's policy. Troops were ordered back into Scotland, under the command of the Governor, Q. Lollius Urbicus. A second wall, which we call the Antonine Wall, was built between the Forth and Clyde around AD 142. A single sentence in a much later biography of the emperor Antoninus notes the Wall's construction. Scotland was occupied until around AD 165.

3. The Severan period (after the family name of the emperor Septimius Severus, his sons and successors, AD 193–235) witnessed the arrival of the emperor Severus himself in Scotland. Severus led a huge force northwards in AD 209. Roman historians record the difficulties encountered and the slow advance in horrible terrain, the backward natives and the dreadful climate. A beginning was made on the task of permanent reoccupation of North Britain but it was prematurely ended by the death of Severus himself, at York, early in AD 211.

MILITARY INSTALLATIONS

Evidence of the Roman army's activities in all three phases can be found in the Borders, which hold rich remains in the form of camps, forts and fortlets, minor installations, and roads. Many survive as upstanding field monuments, and repay a visit. Roman sites began to be identified in the Borders by antiquarians in the early 18th century, and from the mid 1930s onwards aerial reconnaissance has added enormously to our knowledge, by pinpointing from the air many sites visible as cropmarks in ripening fields, where nothing can be seen at ground level.

Camps

When a Roman army moved across the countryside, it was already thinking of its halting place for the night; regulations demanded the digging of a ditch, the piling up of a rampart, whatever the circumstances. For example, the modern visitor can follow on the ground today the ramparts and ditches of camps at Pennymuir beside the Kale Water, and at Chew Green, close to the present day Anglo-Scottish Border, where the earthworks of Roman camps stand boldy against the surrounding landscape.

A series of very large camps of 65 hectares, which could have contained a large part of the army of Roman Britain, have been identified from the air at regular intervals from the Tweed northwards through Lauderdale (Figures 6 and 7). Parts of one of these camps are visible at Channelkirk near Oxton (Plate 7). It has been suggested that the camps mark the progress of the army of Septimius Severus in AD 209–210. Other camps cannot be assigned to particular high profile campaigns – smaller examples may mark the movements of work parties, of reinforcements for a particular garrison or units on the move between postings. Other camps lying adjacent to forts may simply have housed their construction parties.

Some camps may have been used in troop training, as the army practised route marching and camp construction. However, at Woden Law hillfort (Figure 8), south of Pennymuir, lines of fortification long ago identified as belonging to Roman siegeworks are now more plausibly viewed as defences prepared by the users of the hillfort itself.

Forts

Once the campaigns were over and the 'front line' had moved forward, forts were built to secure the areas overrun. These were normally placed along lines of communication, which regularly followed river valleys, and might be set at the junction of a river and a tributary.

A glance at a map of Roman sites in the Borders will show the important routes for the occupying forces – Redesdale, Tweeddale, Teviotdale, and Lauderdale (see Figures 6 and 7). The system of control seems to demand a fairly regular pattern of control points. If so, there are many gaps in it, for example at Berwick, where a Roman road heads northwards towards the modern town, but no fort is known. It could lie undetected either south of the river's mouth at Tweedmouth, or below the town of Berwick itself.

Figure 6

Roman Sites in the Borders: Upper Tweeddale, Lauderdale and the Lothians

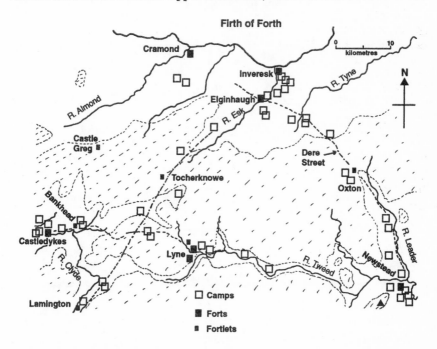

Each fort normally housed a single regiment of auxiliaries, and contained everything that a group of between five hundred and a thousand men needed for survival in a potentially hostile environment. Most of the space was taken up with barracks, stables (if cavalry were present) and granaries to house the vital food reserves; centrally placed were a headquarters building and a commandant's house. Sometimes the buildings were of stone, but most of them were of timber. These buildings lay within a rampart made of turf, clay or stone and further defended by ditches. Immediately inside the rampart, or in a fortified annexe next to the fort, was a small stone-built bath-house. In many cases the sites occupied in the wake of the first advance, the Flavian period, were rebuilt on the same or an adjacent site in the Antonine period.

Figure 7
Roman Sites in the Borders: Redesdale, Teviotdale and Tweeddale

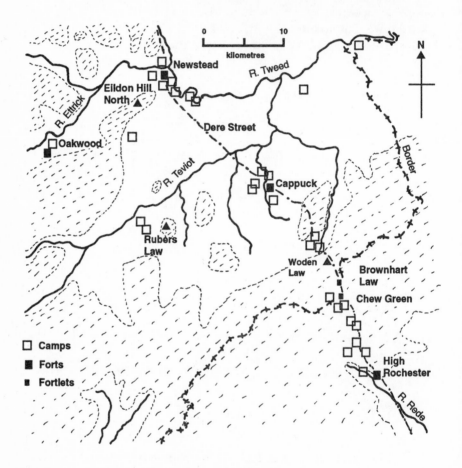

Roads

Road building went hand in hand with conquest. The builders of roads were normally the soldiers themselves. Roads were constructed over long distances, often with straight stretches as the topography allowed. They normally consisted of carefully built cambered mounds of broken stone, topped by layers of gravel, and were flanked by drainage gullies. Many stretches can be seen in the Borders today. Often they remained in use into the Middle Ages and beyond.

Dere Street, running northwards from York, first to Corbridge on the Tyne, then to Newstead on the Tweed, and finally to Inveresk on the Forth, was the most important artery of Roman control in North Britain. Along its line are many camps, testifying to the movements of troops, and forts and fortlets serving to confirm Roman control. In addition to a large fort at Newstead (for which see below) there were forts at Risingham and High Rochester (south of the Border, in Redesdale) and a fortlet at Brownhart Law, near Chew Green, a small fort at Cappuck near Oxnam, and a fortlet at Oxton near Channelkirk (Plate 7), where the large fortified annexe, much larger than the fortlet itself, must have served to shelter troops or wagons halting for the night before attempting the long climb over Soutra Hill. Dere Street itself can be followed on foot today over long stretches as a cambered grassy mound, for example north from Pennymuir (Figure 8) to Whitton Edge, or with its line preserved by farm tracks or minor roads, for example over Ulston Moor. Dere Street is the ancient equivalent of the A68 trunk road, whose course matches it closely.

An east-west artery followed the line of the Tweed westwards from Newstead, via forts at Lyne near Peebles, Castledykes near Lanark and Loudoun Hill near Galston, to reach the Firth of Clyde near Irvine. Several camps have also been identified on this route. An eastwards extension from Newstead to the mouth of the Tweed at Berwick can be assumed, though no trace has yet been found; the general line, on the river's south bank, can be inferred from camps at Dryburgh, St. Boswells and Maxton, and others farther east at Carham near Coldstream, Wooden near Kelso and Learmouth near Cornhill-on-Tweed.

Other routes linked the Tweed Valley to the south-west, first via the Ettrick Water past a fort at Oakwood near Ettrickbridge, then via the Moffat Water to the Annan Valley at Milton near Beattock. A second road followed the Teviot and the Borthwick Water, across Craik Cross Hill to the Esk at Raeburnfoot. Its cambered mound can be followed over many miles.

The route along the southern flank of the Pentlands, running north-east towards the Forth, has yielded recent discoveries; camps at Kirkhouse near Dolphinton, at Kaimhouse near West Linton, with a fortlet nearby at Tocherknowe. Many other roads doubtless remain to be discovered either by ground observation or aerial reconnaissance. Sometimes the course of a road which itself has been totally removed or ploughed away can be detected from the air by the presence of quarry pits flanking its route, from which material was dug to permit resurfacing.

Bridges were built to carry the roads across major rivers. Usually they were of timber, on stone piers. Dere Street crossed the Tweed on a bridge just west of Newstead fort.

Figure 8

Earthworks at Pennymuir (Camps A–D) and at Woden Law hillfort.

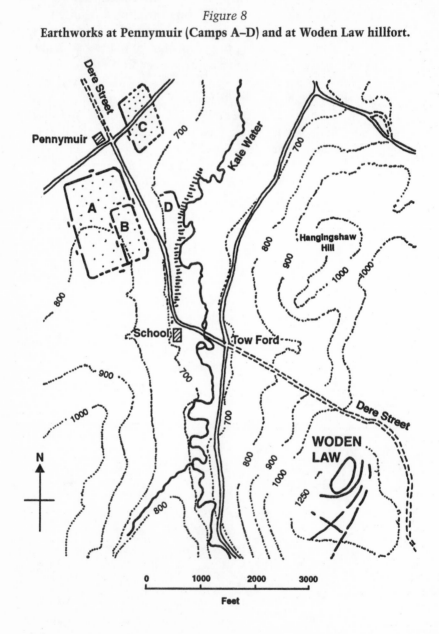

RCAHMS (Reproduced by permission).

THE LOCAL PEOPLE

The Borders was of course an already populated region by the time the Romans arrived. The preceding chapter has demonstrated developments in agriculture, housing, society and economy over several thousand years. Information on the peoples and places overrun was later incorporated in a map of the Roman world prepared about AD 150 by Ptolemy of Alexandria. Ptolemy names the *Novantae*, the *Damnonii*, the *Selgovae* and the *Votadini*, with some indication of their tribal area and several placenames in the territory of each. The *Votadini* probably occupied the Lothian plains and Berwickshire east of Lauderdale, together with part of Northumberland; The *Selgovae* held the central uplands between Lauderdale and Clydesdale, the *Novantae* were in Dumfries and Galloway and the *Damnonii* in the Clyde Estuary and the central belt of Lowland Scotland. The precise dividing lines between the tribes are not known. Ptolemy also lists a small number of placenames under each tribe. Among the Selgovae he names *Trimontium* which we can place at the Eildon Hills, and the unidentified *Carbantorigum*, *Uxellum* and *Corda*. Among the Votadini were *Curia*, *Alauna* and *Bremenium*, the latter identifiable as High Rochester fort south of Carter Bar.

The seeming absence of military installations and roads located from the air or by ground observation in lands thought to be Votadinian has led some to suppose a long-standing pact or treaty between the Romans and that tribe. Certainly their hillfort at Traprain Law in East Lothian continued to flourish throughout the Roman period and achieved some success as a manufacturing centre of trade-goods likely to appeal to the resident occupying forces.

To try to picture the Borders on the eve of the Roman occupation is a difficult task. There was clearly a substantial Iron Age population. The area abounds in hillforts, some very large, which at one time served as centres of population or defence, defended by stone walls and multiple ditches. But modern opinion has it that they were mostly long abandoned and that the tribes were living in smaller communities, in circular timber-built or stone-built houses, sometimes in undefended settlements, or homesteads protected by a palisade or a stone wall. Many such sites have yielded Roman material: jewellery, coins and pottery, the products of trade – or loot. The native community on Eildon Hill North could have numbered several thousand in its heyday, but it is not clear that the place was occupied when the Romans arrived. Certainly a Roman watchtower was subsequently positioned on its summit to act as the 'eyes' of Newstead fort below. A few brochs were built in the Borders in the early centuries AD. Some suppose that they were occupied by a population introduced by the Romans from the North; alternatively, their builders may have intruded into the area in the immediate aftermath of the Roman withdrawal. A souterrain built close to Newstead incorporated stonework likely to have been robbed from the fort after abandonment.

What impact did the Romans have on this population or its lifestyle? On the one hand the arrival of the Romans undoubtedly represented a fillip to the local economy – the garrisons needed fresh food and locally available supplies, the soldiers had pay to spend, trade goods were available in abundance to enhance farming practices, alter eating habits and so on. But for many, perhaps most of the population, life went on as before.

NEWSTEAD

Roman troops heading northwards, topping the rise at Lilliardsedge, had directly before them the distinctive profile of the Eildons. The nickname *Trimontium*, 'the place of the Triple Peaks', presumably given to the hills themselves, or the native site on the summit of Eildon Hill North, soon became attached also to the major fort which was quickly built in the lea of the Hills, just east of the present day Newstead village. The fort was constructed by Agricola's forces, rebuilt at the beginning of the Antonine period, and in use again as a staging post on the campaign route of the emperor Severus in AD 209–210.

Newstead Roman fort is (Figure 9) at 4 hectares the largest fort known in Lowland Scotland. It had all the standard components – headquarters building, commandant's house, barracks, granaries, bath-house. Beyond its stone wall and gates were fortified annexes to the west, south and east. The sloping ground to south and east also served to house camps containing troops on the move, which had stopped for the night beside the fort for safety, supplies and a little socialising. The camps were identified by aerial reconnaissance, initially undertaken by the late J.K. St. Joseph (Cambridge University), continued by Colin Martin (St. Andrews University) and by staff of the Royal Commission on the Ancient & Historical Monuments of Scotland; new elements are still being added. A recent theory that an amphitheatre lay north of the fort beside the Tweed has still to be tested by the spade. The site was first identified as a Roman fort in 1846, when the North British Railway, heading for Edinburgh, bisected the south annexe. The site was the subject of extensive excavation directed by local solicitor James Curle in 1906–10, promptly published in magisterial form, as *A Roman Frontier Post and its People* (Glasgow 1911). Curle's investigations were supplemented by further trenching in 1947. The site is protected or 'scheduled' as an ancient monument, and continues under the benevolent eye of local antiquarian Walter Elliot who has regularly fieldwalked the site and recovered material turned up by the plough. The recently implemented proposal to redirect the A6091 (the Newstead Bypass) along the now abandoned railway cutting through the fort's south annexe caused widespread alarm and brought into being the Trimontium Trust, whose members curate the museum at the Ormiston Institute, Melrose, and keep both local and national awareness of Newstead's importance at an impressively high level.

Figure 9
Newstead Complex

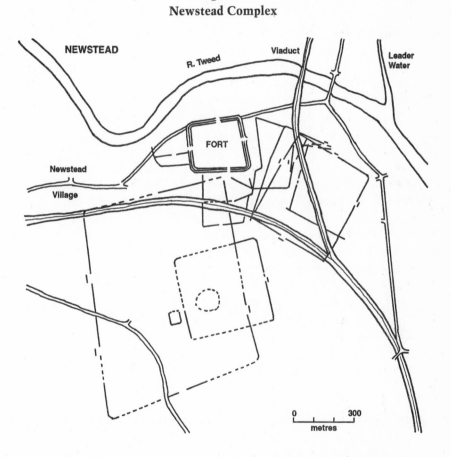

At much the same time, a renewed programme of excavation at Newstead was initiated by the National Museums of Scotland, which houses the mass of the finds from the site, in partnership with the University of Bradford, with work directed by Dr Richard Jones. The results of this work in 1988–93 have provided an increased awareness of the sophisticated lifestyle, economic and manufacturing activity, the bustling nature of the base, with soldiers negotiating with incoming traders and local populace, exchanging goods and transporting them to new markets. Small-scale industrial activities were concentrated in the south annexe, where iron, bronze, glass, tiles and pottery were being produced. Doubtless woodworking, textile making and glassblowing were also in progress. Other goods and services were bought in from farther afield: wine, olive oil from Spain, fish sauces and fine pottery from France and the Rhineland. In the later Antonine period, the fort itself seems to have been divided in two, when a stone wall separated the garrison from industrial activities inside the ramparts.

Of particular importance have been the finds from a large number of deep pits, many located during the 1905–1910 excavations and others during recent excavation (1994) in advance of the bypass. Some of the pits were evidently wells associated with industrial activities, while others were intended to receive religious offerings. The superb collection of small finds from Newstead is unparalleled in Scotland, both in quality and quantity. It ranges from parade helmets, tools and agricultural equipment, weapons, horse harness, leather tents and shoes, to bronze jugs, fine glass vessels, coins, pottery and wagon wheels. A few finds can be seen in the Trimontium Museum, Melrose and others in the Commendator's House, Melrose Abbey, but most are in the Royal Museum of Scotland, Edinburgh.

The garrison of Newstead in the Flavian period is not certainly known, but was probably a regiment of cavalry. In the Antonine period, legionaries from XX *Valeria Victrix* were based there, together with the *Ala Vocontiorum*, a cavalry regiment of originally Spanish origin. We know of the centurions C. Arrius Domitianus and L. Maximius Gaetulicus, both serving in Legion XX. A recently published writing tablet at Carlisle is a letter addressed to Julius Martialis, probably a legionary, whom the sender expected to find at either *Luguvalium* (Carlisle) or *Trimontium* (Newstead). The presence of legionaries and a cavalry regiment testifies to the crucial importance of the site as a control point for the occupying forces, halfway between Hadrian's Wall and the Forth-Clyde isthmus.

CONCLUSION

When the Romans first came to the Borders, they were on a mission to conquer all of northern Britain. As such they were passing through and consolidating their control over the area as a prelude to further advance. But their hold on areas farther north was only brief. After a withdrawal from all installations north of the Forth in AD 86–90, the Tweed Valley probably served as a border land between Rome's British province and unoccupied lands beyond, in the period 90–100. In the mid second century AD the Borders lay to the rear of the formal frontier line on the isthmus between the Forth and Clyde. But as soon as the Antonine Wall had been abandoned in the 160s AD, it is possible to envisage the Borders as marking the limits of the province which extended at times northwards only to the Tweed, and sometimes only to the Cheviots.

In the third and fourth centuries the Roman province was increasingly troubled by raiders from the sea and by land, though we are unable to document their passage through the Borders. The Romans dealt with various kings and chiefs for as long as their power lasted. After the campaigns of Severus in AD 208–210, direct Roman presence in the Borders was probably over. Certainly Hadrian's Wall was maintained, though with weakened garrisons, down to the end of the 4th century. Roman governors and indeed sometimes emperors made demonstrations of their power beyond it – for example, Constantius Chlorus, father of Constantine the Great, in AD 305. But increasingly the emperors were distracted by more pressing threats and commitments nearer to the Empire's heartlands.

Though the picture presented here is detailed and specific, it must be made clear that it is far from complete. A glance at the map of Roman Scotland shows gaps in the regular spacing of forts. Many apparently isolated finds of Roman material have been made. For example, fragments of three altars found embedded in the masonry of Jedburgh Abbey could suggest the presence of an unlocated fort at no great distance. Further discoveries can be confidently predicted to add to our awareness of this short but action-packed interlude in Borders history.

FIVE

THE EARLY HISTORIC PERIOD

The Borders are recognisable today as a physical and political entity, although they are, of course, a developed product of Anglo-Scottish politics during the tenth and eleventh centuries. It can be suggested that the region existed as an entity whose exceptional character clearly set it apart from the rest of northern England and southern Scotland long before a political boundary between Scots and English was ever considered. It must be stressed that the development of Anglian settlement, shires, estates and patterns of land use in the period after the battle of *Degsastan* fought in 603 represented no more than a partial Anglian 'veneer' on the 'slab' of native settlement and society persisting in the region prior to that date. Central to an evaluation of Anglian society, and the development of the region, must be a consideration of the extent to which this Anglian society developed in relation to the prevailing character of native settlement. Thus, to understand the Anglian 'veneer' it is essential first to comprehend the underlying native 'slab'.

THE BRITISH BACKGROUND

Native and Roman Interaction
Native society has its origins in the late pre-Roman Iron Age and it is crucial to consider the way that this society may have developed during the Roman period, and into the sub-Roman period. Traditional views of Roman and native see the native population of what became the eastern Scottish Borders, as falling within a broader region which was subjected to tight military supervision. An alternative view propounded by the writer is that an autonomous native society persisted in the region.

Although the Roman intervention was distinctly short lived, it is quite likely that it offered a positive boon to the native landscape. From this it might be inferred that British society would have owed a greater debt to the legacy of pre-Roman settlement and land use practices already long established. It is axiomatic that Roman monuments are few in number, and the *raison d'etre* would invariably seem to lie farther to the north. The Roman fort at Newstead, the camps at Pennymuir, Chew Green and Channelkirk are therefore staging posts, not necessarily to be seen as holding the line of the Roman road north, but rather as a critical springboard, maintaining the potential for mounting an advance to north of the Forth. The military concern may only ever have been focused, in a disruptive sense, immediately upon the eastern Scottish Borders, for a period not exceeding twenty five years out of over three hundred years during which time military activity either fell back or came to focus upon a forward military zone.

It can be argued that the larger settlement sites could have continued in use during the period of Roman jurisdiction. It is surely significant that in Peeblesshire only five out of eighty native defended settlement sites recorded by the RCAHMS* display incontrovertible evidence for disruption attributable to this period. Also, clearly the lack of defences need not preclude continued occupation. For instance, at the Dod, a multi-period settlement in the foothills of Teviotdale, Roxburghshire, following a late pre-Roman Iron Age settlement, occupation or activity continued within the site's perimeters, although its ramparts had apparently fallen out of use early in the site's history. It follows that the location of Roman signal stations within native settlements need not preclude continued occupation by the native population. However, not *all* pre-Roman Iron Age sites continued in use, and some sites underwent fundamental change, or were even wholly abandoned for a period.

With the population neither depleted nor deported, and resident still in its pre-Roman settlement sites, what can be said about the character of native society and its probable relations with the Roman military? From the outset it appears to have been a society capable of producing an agricultural surplus – itself fundamental to the maintenance of a social hierarchy. The presence of this hierarchy is inferred from the broad range and hierarchy of native settlement types present in the region: from the single homestead groups to settlements covering several hectares in total interior area. The presence of these larger sites is of a particular interest. The term *oppida* might be applied to North Eildon Hill, Ruberslaw, Yeavering Bell and White Meldon, with the implications that they were central places within developed and well-defined territories. They would have supported resident populations, and have been dependant upon a diverse and mixed economy; but they were also capable of producing goods surplus to their needs and able to support specialist craftsmen. Coercive power by a select group, mustering labour and manipulating the use of surplus to bring about social and economic change is a further corollary.

The presence in the eastern Scottish Borders of a hierarchically-defined native society, based upon a developed landscape, and able to achieve trade relations over long distances, may have constituted a viable threat to the

* The Royal Commission on the Ancient and Historical Monuments of Scotland

establishment of a military frontier. Alternatively, it is conceivable that it could have been in military interests to co-operate with a semi- if not wholly-autonomous native state lying immediately to the north. Furthermore, this state was singularly set apart from the rest of southern Scotland or northern England by the encircling hills of the Southern Uplands. To maintain the native state would make sense in terms of frontier policy. There is, after all, little point in destroying the fabric of native society and its economic framework, and then expecting that same society to fulfil, effectively the role of a buffer zone. Far from merely surviving during the period of Roman jurisdiction it is possible, perhaps in this region alone, that native society was able to develop, prosper and conceivably evolve into the form of society ultimately represented by the documentary sources of the sub-Roman period.

The emergent British kingdoms

In attempting to define something of the structure of the British landscape, the forts offer a firm line of enquiry. On the basis of those which RCAHMS infer, with varying degrees of confidence are 'Dark Age', or are forts that are at least 'unprehistoric', a relatively complete picture can be proposed. Circles drawn around the forts may tentatively indicate the resource zones attached to each, a hint perhaps of an estate structure embracing the greater part of the region, but for one notable gap, probably filled by *Coed Celyddon*, the Wood of Celyddon, later Ettrick Forest.

It is possible that some sites, classified as Romano-British, may have been retained well on into the sixth century, and quite possibly later. A glass bead from Bonchester and a clutch of later artefacts from the homestead at Crock Cleugh, including a bronze annular brooch of Germanic type, might support this. However, this is a very fine thread on which to hang a case for continuity, and we must probably admit that the evidence for rural settlement of the British period eludes us. At the Dod, there are three last phases of rectangular buildings (out of twelve in all), represented by rafts of compacted rubble, probably the stances for buildings of sill-beam construction. They follow upon a complex sequence of timber round houses, rebuilt in stone. Analogies can be drawn with similar 'buildings without walls' identified by Hope-Taylor within the hillfort on Yeavering Bell (of third and fourth century date) and by Hill at Whithorn (of later fifth and sixth century date). Pollen evidence, too, in Teviotdale, suggests phases of increased clearance activity within the context of a progressively deforested landscape. Not all evidence is compatible, however, with this for at *Gefryn* the Anglian farm was laid out over a Romano-British field-system already long abandoned, and at Thirlings there is no immediate evidence for activity on site until the Anglian period.

The tentative territorial framework of the British period sits within a reconstruction that can be put forward of the political geography of the region, postulating three 'lost' British kingdoms. These are: to the west in Tweeddale, perhaps the kingdom of *Goddeu*; its neighbour, the kingdom of Cadrod Calchvynyd; and, to the east, British **Bernaccia*, the forerunner of *Berneich*, Anglian Bernicia. The boundary to the north, between Bernicia and Gododdin, would seem to be the Lammermuirs (*not* the Tweed: *pace* Hope-Taylor) and to the west Dere Street was probably the boundary between Cadrod's kingdom and Bernicia. The adoption by Angles of Brittonic place-names – such as *Din Guoaroy* at the coast, *Maelmin* and *Gefryn* inland, indicates the identity of the predominant cultural grouping within Bernicia, even in the sixth century and one must keep an open mind as to whether Bernicia at any stage in the sixth century was in any formal sense 'Anglo-British', as argued so forcefully by Hope-Taylor, rather than primarily British, with some Angles present.

The Early Church in the Eastern Borders

Within this area as a whole, the persistence into the sub-Roman period of an autonomous and evolved native state provides the key to the previously elusive mechanism by which Christianity could have become established and have survived in an area which was apparently outside the sphere of the Ninianic and Columban missions. The regnal lists of the northern kingdoms appear to indicate that a sector of native society had become Christianised and adopted Romanised names in honour of the new religion (Clemens, Paturnus and Qunitilius). The unique occurrence of a dedication to a fourth century martyr, St. Gorgian, preserved at a remote site at Kirkhope in the upland valley of the Manor, could conceivably also belong to this period. An Early Christian memorial stone for other members of the élite (the sons of Liberalis) is to be seen *in situ* near the church of Yarrow, Selkirk and Professor Thomas has used a series of stones in Peebles to argue for the presence of a diocesan structure based here for the Upper and Middle Tweed Basin. They are inscribed '*locus sancti Nicolai episcopi*' and '*Neiton Sacerdos*'. It could perhaps be suggested that a *paruchia*, rather than a diocese, might be a better term, in order to stress that this was, first and foremost, a church of distinctly native character.

The *Eccles* names provide further evidence for Christianity having been established in the region prior to the late sixth century. Ecclaw, near Duns, Eccles near Coldstream and *Eccles Cairn* on the boundary of Yetholm Parish, indicate Christian enclaves or foci recognised by the Anglians during the initial phases of settlement. An iron-clad bronze-coated hand-bell from near Ednam, Berwickshire, and an east-west orientated masonry long-cist from Castleton join with the placename *Annat* (perhaps denoting the site of a founder's church, or a church within which the founder's remains were preserved), in indicating an evolving Christian infrastructure in this region, supported by a cohesive native society. Further, a topographical name at Old Melrose, the later Anglian foundation, is alluded to by Professor Thomas as of some importance as a sub-Roman British Christian locality.

THE ANGLIAN PERIOD

The political background

The Anglo-Saxon literary evidence of the eighth and ninth centuries unfortunately reveals nothing of the process of Anglian settlement in Bernicia before the late sixth century, and the British/Welsh literary tradition offers a spotlight on events in the 570s, but this is devalued by the distance in time of the writer from the events noted and the ill-understood means by which the material was transmitted from the sub-Roman North to medieval Wales.

Following the accession of Ida to the northern kingdom in 547 and the alleged recognition of *Din Guaoaroy*, or Bamburgh, as the principal royal stronghold, along with *Medcaut*/Lindisfarne, there was Anglian penetration of the British kingdom of *Bernaccia*, perhaps represented symbolically by the inland sites of Gefryn and Maelmin. However, the presence of a palisade at Gefryn, the buildings of whose first phase have now been re-interpreted by Scull as Anglian, does suggest that the success of this Anglian colony so far inland, at the archaic core of the British Kingdom was less than certain. Indeed the Welsh heroic poetry, in describing the siege of *Medcaut* by Urien of Rheged and his allies in 572–9, suggests that Bernicia was probably no different from any of the other British polities in being prone, from time to time, to assault by neighbouring warlords. Urien had also raided the Gododdin, and there was a struggle for Gwenddollau's kingdom at Arthuret *(Arfderydd)* about 573.

The ninth century *Historia Britonnum* noted that there were settlements by Octha and Ebissa 'as far as the borders of the Picts' (presumably the Firth of Forth) and the first battle recorded in it between Britonnic and Germanic forces was in the north at the mouth of the Glen, in Glendale (that is, at *Gefryn*); the seventh was fought in *Coed Celyddon*, probably the Forest of Ettrick. This might provide a context for Germanic activity in the eastern Borders in the mid to late fifth century onwards, although really there is not a shred of evidence for this. It is, certainly a possibility that lands on both sides of the River Tweed may have been in a state of incipient transition by the later sixth century, and Anglian interest increasingly apparent.

The battles of *Catraeth* (perhaps a surgical strike by Goddodin on the eastern march of Rheged), at the juncture of Bernicia and Deira, and *Degsastan* (fought between Aedan mac Gabran king of the Scots and Aethelfrith king of the Angles in Bernicia), probably at Addinston ('at Aedan's stone') at the head of Lauderdale on Dere Street, at the fulcrum of the crucial inter-dynastic boundary, perhaps relate – as proposed by Hope-Taylor – to a northern battle zone for the later sixth and earlier seventh centuries. At *Catraeth* (c.600), British hopes evaporated, and *Degsastan* (603) established Anglian military supremacy over the Scots and British. Bede tells us that:

He (Aethelfrith) overran a greater area than any other king or ruler, exterminating or enslaving the inhabitants, making their lands either tributary to the English, or ready for English settlement.

This supremacy was to survive little challenged for nearly eighty five years. Anglian takeover of lands on both sides of the River Tweed seems to have closely followed success at *Degsastan.* The eastern Scottish Borders were now opened up to the spread of Anglian settlement, as a logical and natural extension of Bernician territory.

The Anglian takeover

The English settlement seems to have developed by stages – the first being marked by the actual military takeover and the setting of bounds. The archaeological evidence for this is perhaps to be seen in sunken-featured buildings at New Bewick, Thirlings, possibly Dunbar, and most notably at *Maelmyn*, where there could be as may as sixty. Also, some sparsely-furnished inhumations containing Germanic grave-goods of the late sixth or early seventh century date may represent the movements of settlers from north Northumberland into the annexed territories. Perhaps, also, the folknames formed with personal names at Sprouston, Simprin and *Colodaesburg* refer to firstly the communities of people and then the districts which they settled. Probably characteristic of this distinctly military phase are a number of substantial palisaded forts: *Maelmyn*, *Gefryn*, Sprouston, *Colodaesburg* and, perhaps, too Hogbridge and the timber defences at Bamburgh. These would seem to have been a short-lived phenomenon, their function probably declining with the emergence of the townships which grew up alongside, as at *Gefryn* and Sprouston. The abandonment of *Gefryn* some time before 633 and the granting of the vacant fort at *Colodaesburg* after 643 perhaps give us an approximate date for the second phase of Anglian settlement.

Anglian consolidation

The second phase was one of consolidation, seen most clearly in a group of characteristic place names. Excluding (because of the difficulty of knowing to what part of the framework they properly belong) the most prolific place name element, *tun*, the pattern revealed is essentially that of the Anglian advance across the Merse. Simprin (an-*ingas* name) and *Colodaesburg* on the coast and Coldingham, a little way inland, may represent a first phase of Anglian centres. The second phase is represented by the – *ingatun* names, infilling to the west of both Simprin and Coldingham and on both sides of the Tweed. Names formed with the suffix endings -*ham* and -*worđ* probably mark a phase of consolidation, perhaps in the eighth century, essentially only as far as Dere Street. The advance and takeover of former British estates would seem to have been on the pattern of protracted encroachment from two initial centres and extending westwards with successive phases infilling and developing on gains already made.

Although this will not be entered into in any detail here, the place names, especially in relation to land utilisation, may be used to deduce a pattern of territoriality. Assuming the forts to be *caputs* of the British estate infrastructure, it can be argued that there are Anglian townships and farms located at a discrete distance from these earlier centres (usually about 1.5 to 2 km), but nevertheless occupying on a one-to-one basis the former British estates (see Chapter 15).

The structure of settlement

As argued elsewhere, Sprouston appears from a palimpsest of crop-marks to have all the attributes already recognised at Yeavering south of the Tweed as marking the presence of an important religious, ceremonial and market centre: a substantial palisaded enclosure; halls of greater and lesser extent; and ancillary buildings, *grubenhäuser* and barns. Given the description of Yeavering as a *villa regis* by Bede and Stephen, and the overriding similarities with Sprouston, it, too, should be recognised as a *villa regis* with subsidiary *viculi*. Lower down the scale, *villae* north of the Tweed may perhaps be recognised from aerial photography at Philip Haugh and possibly at Whitekirk in East Lothian, but they are a scarce commodity in this region. Doon Hill might best be interpreted as the suitably enclosed residence of a thane, perhaps charged with the oversight of the *urbs* of Dunbar.

Nevertheless, the *villae regiae* seem to have been a relatively short lived phenomenon and they perhaps reflected a period when the maintenance of the ruling house required royal progresses and nodal centres: a phase of transition. Once a wider settlement structure had become established, with the affairs of the emergent communities now dealt with by others such as *praefecti* and thanes, the king, now attending principally to the affairs of state, might be seen more often at the main royal fortresses.

Shires and estates

Within a couple of generations, at most, from the Anglian advance
initiated by Aethelfrith, between about 630 and 650, there would seem to
be the critical threshold for the emergence of the Anglian shires in the
eastern Borders. It should be noted that attribution to Anglian settlement,
rather than earlier British presence, is crucially dependant upon
recognition of an interval after the Anglian advance. The shire would then
emerge as a logical corollary of Anglian settlement structure with the
grouping of *vills* into administrative units for the purpose of rendering
services to a lord or thane. It is typified by the presence of a central place,
which might also be the site chosen for a mother church, and a number of
outlying dependencies, some of which lay at a considerable distance from
the shire centre. Shires have been mapped by Professor Barrow from
Berwick, Coldingham, Norham and Holy Island as well as the lost shire at
Yetholm; further evidence for a shire system has been well demonstrated
by Dr Aliaga-Kelly in the Lothians.

The Anglian Church

Of interest in the case of the shire of Berwick is the suggestion that the
shire centre was probably not at Berwick but farther to the west, and that
the mother church of the Anglian shire appears to have been Eccles, a
name which – as noted above – implies the presence of a British Christian
community. This perhaps reflects a clear wish that the Anglian minster
should be tied to a centre with an established (British) Christian tradition.
Alongside such a proprietorial system, within thirty five years of the battle
of *Degsastan* a distinctive type of site had appeared in the Border
landscape, the Anglian monastery. Old Melrose, Coldingham and possibly
also Norham were founded subsequent to the foundation of Lindisfarne by
St. Aidan from Iona at the bidding of Oswald, king of the Northumbrians.

The monastery at Old Melrose, transplanting perhaps the site of an
earlier British monastery (it has a topographical name as of some
importance as a sub-Roman British Christian locality), occupied the
plateau of a steep sided promontory formed by the tight meander of the
River Tweed, with the neck of the promontory effectively cut off by a
substantial bank and ditch, the *vallum monasterii*. The buildings at Old
Melrose, like those at Coldingham, appear to have been of timber, for the
monastery was burnt by Kenneth MacAlpin, King of the Scots, in 849.

The double monastery at *Colodaesburg* was founded by Aebbe, aunt of
Ecgfrith, on one of the coastal promontories of St. Abb's Head in
Berwickshire. A particularly marked promontory, similar to the terrain of
Old Melrose, with its landward approach separated from the mainland by a
substantial rampart, it is generally considered to be the site of the
monastery. Recent excavations by Professor Alcock would suggest Kirk

Hill as the more likely site, though that might be better seen as the focus for primary secular settlement, the *Coludi Urbs* of Bede. The monastery was destroyed by fire and apparently abandoned, though archaeological evidence suggests that the focus of ecclesiastical activity moved into the vicinity of Coldingham Priory and was well established by the ninth century when the monastery was again destroyed by fire, this time by the Vikings.

The status of the monastery at Norham is less clear, though the presence of conventual buildings is implied by the transference here, sometime before 875, of the see of Lindisfarne accompanied by the reconstruction of Aidan's wooden church, and the translation there of the bodies of St. Cuthbert and King Ceolwulf.

The nature of British survival

Although the Borders can be recognised as an entity, as noted above, this is a developed product of the politics of the tenth and eleventh centuries. It seems evident that prior to that time there was a crucial east-west boundary. The two halves of the area may be regarded as each being a mirror image of the other. Drawing together the evidence, it may be argued that there was a broad cultural schism between the development of an Anglian polity in the east, and the persistence of a more native society in the west. The boundary is in fact more closely definable and is supported by the distribution of the pre-Conquest Lindisfarne estates. A line drawn along Dere Street, north of the River Teviot, is seen to be critical. This boundary is respected throughout by *terra Lindisfarnensis* north of the Tweed, and is marked too by the most westerly extent of Anglian sculptural types, and the distribution of all but the latest Anglian place-names. The *chester* names, representative perhaps of native sites, defensive in character, either still occupied or abandoned during the opening phases of Anglian settlement, are particularly worthy of note. Their most westerly distribution coincides with the line of Dere Street north of the Teviot where they appear as satellites to the boundary.

West of Dere Street, there is a strong presumption that there were areas which remained to all intents British. In eastern Dumfriesshire, two *w(e)alh* place names in Langholm Parish suggest the presence of a discrete British community happily co-existing within an Anglian domain. In Tweeddale, perhaps typical of the Brittonic territories, the evidence points to the maintenance of a system of *maenors*, typified by the grouping of *vills* in relation to a central place (the *maerdref*). In the case of the Parish of Manor (where the place-name may preserve the memory of this administrative system), on the basis of territorial analysis and drawing upon the widest body of evidence, the development of the component estate units of this system can tentatively be traced from the mid to late first millennium BC to the division of the barony in the early fourteenth century. If the evidence from Manor is typical, this would seem to raise the possibility that patterns of settlement and land use in the British territories proved more conservative to change, and were of as much lasting significance, as those imposed by the structure of English settlement in lands to the east and farther afield.

CONCLUSION

It has been argued elsewhere that for the later Anglian period, similarly, an analysis of settlement and land use would appear to indicate that, despite political isolation and economic instability, the region maintained its identity and continued to reflect the changing cultural influences in Northumbria. A hierarchy of site and settlement types, both ecclesiastical and secular, developing within a framework of estates and a shire system, is the picture that seems to emerge. Significant native survival is apparent in both the uplands and the lowlands, though in the uplands, and as illustrated by the Manor valley, native traditions may have been more resistant to any changes brought about by the emergence of English settlement. By contrast, in the lowlands, if Sprouston is typical, English settlement developed with little or no regard for pre-existing native settlement.

Many of the arguments employed here (and in greater detail elsewhere) for the British background and Anglian settlement are conjectural, and will remain so until tested against a refined archaeological settlement chronology and a more detailed understanding of the character and development of individual sites. Similarly, nothing less than a comprehensive programme of selective excavation, and environmental sampling, is needed to establish the balance between urban and rural landscapes, and to define the function and hierarchy of late Anglian settlement types in the area. The Early Historic period has yet much to gain from the methodology of archaeology, and much potential remains to be unlocked.

Note
* This summary chapter has been created by Christopher D. Morris from the views expressed in a number of papers by Ian M. Smith. The very nature of this chapter makes it inevitable that a critical apparatus cannot be provided; for this, the reader is referred to the articles mentioned below. The editor is only too well aware that, as a posthumous creation, it inevitably suffers from a lack of immediacy which only the author himself could have brought to the work. Those who attended either of his lectures

at Glasgow in December, 1993 or Edinburgh in May, 1994 will, I hope, recognise here the issues he addressed on those occasions, but will miss the panache and brio he brought to his presentations of academic papers at conferences. Ian Smith's tragic death in July 1994 came at a time when he had been working on a number of inter-related themes, but before he had created the commissioned chapter for this book. He had given the general editor an outline for the chapter, and as far as possible this has been adhered to. The reader is directed to Dr. Smith's detailed studies of a number of issues dealt with here, most notably the following:

Recent Excavations at the Dod, in D.W. Harding (ed) *Later Prehistoric Settlement in South-East Scotland*, Edinburgh 1982, 129–35.

Brito-Roman and Anglo-Saxon: the Unification of the Borders, in P. Clack and J. Ivy (eds) *The Borders*, Durham 1983, 9–48.

Patterns of Settlement and Land Use of the Late Anglian Period in the Tweed Basin, in M. Faull (ed) *Studies in Late Anglo-Saxon Settlement*, Oxford, 1984, 177–196.

Sprouston, Roxburghshire: an early Anglian centre of the eastern Tweed Basin (Chalmers-Jervise Prize essay), *Proc Soc Antiq Scot* 121, 1991, 261–294.

The Early Church in Southern Pictland, forthcoming.

The Structure of Anglian Settlement in Southern Scotland, forthcoming.

It is to be hoped that other parts of his comprehensive survey, in a Durham University doctoral thesis, will be published, in conjunction with his supervisor Professor Rosemary Cramp:

The Archaeological background to the emergent kingdoms of the Tweed Basin in the Early Historic period, 1990, University of Durham, Department of Archaeology.

Six

The Early Medieval Period in the Borders: 1000 AD – 1296 AD

It is not possible to look at the history of the Borders in isolation. Nor is there a sudden ending of the dark ages and the start of the medieval period. The battle of Carham on the Tweed in 1018 AD, is often taken as the starting point of Scottish medieval history. But this was not as conclusive in settling the land border between Scotland and England as many historians have claimed; the question is much more complicated than that. It is equally difficult to look at the history of the Borders Region as a whole since it covers an area of nearly 2000 square miles making the story of Berwickshire differ considerably from that of Peeblesshire. There is a lack of much archaeological evidence or enough reliable documentary sources; the few documents of the period have usually been written by clerics who could be biased in their recording. So, educated guesswork makes up much of the initial history of this time while the fascinating study of placenames allows us to build up some idea of the past.

Setting the Scene

For around two hundred years prior to the battle of Carham, the question of claim and physical possession of the lands of Lothian and the Merse was one of ebb and flow depending on the strength or weakness of the claimants (see Chapter 5). At the turn of the millennium, the Tweed basin lay within the Anglian kingdom of Bernicia. Even this area could be divided into two distinct folk groupings: the Anglian settlers, initially from Northumbria, had possession of the more fertile lower lands while the original Celtic inhabitants of the area occupied the hillier land at the heads of the valleys. It was a wild land with wide wastelands of bog and moor with rough forests of scrub timber.

The Anglians

The influence of the Anglian kingdom of Northumbria has been the most lasting. At the start of the 11th century, early English was the common tongue of the people of the Lower Tweed and their physical characteristics would not differ much from that of their neighbours in Northumberland. In effect, the people of the Merse were English in their language, customs, methods of land cultivation and way of life.

They lived in small village communities dotted amongst the fertile lower lands of the Tweed. In the village, one could own a house and the large garden in which it stood; the surrounding land was held communally and individual fields were balloted for annually depending on status within the community. With no certainty of getting the same field in successive years, there was little incentive to improve the fertility of the land and this could lead to ground exhaustion. Within the village, the wealthier class of villager had the use of twenty six Scots acres with an additional oxgang of thirteen acres for grazing two oxen. Each holding could consist of several rigs scattered round the cultivated area. (These were the husbandmen and their land holding was a husbandland.) The poorer, labouring class were called cottars, with a land holding of one to ten acres depending on the area and location; they had no plough animals. Both classes had a share in the common grazing lands of the village and the use of certain wild woodlands and natural resources. On the flatter fields the incoming settlers had introduced a new form of field cultivation by the use of the ox plough. This form of tillage destroyed the small patchwork Celtic field system. A common method of working the land was for four husbandmen to share a plough and each would supply two oxen for draft animals. The heavy oak plough with four, or sometimes six pair of oxen in harness extended to some ten to fifteen metres in length and this made turning the plough very difficult. Consequently, the Anglian fields or rigs tended to be long and narrow and often had a sweep at the lower end where the cumbersome plough turned out of the furrow. The long narrow rig fields could be seen around many of the Border villages until recent times.

The land that a single eight ox plough was able to turn over in any one year was reckoned to be one hundred and four Scots acres and this became a standard unit of Scots land measure, the ploughgate. As this was the worked land of four husbandmen, a quarter of it became a 'husbandland', twenty-six Scots acres. Wheat, oats, rye and bere were grown on the ploughed fields but the Anglian economy did not depend entirely on arable farming. Cows and sheep were kept on the common grazings with pigs finding their food in the beech and oak woods.

Anglian villages had a distinctive layout. They started as either a single street with houses on either side as in Lauder or Lilliesleaf or were triangular like Melrose, Selkirk, Midlem (Plate 8), Bowden or Sprouston. In each case, houses were built on or near the street within a large yard/garden area. There was a back road for servicing which often grew into a street in its own right if the village expanded. The market place was within the triangular space or, in single street villages, in a place where the street widened out as in the case of Lauder.

Stone houses were not common and the Anglian villagers lived in wooden houses in a thick layer of wattle and daub. There was seldom any defensive structure round the villages. Livestock was kept in a wooden palisaded enclosure nearby when not out grazing under the eye of the herdsman. Given the fact that few Anglo-Saxon coins have been found in the Borders, we can infer that they used a barter economy and had a way of life probably just above the subsistence level.

THE CELTS

In the upper regions of the Tweed basin, the picture was different. Deprived of the richer lands of the lower Tweed which they could not till anyway, the dwellers of the upper valleys of the Tweed and its tributaries were pastoralists. It has been suggested that the bulk of their food was provided by their flocks and herds with some supplementary meat coming from hunting wild animals. This is not the whole picture, as terraced fields were constructed on many of the lower upland hills and these can only have been made for the express purpose of cultivating crops. This is likely to have been done primitively by spade or man-hauled plough. Further evidence that some form of cereal was grown, is that many querns for grinding corn have been found in and around the hill settlements.

The houses of the Celtic hill folk were usually circular, made of stone and with an inferred thatched roof. In the hills, stone is plentiful and they made bountiful use of it in their houses and stock pens. They lived in extended family groups in settlements which were fortified by a mound and ditch or several ditches. The fortification would serve as a place of safety for stock as much as a barrier against human enemies.

With stone as a favoured building material, many settlements can still be seen in the upper parts of the Tweed valley. However, an added complication is that this type of dwelling has been used since Roman days and was occupied well into medieval times. In the absence of archaeological excavation, there is little chance in the near future of defining the periods of occupation.

THE SCOTS

When Malcolm II ascended the throne of what was then called Alba in 1005 he was king or overking of Strathclyde and Lothians. He was ambitious and began his reign by making a foray into Bernicia in the following years with a view to extending the kingdom as far south as the rivers Ribble and Tees. He was repulsed with heavy losses by Northumbrian forces under the command of Earl Uhtred of Bamburgh. In 1018 he tried again and defeated the army of Earl Eadulf of Bamburgh at the battle of Carham. His aim was to be overlord of Bernicia which had once stretched from the Tees to the Forth. However, this was not to be, for Cnut the Danish king of the English invaded northwards in 1031/2. Malcolm was forced to submit but still managed to retain the Tweed valley for himself. When Malcolm died in 1034, he was described as 'king of Scotia', the name which had replaced the older Alba. It is about this time that Gaelic names appear as overlords in certain parts of the Borders and from the study of Gaelic placenames, Gaels appear to have been given lands in the upper valleys of the Tweed and its tributaries.

The English population in the lower reaches of the Tweed seem to have been left in possession of the land while the Gaelic speaking Scots were given vacant hill lands. It is doubtful if there was a significant folk movement within the area. The retention of Anglian placenames suggests that the transition was comparatively painless.

THE NORMAN CONQUEST OF SCOTLAND

The Norman invasion of England in 1066 caused many of the Anglo-Saxon nobility to flee to Scotland. Instability in the north of England gave Malcolm III, King of Scots, the opportunity to acquire Northumbria and Cumbria. To legitimise his claim, Malcolm had married as his second wife, the Saxon princess Margaret who had fled to Scotland, which had become a refuge for those who opposed William the Conqueror. This marriage produced two daughters and six sons, three of whom became Kings of Scots.

William was not slow to retaliate to the invasion of his northern counties. In 1072 he crossed the Tweed and the Lothians with a large army and a fleet in close support. Malcolm used guerrilla tactics, yet William reached Abernethy before a peace was concluded. Malcolm still had territorial ambitions and invaded again in 1079 when Norman authority in the northern English Counties was weak; William's forces again invaded Scotland. The same scene was played again in 1091 with similar results. Malcolm's fifth attempt in 1093 ended in disaster when he and his son Edward were killed in an ambush near Alnwick.

It has been said that the reign of Malcolm III (1058–1093) began in obscurity and ended in chaos. For the next four years, the throne of Scotland was occupied by Donald Ban, Malcolm's son by his first marriage and then by Edgar, son of Margaret who was placed on the throne by the Norman forces of William Rufus. From here on Scotland took a pro-Norman stance.

The medieval period really began in the Scottish Borders in the year 1113. In that year David, the sixth and youngest son of Malcolm III and Margaret became Earl David and was given lands and power in southern Scotland. He was to have more influence on the Scottish Borders than anyone before or since. His brothers, Edgar (1097–1107) and Alexander (1107–24) had depended on the Norman kings of England to take and retain the throne of Scotland.

On the death of Malcolm and Margaret in 1093, their young family had sought refuge in England and were brought up at court, becoming French-speaking with ideas of Anglo-Norman feudalism as the accepted form of Government. The reign of Edgar seems an unremarkable ten years, with a grant of land at Coldingham given to the monks of Durham being one of the few items of Border interest. Alexander reigned for seventeen years but his interests and religious foundations were largely directed to the northern areas of his kingdom while David as Earl held the south. During their reigns Scotland enjoyed a period of comparative peace, in contrast to the civil wars in England.

David the Earl
Earl David had spent his adolescence as a member of the Anglo-Norman royal household, travelling on the Continent, seeing at first hand the new religious houses and how a stable society produced trade and prosperity for all. When he was Earl of Cumberland with control of most of southern Scotland, he introduced some of these people into the rough Borderland. With them came a new feudal system of land holding, the raising of townships to free burgh status and the foundation of new religious houses, which are examined in detail in other chapters but it is impossible to ignore them here.

In 1113 David brought thirteen monks from the newly founded monastery of Tiron in France and with them, founded a monastery near Selkirk. His generous provision for them in lands and rental gifts would amount to around three million pounds in 1994 prices. The Tironensian monks were working tradesmen as well as writers recording the deeds of the times. From the church, the medieval kingdom drew its civil service.

In 1114 David married Matilda the widow of Simon de Senlis and through her acquired the earldoms of Northampton and Huntingdon. While still Earl, he was virtual overlord of the northern regions of England where there was already a number of Anglo-Normans. With the Lothians and Tweeddale under his control, he was able to bestow lands on the younger Anglo-Norman sons and through them a different system of government was established – feudalism. The new landowners were French-speaking feudal owners parcelling out their new lands in return for rent in service or in produce and owing their own-man service to their patron, David. This made for an interdependent class society.

Law was enforced by another introduction, the office of sheriff, who acted as administrator and justiciar on the king's behalf. The concept had been taken from English examples and the first definite mention of a Scottish sheriff can be found in the charter of foundation of Selkirk Abbey *c* 1119, when 'Conspatric the sheriff' is cited as witnessing the charter. It is interesting to note that, included in the many Norman witnesses, is the name of 'Robert of Bruis'.

David the King

Earl David became King of Scots in 1124, when he was in his early forties. He was to reign for almost thirty years, introducing reforms and bringing his Dark Age kingdom into medieval times and practices.

One of the first charters of his reign was to give 200,000 acres of land in Annandale to a Norman Knight, Robert de Brus; only one of the witnesses was not a Norman knight. This was to be but one of the many land grants to Normans throughout the Borders.

The spread of the Anglo-Normans can be traced by a new type of building – the motte. This was an earth mound, usually on an improved knowe and incorporating a timber tower on the top. It was the defensive stronghold of the Anglo-Normans and appeared throughout southern Scotland. In Peebles, Selkirk, Coldstream and Hawick, they probably formed early royal administrative centres. Mottes were to remain in use in the Borders well into the fourteenth century.

David I was generous to his Norman friends but he balanced their increasing power by boosting the position of some of the Border communities, into burghal status. By increasing trade potential within the new burghs, he received additional taxes and tolls as well as a power counterbalance to the nobles. (The role of burghs is examined in detail in chapter 14).

In 1136, David I became the first Scottish king to strike coins. It is interesting to note that they were struck at Berwick, Roxburgh and Carlisle while his son, Henry, now Earl of Huntingdon and Northumberland, struck coinage under his own name at Carlisle, Corbridge and Bamburgh. English coins would already be circulating in southern Scotland as the use of coinage made for easier trading conditions.

The twelfth century was a time of trading expansion in Europe. The export of Cheviot wool through Berwick made it the greatest port in Scotland; domestic pottery was imported from the north of England and the Continent. Other than the regular wars and revolutions, Scotland never had it so good.

Religious houses grew in number through the land. Selkirk Abbey was moved to Kelso in 1128; Melrose Abbey was founded in 1136; Jedburgh Abbey was founded about 1138 on the site of an earlier church and Dryburgh Abbey in 1150. The abbeys were given wide lands with scattered granges throughout the Borders. Their well tended flocks made money for their abbeys, the king, the ports and the people.

David the Legend

David I was a legend, if not in his own lifetime, then at least in the writings of his historical biographers. It does not detract from his achievements to point out that most of the biographers owed their position to his benevolence. Yet, his defeat at the Battle of the Standard inflicted one of the greatest defeats suffered by a Scots army and there were four or more serious rebellions during his reign.

In 1152, the death of Prince Henry, his only surviving child, left the aged monarch with an eleven year old grandson, Malcolm, as his heir and his younger brother William, as Earl of Northumberland. David died a year later and within four years, Northumberland and Cumbria had returned to England leaving the border settled on the line of Tweed and Solway.

AFTER DAVID

The Scots kings following David continued his policies. In the Borders, religious houses flourished; Norman settlement provided an orderly rule without too much displacement of the native Anglian/Celtic inhabitants. There were some wars and cross-border raiding but this era was later to be looked on as a golden age.

To condense Scottish history into a short chapter, we will look at how some aspects of each king's reign affected Borders history.

Malcolm IV 1153-65

The reign of Malcolm 'the Maiden' highlights the troubles of a king in his minority. This was to be the Curse of Scotland in successive reigns. In the Borders, Malcolm was as generous a patron as his grandfather, giving Melrose Abbey 'the Forests of Selkirk and Traquair, all the pasture upon Gala water, a fish trap at the Yair, and a byre for a hundred cows at Colmslie', to cite but one example.

He also gave the rights of sanctuary to the church of Innerleithen 'where my son's body rested the first night after his decease'. Malcolm never married and left no legitimate heir.

William the Lion 1165–1214

William reigned from 1165–1214 being one of the longest reigning Scottish monarchs. His reign was to be a period of acquisition and consolidation by the Norman settlers in southern Scotland and revolt in the Celtic north and west. William was the most Anglo-Norman of the Scottish medieval kings and an English chronicler, Walter of Coventry, notes that he and Malcolm 'profess themselves to be Frenchmen both in race and in manners, language and culture'.

William invaded the lost territory of Northumberland in 1174 with a view to regaining it for the Scottish crown. Embarrassingly, he was captured while besieging Alnwick Castle and the price of his ransom was that he would do homage to the King of England for the whole of Scotland and would hand over the castles of Berwick, Roxburgh, Jedburgh, Stirling and Edinburgh. Jedburgh and Stirling did not change hands; Edinburgh was retrieved as part of William's marriage dowry while Berwick and Roxburgh together with Scots independence, were bought back for 10,000 merks when Richard the Lionheart needed money to go on a Crusade.

William seems to have spent much time in the Borders, Selkirk being a favourite residence since many Acts of Government were passed 'before his full court assembled at Selkirk'. Roxburgh and Berwick, although in English hands from 1174 to 1189, were the most important burghs in Scotland; Roxburgh was the biggest trading burgh with five moneyers striking coins there during his reign. Berwick remained the major port.

Alexander II 1214–49

Alexander II came to the throne in 1214 at the age of sixteen. In October the following year he set about recovering the lost territories of Northumberland; here, he was taking advantage of the civil war raging in England between King John and his revolting barons.

King John retaliated in January 1216, burning Berwick and Roxburgh and devastating the Eastern Marches. Alexander returned the compliment by raiding Cumbria. Between 1215 and 1217, Alexander invaded the north of England five times in attempts to regain Northumbria and Cumbria. In 1221, when Alexander married Joan, the sister of Henry III, Anglo-Scots relations became less strained, especially as Alexander had regained the Earldom of Huntingdon in the marriage settlement. Alexander was less of an Anglo-Norman than his immediate predecessors and had partly succeeded in uniting the diverse cultures of his kingdom into a unified nation.

Alexander III 1249–86

Alexander III succeeded to the throne at the age of eight. Unusually, there was no struggle to exploit the young king but rather a consensus amongst the greater nobles for his protection.

Additionally, the kingdom was prosperous. The Border abbey flocks were increasing as uncultivated lands were brought into production; wool and hides were being increasingly exported to the Continent; burghs were expanding their economies through trade. Moreover, a system of thirty sheriffdoms made for safety in the realm.

There was peace between Scotland and England for most of the reign. Alexander had married Margaret, the daughter of Henry III in 1251. In 1255, Henry with a large retinue of nobles, took up residence at the Border village of Sprouston while he awaited the arrival of his son-in-law, Alexander with a deed designed 'for the peace and government of

Scotland'. Henry took a great interest in the affairs of Scotland and made many suggestions for its government. Historians have tended to look on him as an innocent mischief-maker but it must be noted that the bulk of this evidence comes from English written sources.

Much of the prosperity came through the port of Berwick. The lucrative wool trade went out bound for the Low Countries and for Italy, both having a burgeoning textile industry; Italian merchants were also bankers and handled most of the monetary transactions for the Border Abbeys. Imports into Berwick included sugar, currants, onions, garlic, pepper, cumin, ginger, almonds, rice, basil, alum, dyestuffs, pans, cauldrons, locks and raw materials like timber and iron. However, the greatest import was wine and of varieties which would please the connoisseur. In 1263, Alexander III brought 178 tuns of wine through the port of Berwick and in those days, a tun was reckoned to hold 252 gallons. This amount was for the royal household but where a king leads, many of his subjects follow.

Meanwhile, the Anglo-Normans were integrating into the Borders community. Many had married into local landowning families and a third of the Anglian/Celtic earldoms in the whole of Scotland were held by men of Norman descent. Some held lands equally in Scotland, England and parts of France and sought peace for prosperity on their lands.

Alexander had married his daughter to the King of Norway and concluded a peace treaty with Norway while the new King of England, Edward I, was his brother-in-law. The country was secure and prosperous. This was brought to an abrupt end when Alexander fell over the cliff at Kinghorn in 1286, leaving a small girl in Norway as heir apparent.

The Troubled Times

With an infant Queen of Scots, 'Guardians' of Scotland were appointed and the jockeying for power started. In the Treaty of Birgham (1290) the Guardians set out terms for a future marriage between the infant Queen and the eldest son of Edward of England. This was voided when the Maid of Norway died in Orkney in the September of that year.

An Interregnum took over the affairs of Scotland until a successor was found. There were four serious contenders and Edward I of England was asked to make the choice as an unbiased judge. Edward saw his chance to acquire Scotland and in 1292, chose John Balliol to be King of Scots after having first made all claimants swear that he, Edward, was their overlord. This did not please many Scots and the Borderers not at all.

Edward considered that Scotland was now his as the demand for a rent of £28 was made to the tenant of Selkirk Mills in 1292, stating that this sum be paid to 'the chancellor of OUR kingdom of Scotland'. Edward stripped dissident Scots nobles of their English property.

There had been severe crops failures in both countries for several years. In 1294, the mayor and community of Berwick appealed to Edward to stop the seizure of their grain ships which were being captured and taken into English ports. The appeal might have been more successful had not the Scots massacred English sailors in Berwick.

ENGLISH OCCUPATION

In March, 1296, Edward crossed the Tweed with an army of nearly 30,000 veterans from the Welsh wars. They took and sacked Berwick and butchered all the male inhabitants, including thirty Flemings in their Red Hall. From there, he defeated a Scots army at Dunbar and then proceeded as far as Banff, meeting little opposition; the Scots simply could not muster enough men to oppose him in battle. Many of the nobility held lands in England, Scotland and France and were reluctant to compromise any of their holdings.

During this expedition, Edward made a point of exacting an oath of fealty from every person of note. Among those professing loyalty to Edward on the infamous Ragman's Roll, were 174 names from the County of Roxburgh, 40 from the County of Peebles and 9 from the County of Selkirk. Future events would suggest that many had their fingers crossed behind their backs when they made the pledge.

SEVEN

WAR OF INDEPENDENCE TO THE UNION OF THE CROWNS: 1296–1603

If Edward I had played his cards right, he might have been accepted as overlord of Scotland as well as King of England. The mainly Norman nobility had lands in both countries as well as in the English dominions of France, Ireland and Wales; so they had conflicting loyalties. The burghs were interested in keeping the lucrative trade links with the Continent and England. The Church as an international organisation, was both landowner and trader.

Edward had been having a bad time in the early 1290s. There was a revolt in the English dominion of Gascony in 1294 which had blown up to a full scale confrontation with France; there was a Welsh uprising in 1294/5 and Ireland was revolting as usual. The Scots confrontation was merely the final straw because the separate political existence of Scotland was a constant threat to England, the more so since they were physically joined together.

In the end, it was a battle between the English nationalism of Edward and the Scottish nationalism of the bulk of the Scots nation. Edward made a point of removing the records and relics of the conquered to destroy reminders of national identity. When the English army removed the Stone of Destiny, the Black Rood of St. Margaret and loads of documents from Scotland in 1296, they were taken 'as a sign of the resignation and conquest of the kingdom'.

It is questionable if the bulk of the Borderers cared much about the Stone of Destiny; they had little interest in holy relics and couldn't read anyway. What they didn't like was the assumption that they fight Edward's foreign wars for him; and the aristocracy were upset when Edward started giving their lands to his English nobles. The burghs didn't like paying tolls to Edward since he gave them little trade in return. The Scottish Church had close connections with the papal court and were displeased when they were informed that they would be subordinate to the English Church.

Edward had found that it was easy to conquer Scotland with his superior forces; it was less easy for him to hold it. English forces could control parts of the Border country by garrisoning the castles of Roxburgh, Berwick, Cavers, Selkirk, Jedburgh, Wark, Biggar and Oliver Castle. But these were isolated strongholds which needed food and supplies and Edward soon found that an army of occupation was an expensive business.

In April, 1296, Sir Robert Clifford was collecting hostages from Selkirk Forest but by the 23rd July 1297, an English report states that Sir William Wallace 'lay with a great company in the Forest of Selkirk'. Before action could be taken, Wallace had raised enough fighters from the forest to join Sir Andrew Murray and win the Battle of Stirling Bridge. This victory was a fluke brought about by bad English generalship. In 1298, Wallace was proclaimed Guardian of Scotland in 'the forest kyrk' which is thought to be Selkirk although some historians suggest that the kirk of St. Mary's Loch is another possibility. Wallace kept his forces in the security of Ettrick Forest while besieging Roxburgh Castle.

The English had the manpower to win battles while the Scots had to adopt hit-and-run tactics. So, at the set Battle of Falkirk in 1298, the Scots were soundly beaten. The Ettrick Forest archers fought on the losing side. On the other hand, the burgh Borderers seem to have supported, or been forced to support the English. The burgesses of Roxburgh sent a plea to Edward to 'save them from the brigand Wallace' and later on, those of Selkirk helped the English to burn the lands of Sir Simon Fraser who had previously been the English-appointed Keeper of Ettrick and Traquair Forest but had subsequently changed sides.

The Borders were split in their allegiance with the flatter and most accessible lands of the Merse supporting or being forced to support the English forces while the hillier and roughly forested west was for Wallace and his Scots outlaws. About half the Norman nobility supported Edward. On the English side was the Lovel family who held the estates of Hawick and Branxholme and other land in the area. This kept them relatively safe when the English were in control but less so when the Scots were dominant. The barony of Hawick was given to Sir Henry Balliol by Robert the Bruce when he gained the Scottish throne.

Edward's ambition was to have a united Britain and the majority of Scots were determined to retain national independence. The result of those opposing forces was to ensure that there would never be total peace on the Border as long as the two countries remained separate. For the next three hundred years, turmoil and anarchy were to prevail, while raiding and spoiling became a way of life.

AFTER BANNOCKBURN

Robert the Bruce, afterwards Robert I King of Scots, was a gambler taking the opportunity when and where he saw it. He risked life and lands by renouncing fealty to Edward and claiming the crown of Scotland. He was also a good fighting man and brilliant general with both charisma and good contacts. His victory at Bannockburn with a small army saw a totally dispirited English retreat in disarray even although their retreating army had twice the number of uncommitted men as was contained in the whole Scots force.

This victory caused havoc in the north of England. Scots raided in force into Northumberland, Westmorland and Yorkshire burning and looting as they went. Durham and Cumbria escaped only by paying large sums in tribute; towns paid or burned. The Bruce gave a fine example to the successive generations of Border thugs by demanding protection money in exchange for immunity. If Edward was the hammer of the Scots, Bruce was the Mell of the English.

The War of Independence had left both sides of the Border devastated. Adding to the misery was the unusually heavy rainfall in 1315 which rotted crops and killed most of the stock which had survived the war. Things were so bad on the English side that many English Borderers gave up their own king's protection and joined with the Scots who raided farther southwards. This was to set the precedent for future dealing between the Scots and English Border reivers.

THE REIVER ECONOMY

Nobody ever won the Border wars; they simply kept on repeating and repeating, often with different results but never with total victory to either side. There were and are really three countries in the island called Great Britain – England and Wales is one; Scotland is another and the Borders which covers the northern part of one and the southern part of the other forms a third separate entity. For the three hundred years covered in this chapter, the Borderland was devastated by Scottish and English armies marching over, plundering and burning in time of war. Times of reputed peace between the nations made little difference, for the people had learned to adapt to a reiving society. The story about the much publicised Wat o' Harden lamenting that an English haystack did not have legs otherwise it would have been added to his stolen cattle, was apocryphal, but summed up the philosophy of the reiver.

The Scots were usually outnumbered; so when an English force was seen to be approaching, the Scots Borderers would drive their stock into the hills and burn their houses and crops to deprive the enemy of food and comfort. This scorched earth policy was so successful that many English raiders had to turn back for lack of food; the official reason often given in reports to the King of England was 'through lack of beer'. This was the well worn excuse by English commanders for not advancing into Scotland.

The conflict was not so one sided as might be thought. Scots Borderers could and did raid into England, sometimes in surprising numbers and over great distances. The ruination south of the border was just as great and the consequences much the same. So there evolved in the Border counties a guerrilla mentality and existence. There was no point in tilling the fields to grow corn because somebody would just come along and burn it; to raise cattle was just to get them stolen; leave that to others and then steal them yourself; why bother to build a permanent house when you would either have to burn it yourself or have it shelter your enemies; anyway, an adequate shelter could be built in a few hours. The best possessions were a sharp sword, a swift horse, some strong followers and a fastness in the hills where cattle could be held in relative safety. People put little faith in stone and lime for defence but used hill and forest to advantage. It made for rough living but it honed hard people who could survive; the object was to survive. Robbery was more profitable than industry.

Even in the worst of the reiving times, the Border burghs could look after themselves. Burgh Court records of the sixteenth century show that burgh law was obeyed and trade continued. Burghs had enough manpower to defy casual raiding bands but vacated the premises when an English army appeared. When the army left, business was resumed as usual.

Both Edinburgh and London, as the central authorities, ostensibly tried to bring the Borders 'into the kingis lawis'. Rules were made for the governance of the Borders and Wardens were appointed by both sides for each of the three Marches. The Warden was supposed to keep the peace but as he was often from a Border family, the appointee used his office to the betterment of his own pocket or to pay off old feuds and debts. There were notable exceptions but largely the Warden was the most successful rogue in the March, though now with a semblance of legality.

Edinburgh and London made constant angry protests to each other about crossborder reiving. These were largely the 'keep your Borderers in order or else you will be sorry' variety. In fact, both were glad to exploit the Borderers as a convenient and willing source of superb fighting men. In time of war, they were the first shock troops in either defence or attack; in time of peace, the Borders provided a buffer state which no invader could cross unnoticed.

Despite almost continual warfare, the Borderers from both sides maintained a healthy respect for each other, almost a liking formed by shared hardship. This Mafia-like bonding was to make for some peculiar alliances during the three hundred year 'riding times'.

AFTER INDEPENDENCE

We now return from the generalities of reiving to the particulars of Border history after the War of Independence. When Robert the Bruce became a de facto monarch, he followed the sound policy of rewarding his followers with land and honours. Sir James Douglas who had captured Roxburgh Castle in 1312, was given the forests of Selkirk, Ettrick and Traquair in a charter of free barony dated 1321/2; this, together with other lands throughout the Borders being given to Sir Archibald Douglas, Sir Thomas Randolph and Robert the Stewart made a block of Bruce supporters on the Border. It proved a sound strategy, for Sir James was called on to defend Teviotdale from an English invasion of 10,000 men in 1326. This force he defeated and turned back at Linthaughlee near Jedburgh.

At the Treaty of Edinburgh in 1328 'perpetual peace' was made between the two countries and Robert was acknowledged as King of Scots. The perpetual peace was short-lived. Robert the Bruce died on the 7th of June 1329. It had always been his intention to go on a crusade and by his wishes, Sir James Douglas set sail from Berwick with Bruce's heart in a silver casket bound for the Holy Land to fight the infidels. Douglas never made it because he stopped to fight the infidels more conveniently in Spain where he perished in battle.

Sir Thomas Randolph, the last of the great captains, took over the government of the realm until Bruce's son, David II was of age. However, Randolph died three years later, probably by poison and two years after that, Edward III of England disavowed the Treaty of Edinburgh on the grounds that he was under age when he signed it and that it was an illegal government which made him do so. It was back to square one as the protagonists lined up to renew the conflict with, as usual, the Borders in the middle.

Edward III of England had the martial ability and vigour of his grandfather Edward I. Using Edward Balliol the son of John Balliol and the nobles dispossessed of their Scottish lands by Robert I, he tried to destabilise Scotland. In 1332 a campaign by the dispossessed succeeded in having Edward Balliol crowned at Scone and in December, he renewed his allegiance to Edward of England at Roxburgh. However, Balliol and supporters were driven from Scotland a few days later. Edward of England invaded Scotland with a large army the following year, officially on behalf of Balliol. He besieged Berwick and executed two hostages per day within sight of its walls. A Scots army moved to relieve the siege but suffered a disastrous defeat at Halidon Hill just outside Berwick, proving yet again that a small Scots army could not defeat a large English one in set battle. So great was the slaughter that English opinion was that the Scots wars were finally over; Scotland was completely conquered. Balliol was installed as a puppet king and Edward embarked on a war of attrition to stamp out any faint sparks of resistance which might exist. The Lothians and Borders were comprehensively looted with anything of value taken away and the rest burned or otherwise destroyed. The victors wished to create a desert rather than a colony.

Edward Balliol had to pay a price for English aid and in 1334, ceded the seven southern counties of Scotland into English hands. The area was administered from Berwick with sheriffs there and at Roxburgh, Dumfries and Edinburgh. Their exchequer accounts show several other English garrisons in the Borders in or near the Forests of Jedburgh, Selkirk and Ettrick.

It is doubtful if the English garrisons controlled much of the area other than the land immediately adjacent to the garrisons. Some burghs were compelled to pay taxes but landowners were either unwilling or unable to pay; the burnt-earth policy was rebounding on the perpetrators. It cost five times more to maintain the garrisons than was being collected in revenue. The Borders may have been an occupied territory but the population was restive.

The spirit of Scotland still lived when, appropriately on St. Andrew's Day 1335, Andrew Murray son of Wallace's companion and himself Guardian of Scotland for David II, defeated a Balliol supporter near Ballater. A massive English force was assembled in 1335 and campaigned in Scotland over the next three years. However a war with France turned Edward's attentions to the Continent. By 1342, the English held only Berwick and Lochmaben. David II returned from France where he had been sent for safety and started launching large scale raids into England. On the fourth, the Scots were defeated at the Battle of Neville's Cross in 1346.; David was wounded and captured along with a number of his leading nobles. Again, much of the Borders was overrun and burnt by an English army which re-garrisoned the strongholds.

This time, Edward played it differently, offering security of life and property to any who would swear fealty to him. Many from all parts of the Borders did, especially those like the Lovels who regained the barony of Hawick and Branxholme by doing so. Border merchants were given safe conducts through England and all was seemingly well on the border. Edward did not find much support and decided to cut his losses and settled for a ransom for David in agreeing to the Treaty of Berwick in 1357.

THE BLACK DEATH

With starvation and deprivation widespread in the Borders counties, it is no wonder that the Black Death swept through the land in 1349/50. Here it was called 'the foul death of England' or 'the English Pestilence'. In England, nearly a third of the population had died although this death rate may not have been so severe in the Borders. Here the population was more scattered and thus less prone to becoming infected; but labour became scarcer, rents fell and wool production dropped. For those left there was 'an abundance of provisions in the kingdom'.

Further outbreaks of the plague were in 1361/2, 1379, 1392, 1401/3, 1430, 1439 and 1499. War and plague had kept the population of the Borders fairly stable for a century and a half.

MEANWHILE

From the death of Edward III in 1377, the next ten years were spent by the Scots in recovering most of the land of the Borders. Despite the peace treaty of 1383, the English had raided as far as Edinburgh leaving the eastern Borders a mass of smoking ruins. In 1384, Earl Douglas retrieved his lands of Teviotdale and went on to capture Wark and parts of Northumberland. In 1385, Richard II of England led 14,000 men into the Lothians, defacing the Abbeys of Melrose and Dryburgh, burning Edinburgh and generally creating havoc. They were forced to retreat since they could not find enough provisions for man and horse. Three years later, Earl Douglas, decided to mount a raid into the north of England by way of returning the compliment. This was not a good move on his part as he was slain at the Battle of Otterburn.

In 1402, the Scots launched another full-scale raid into England but were brought into battle at Homildon Hill with the usual results – the 'flower of chivalry of the realm' captured or killed. The King of England, now Henry IV, granted the Earl of Northumberland and his son Henry Percy all the Douglas lands in Scotland which included the whole of Teviotdale, Selkirk and Ettrick Forest. The Earl of Douglas had lost an eye, received five wounds and been captured at Homildon but received such kindness during captivity that he joined the Percies in an English rebellion against Henry. The Border Mafia was working well! However, Douglas was captured again at the Battle of Shrewsbury, which the Percies lost, and remained in English captivity until 1407.

In 1408 Sir William Douglas of Drumlanrig stormed the castle of Jedburgh, which had been in English hands for nearly a hundred years. It was decided to raze it to the ground in order to deny any future English occupation. The walls were so thick and the masonry so strong that the cost of levelling it would be two pence per household throughout the land. The Regent Albany decided to pay it from the royal treasury rather than become more unpopular. The Regent had also been stalling on getting the boy king, James I, back from English captivity.

In 1411, the same Sir William Douglas raided and burned the town of Roxburgh which was in English hands. In retaliation, Sir Robert Umfraville, who had just been appointed Keeper of Roxburgh Castle, seized and destroyed Jedburgh on a fair day. In 1418, Albany raised an army and besieged Berwick and Roxburgh but fled on hearing that a larger English one was approaching. The following year, Umfraville invaded the

Borders from the east, taking and burning Hawick, Selkirk, Jedburgh, Lauder and anything which got in his way.

THE FALL OF THE BLACK DOUGLASES

When Archibald the Grim died in 1400, his Black Douglas branch of the family and its retainers held most of the Borders. Their lands included the Forests of Ettrick and Selkirk, Sprouston and Browndean, Eskdale, Lauderdale and much of Teviotdale. With so much feudal land at their disposal, other families rose in importance under the Douglas banner; the Homes spread over the Merse, the Hoppringles in Lauderdale, while Kerrs and Scott had holdings in Teviotdale. When Archibald the fourth Earl was killed at the Battle of Verneuill in France, there were many Borderers under his banner; among those who fell was Robert Hoppringle of Galashiels and Smailholm.

The return of James I from captivity in 1424 was the beginning of a struggle with the Douglas faction. James wanted to decrease the power of the nobles and increase that of the crown, an ambition which led to his assassination in 1437. James II eventually had the Earl of Douglas attainted in 1455. Many of the Borders families took the hint and switched allegiance from Douglas to the King. The King made an expedition to Ettrick Forest, captured and destroyed a tower at Craig Douglas and recovered all Douglas lands in the Forest. The names of Scott, Kerr, Murray, Turnbull and Pringle appear in the records with greater frequency from this date. Walter Scott of Buccleuch obtained many of the Forest steads in tack with 'certain men of Teviotdale newly brought into the king's service'.

Douglas was not beaten yet for he allied himself with the Percies and with the encouragement of the English monarch, made several strong forays into the Scottish Borders. They were repulsed by a force led by the Earl of Angus, the Red Douglas branch who benefited by receiving much of the Black Douglas land.

At this time, James passed laws for a wapinshaw to be held annually in each parish and butts to be erected near the church for practising archery. Each man had to shoot six shots every Sunday or be fined two pence which was given to the attenders for drink money. Games of football and golf were strictly forbidden. The Border lords were enjoined to keep their towers in good repair and well provisioned. They had a joint commitment to keep a force of two hundred archers and two hundred spearmen on the east and middle marches and one hundred of each on the west march.

In the middle of the fifteenth century, the area around Galashiels seems to have been the artillery arsenal of Scotland. The placename 'Gun Knowe' is likely to date from this time. Exchequer Rolls give proof that guns were either cast or repaired near the mouth of the Gala Water. The abundance of puddle clay and charcoal from the forest would strengthen the argument for casting.

James II took the offensive in trying to drive the English from his kingdom. In 1460 while trying to batter Roxburgh Castle into submission and 'haveng sik plesure in dischargeng gret gunis', James was mortally wounded when one of them split on firing. His Queen rushed to Roxburgh with the nine year old James III. Roxburgh was captured and knocked down while James III was being crowned in Kelso Abbey. Berwick was ceded to the Scots in 1461; the Borders looked secure after nearly two centuries of warfare.

In 1482 Alexander Duke of Albany, who was the brother of James III, returned from exile as a vassal of Edward III of England with a claim as Alexander IV King of Scots. This meant an invasion of southern Scotland and the retaking of Berwick and other strongholds. Meanwhile, James had been seized at Lauder by a conspiracy of his three half uncles and was held a prisoner in Edinburgh Castle. The English party besieged it but finally gave up, while inside the castle, the conspirators fell out over the division of the kingdom. James continued to reign until he was displaced by his son and heir in 1488 after the Battle of Sauchieburn. James III was murdered in rather strange circumstances after the battle.

James IV was a public relations king. He cultivated the warrior king image and liked to be thought of as a King Arthur. He was a hands-on king, a builder both of ships and castles. He was a committed European and wished to lead a European Crusade against the infidel. James supported the pretender Perkin Warbeck and made a swift raid into England on his behalf in 1496. Henry VII was having trouble at home and finally appeased the belligerent James by giving his daughter Margaret in marriage in 1503. At Galashiels, the young Queen was given the Forest of Ettrick and the castle of Newark as dowerlands.

The court of Scotland was a place of culture in the early sixteenth century. The King spoke six languages, fought tournaments, fostered poets and architects, built great ships and castles and encouraged others to do the same. He had gathered his knights into a medieval version of the Round Table. It all fell to pieces when the Queen of France appealed to James as a perfect knight, to advance into England 'one yard for her sake'. France was being pressed by the English and a threat on the Scottish border would remove some of the pressure. James agreed to this plea to his chivalry, gathered the largest Scots army ever to enter England and marched south in a rather holiday spirit, his young knights trying to impress each other.

FLODDEN

The battle of Flodden has been fought so often that it is unnecessary to do so here. There is a romantic version so well written by Sir Walter Scott in Marmion. The brave defiant little nation against a big strong one, the King and his nobles slaughtered almost to a man with the King falling:

> 'And well in death with his trusty brand
> Firm clenched within his manly hand
> Beseemed the monarch slain.'

Great romantic stuff! Total rubbish of course! James had thrown away every advantage. For once the Scots had superior numbers, more and better guns and the high ground. James had ignored the first rule of generalship – if you have to fight a battle, you fight to win. He had refused the Scots' gunners permission to fire down on the English and split their forces. When the English guns got to the bottom of the hill they could fire directly into the Scots ranks but the Scots' guns could not be depressed enough to fire downwards. The Borderers on the left wing under Lords Home and Huntly, did not see much point of this and charged without orders, driving the English right from the field. The English commander won the battle by opposing the advancing Scots Borderers with a force of English Borderers. They stood and looked at each other for the rest of the day. There was a story that they combined forces to strip the dead of anything useful; it might even be true. The Borders Mafia was working again!

James saw the Borderers winning a fight that he wanted to win himself so he set off down the hill with his knights in the middle of the Scots centre. The foot men were armed with fifteen foot pikes and the combination of these and the slippery slope tumbled them down as an easy prey for the English billmen at the foot of the hill. James and his nobles were clad in armour and less vulnerable, so they managed to fight their way into the middle of the English centre where they were surrounded and shot full of arrows like fish in a barrel. However, when darkness fell, both armies withdrew from the field not knowing the result.

Dawn the next morning and a party of Borderers probably under Lord Home, appeared on the brow of the hill, ready to resume the debate. They had been very successful the previous day. The English commander drove them off with his guns and quickly sent dispatches to London claiming victory as he still held the field. With the King and most of the nobility dead, the Scots command fell to Lord Home who was much better fitted for the task than the chivalrous James. As a Borderer, he knew the ground and had a lot of experience in Border warfare. His primary task was to defend the kingdom. Time was not on his side as the Scots volunteer army had served twenty six of their required forty days military service. So he withdrew from the field of battle to guard the fords and hill roads into

Scotland. This left the English in possession of the field and claiming total victory. Less often quoted is the contemporary English historian Halle who relates how the Scots carried off sixty prisoners and that many Englishmen had lost their horses and the stuff in their tents; the thieves of Tynedale and Teviotdale got the blame.

With Scotland supposedly devastated and its total manpower slain, it would be expected that the English commander would press home the victory and invade Scotland. He refused to do this owing to the lateness of the season and probably the lack of beer. However, Home had no such qualms and eleven days after the battle, the Bishop of Durham was writing to Wolsey 'fearing' that they would have to assent to the truce proposed by Lord Home. Two months later, Lord Dacre was reluctantly raiding into Scotland with four thousand horsemen and four hundred foot, when he was defeated at the battle of Sclatterford in Roxburghshire. He immediately wrote to his king saying that he would do no further raiding for fear that the Scots destroy the Middle March in his absence.

Could we consider Flodden a drawn battle rather than a great defeat? Only the nobility were decimated; for the remainder of the Borderers, life went on very much as usual.

Post Flodden

For nearly ten years after Flodden, as uneasy truce was maintained on the border; but there were some incidents. In 1522, Lord Dacre invaded, burning part of Kelso and some towers but was driven back by the Borderers. Surrey came back the next year with ten thousand men and destroyed most of the Merse and Teviotdale. The Scots hit back by raids into England. Surrey came back with six thousand men to take and burn Jedburgh. Meanwhile a French army had landed but did not take kindly to the Scots way of fighting. It was reckoned that they did more damage to Scotland than all the English forces.

The Earl of Angus who had married the Queen Mother less than a year after Flodden, had possession of young James V. James wished to be free from this constraint and appealed to Scott of Buccleuch to rescue him. Angus and the King with a force of Homes and Kers were returning to Edinburgh when Buccleuch with a thousand horsemen attempted a rescue near Darnick. It failed, with the loss of a hundred of Buccleuch's followers. Ker of Cessford was in pursuit of the fleeing band when he was killed with a single spear thrust from an Elliot in Buccleuch's company. This was the start of the Kerr/Scott feud which lasted for generations.

In 1528, James gained his freedom and was particularly anxious that peace reign in the Borders. This was not an easy option. Even Lord Dacre, not noted for his gentle manners, was complaining about the Elliots,

Nixons, Crosiers and Armstrongs who were ambushing and killing his servants while on their lawful occupations like retrieving cattle which had already been stolen. First, James descended on the Borders with 8000 men, hanging Johnie Armstrong at Caerlanrig in 1530 and in 1535 ordered that each man in the Borders with a hundred pounds worth of land was to build a barmkin for safety of humans and stock 'in troublous tyme'. The many Borders towers which dot the countryside either standing or in ruins were the result of this Act. They were strong enough to deter the casual raider but too weak to resist a siege.

James was a supporter of the Border burghs during his lifetime, notably Selkirk, but had managed to offend most of the nobility. He offended Henry VIII by not attending a conference at York and had to gather an army to repel the ensuing invasion. The Battle of Solway Moss was a total disaster with about 14,000 Scots being defeated by a much smaller English force. James died soon afterwards, of a broken heart it was said, leaving a week old daughter as the heir to the throne.

THE ROUGH WOOING 1544–50

In the first few years of Mary's reign, Scotland was divided even more than usual; not only were there pro-English and pro-French factions but also Catholic and Protestant division. Henry VIII was determined to marry Mary to his son Edward and thus unite the monarchies and religions. When this failed, he tried to batter Scotland into submission until the marriage was agreed. The Rough Wooing lasted seven years with the Border counties taking the brunt of the hostilities.

There was no attempt at acquisition of lands but rather a total devastation of southern Scotland. Large English armies, supported by a fleet, went through the Borders, garrisoning strongholds at Roxburgh, Hume, Eyemouth, Ayton, Lauder and Ferniehurst and demolishing others. The Battle of Pinkie in 1547 saw thousands of Scots killed or taken prisoners and Haddington becoming the military headquarters of the English forces.

The Scots were fighting back mainly by sniping at the edges of the English military and they did have some successes. Buccleuch and Angus won the Battle of Ancrum Moor in 1545. English policy defeated itself when Mary was taken to France for safety in 1548 and a treaty of marriage was agreed between her and the young Dauphin. This agreement was in return for French aid against the English. Now the English and French fought on Scots soil rather than their own. The English and French poured money and troops into Southern Scotland with both trying to buy support and loyalty. Borderers accepted money from both and fought for both, but mainly for themselves. The many documents which have survived from this time show that Borderers had very pronounced ideas of self-preservation. Hostilities were concluded with an Anglo-French peace treaty in 1550 and an Anglo-Scots one in 1551.

THE REFORMATION

Peace was ephemeral with the obvious danger of a Catholic/Protestant war. When Mary Queen of Scots arrived back in Leith in 1561 as a young widow, there was, she discovered, an increasingly Protestant population. The Catholic Queen was a patron of the Arts, poetry, music and literature and used to the flowery extravagances of the French Court. This did not please the dour Protestants, especially John Knox, who denounced her as a dangerous Jezebel.

In 1560, Protestantism was declared the official religion of Scotland. By this time many of the Border nobles had become Protestants. At the Reformation, the rich abbey lands were split up and a surprising amount went to local Protestant families. Religion pays if the right one is picked.

In the Borders, the priority was law and order; how to suppress the Liddesdale and Annandale reivers. All landed man were supposed to support the Wardens of the Marches in this praiseworthy task. It seldom worked out that way as the Court Records show. Certainly numbers of Border bandits were quietened by hanging, drowning or being taken to Edinburgh but raids, murders and family feuds continued unabated. To take but one example – John Elliot of Copshaw together with 300 Elliots and Armstrongs raided Torwoodlee near Galashiels in 1568, sacking it and killing George Pringle the laird. Justice caught up with the said John thirty nine years later when he was denounced a rebel. Border justice did not grind small; it did grind slowly, but it ground eventually.

JAMES VI

Mary Queen of Scots was deposed in 1567 and her infant son was crowned five days later. With an unmarried Elizabeth in England, the infant was the heir to both thrones.

The 1570s was a time of rising trade in Europe. Scotland was being effectively ruled by the Earl of Morton who was committed to Protestantism and an English coalition. Both countries were seeking peace and this costly exercise was brought to fruition when the Treaty of Berwick was signed in 1586. The peace may have been uneasy but it did bring some stability between the two countries.

In the third country, the Borders, the tempo of life was hotting up – or maybe it just seems to be because more documentary proof survives. Court records and reports show that the Borders were in turmoil. Border reivers still rode on raids as far apart as three miles from Edinburgh to near York.

In 1525, the Bishop of Glasgow had pronounced a 1500 word 'monition of cursing' on the Scots reivers while the Bishop of Durham did the same for the Tynedale ones with equally little effect; so a mere peace treaty was not going to disturb their way of life. Most lived their lives 'at the horn' ie outlawed. James attempted to curb their worst excesses by trying to get the Border lairds to band together to either capture and hang them or at least to stand surety for their good behaviour. This did not work very well since Borderers tended to look for reasons to quarrel. Sir Walter Scott of Buccleuch, the Keeper of Liddesdale in 1594, had to go back a long way to find a legitimate cause of enmity against the men of Tynedale; they had captured his grandfather, taken his sword and not returned it. His grandfather had died in 1552! This was the same Buccleuch who with eighty Scotts, Elliots, Armstrongs, Bells and a few English Charltons, rescued Kinmont Willie from Carlisle Castle in 1596.

When James VI rode over the bridge at Berwick to become James I of England in 1603, it was probably with relief that he had crossed the border without being killed or captured.

EIGHT

UNION OF CROWNS TO UNION OF PARLIAMENTS: 1603–1707

When James VI entered Berwick to become James I as well, he was presented with £2000 by the English authorities and a sermon by the Bishop of Durham. Well sustained, he pressed on to London. He was now King of Great Britain and did not wish a wild bunch of thugs disrupting the middle part of his kingdom which was henceforth to be called The Middle Shires. The peaceful solution was that the Borderers either behaved or they went into exile or the gallows. To keep the peace, a number of 'reformed' reivers were given the task of hunting down and hanging wrongdoers; mass hangings became the order of the day. There was a fine war going on in the Low Countries and Buccleuch solved a tiny part of the problem by taking 2000 Borderers to fight there.

The more recalcitrant sinners, the Grahams, Elliots and Armstrongs were transported to Ulster where they caused mayhem by dispossessing the native Irish. Some went or were transported to the Americas where any ill-doing was less noticeable. This sustained effort gradually took effect as there were only thirty seven executions in 1637.

When James took the road south, he likened himself to 'a poor man wandering forty years in the wilderness ... now arrived at the land of promise'. He had a great time. The English nobility were less impressed; they saw a short, untidy fellow who spoke broad Scots and whose table manners were rough. They put about rumours that handsome young men were his esteemed companions, often the same ones favoured by his predecessor.

James was an intelligent and educated man who took to the English conception of the Divine Right of Kings like a duck to water. He favoured Espiscopacy rather than Puritanism and encouraged its introduction into Scotland. In 1607, James boasted that he ruled Scotland with the pen while others could not do it with the sword. The Statutes of Iona of 1609 forced Highland chiefs to have their sons educated to 'speak, read and write in English'.

In the early 1620s there were severe harvest failures with one in six people dying in some parts of Scotland. James died in 1625 and Charles I became King of Great Britain and within weeks issued a Revocation which decreed that all grants of land from Crown or Church were annulled. This was not popular. Nor was the new Prayer Book which he foisted on Scotland in 1637. Nor were the Bishops. A National Covenant was drawn up and signed by nobles, ministers, lawyers and burgesses and a riot was carefully planned in Edinburgh in 1637. There were also two anti-Bishop Wars in 1639 and 1640/1.

When the English Civil War broke out in August, 1642, both King and Parliament appealed to the Scots for aid. Eventually a Scots army of 20,000 men crossed the border and helped to defeat the Royalists at Marston Moor in 1644. Under the Lords Buccleuch, Lothian and Cranston, many Borderers besieged and took Newcastle which was being held by Royalist forces.

In Scotland things were not going so well. The Marquis of Montrose had raised a Highland/Irish force and within a year had won a string of battles against the Covenanting armies. He came through the Borders hoping to raise disciplined troops to stiffen his Highland host. He expected support from the Lords Traquair, Home and Roxburgh; However Home and Roxburgh had contrived to get 'captured' by the Covenanters and Traquair came to wish good luck but returned home leaving his son Lord Linton with a few horsemen to serve in the King's army.

Montrose's luck ran out at Philiphaugh on the 13th September, 1645; he had to flee while his army and followers were slaughtered, many after they had surrendered. This was the beginning of the end of Royalist hopes. The victorious General Leslie was awarded 50,000 merks for his service to the Covenanting cause at Philiphaugh; he was to lead the Scots against Cromwell at the Battle of Dunbar and be taken prisoner while fighting for Charles II at Worcester.

The light harvest in 1644/5, heavy taxation and wandering hostile groups returned the Borders to the reiving times. Plague swept through the land and severe penalties were imposed on those who left the parish or employed strangers during harvest time. Part of Kelso was burned when a fire which had been set to cleanse a house of plague got out of control. After the Battle of Dunbar in 1650, Cromwell had spread part of his army over the south of Scotland; each town and village had Cromwellian troopers quartered upon it and were expected to supply their food and shelter. By their demands, the troopers reduced many Borderers to great poverty.

For the descendants of reivers it was like a return to the old days and they took the time-honoured remedies. Parties of sixty or eighty men would ride out to drive off cattle and sheep. Not even the troopers were safe and their horses were stolen on several occasions. When the Burgh of Jedburgh protested their innocence of certain outrages committed, a court-martial of English officers held the burgh responsible and fined them £500. They refused to pay, so the Provost, bailies and councillors were arrested and flung into jail. Jedburgh paid – but not willingly!

THE COMMONWEALTH

The combined effects of war and plague was the price paid by the Scots for the Covenanting revolution. The English campaign led by General Monck had moved relentlessly forward with towns surrendering or being taken by force; Dundee had been stormed and 1000 inhabitants killed in the twenty fours hours of pillage which followed. So when the Border representatives were summoned to negotiate for 'doing away with kingship in Scotland and for uniting that country into one Commonwealth with England', it is no surprise that they voted in favour.

Like English conquerors before him, Monck was soon to learn that Scotland was difficult to hold and disastrously expensive to run with an annual deficit of £130,000 between taxes raised and money expended. It is no wonder that when he marched south in the winter of 1659/60, he had pleas from the burghs for a reduction in taxes. That he stopped in Coldstream to raise the Guards and was to be instrumental in restoring the monarchy is a footnote to Border history. Generals turn their coats as easily as reivers but usually do better out of it !

RESTORATION TO REVOLUTION

With the Restoration in 1660, it was the Royalists turn for supremacy. Episcopacy was in; Presbyterianism out. Throughout the Borders there are recorded instances of petty crimes like the Selkirk man who for having a baby christened by a Presbyterian minister, was stripped of all his goods and thrown into prison.

In 1662, bishops were restored to the Scottish Kirk and an Act of Indemnity and Pardon was passed. This meant that many Borderers had to pay a lot of money or be deprived of lands and goods. From the Restoration until the Revolution of 1688, religious intolerance was to keep the Borders in misery. Conventicles, the open air preaching meetings, were suppressed with violence; of those taking part in conventicles some were executed, some exiled, some fined.

It was to be those exiled or who had fled to Holland to escape persecution, who were instrumental in persuading William of Orange to invade Britain as a saviour. In the first year of William and Mary's reign, all Royal burghs were ordered to elect new magistrates and councils 'by the poll' with the object of weeding out Jacobite sympathisers.

THE DARIEN SCHEME

Scotland had always suffered from a perennial problem – lack of money. The English Navigation Acts of 1660 and 1663 excluded Scotland from the rich trading areas of Asia, Africa and America. So a trading company was formed in 1695 in opposition to the East India Company and the Africa

Company which were English companies. Originally it was intended to be a joint Scots/English company but English merchants brought pressure on Parliament and the King which ruled out any English capital being invested. Scotland would go it alone.

£400,000 Sterling was raised, more than half the money in the country. The Borderers subscribed greatly, Harden £2000, Torwoodlee £1300, Thirlstane £1000, the burgh of Selkirk £500 and so on. The scheme was a total failure through English hostility, Spanish attacks, Scots incompetence and inability to agree. Such was the feeling that no Englishman was safe on the streets of Edinburgh.

UNION OF PARLIAMENTS

In the 1690s, there had been seven bad harvests in a row. The Darien scheme had ruined many. Trade was poor. There were those in Scotland who wished complete Union with England to have access to English markets; and those in England who wished to keep the Scots out for those same reasons. Queen Anne was unlikely to produce an heir to the throne; who would succeed her?

Negotiations on the Articles of Union had been long debated with fire, honour and bribery by the pro-Unionists and the anti-Unionists. Eventually it was a spectacular switch by the Duke of Hamilton which made the Treaty of Union a reality on 16th January, 1707.

NINE

MODERN TIMES: 18TH–20TH CENTURIES

Between the 1790s and the 1830s, the face of the Borders and the lives of the people changed more rapidly than perhaps in any previous period. Access to new ideas and new markets had been triggered by the Union with England in 1707; speed of change accelerated towards the end of the century and continued throughout the 18th and 19th centuries with the coming of steam, engineering, the railways and roads. In the 20th century, the internal combustion engine and electricity have had a profound effect, particularly since World War Two, and more recent technological innovation – the microchip revolution – has led to even greater change in Borders life since the 1970s.

AGRICULTURE

In 1695, the Scots Parliament called for the redivision of runrig land to encourage enclosure and improvement, and the division of commons and wastes. General Roy's Military Survey (1747–55) shows, however that by mid-century there was a long way to go. Relatively few Borders' landowners had begun the process, and enclosure was restricted mainly to the policies and lands immediately adjacent to their houses. Most of Peeblesshire was unaffected, for instance, other than for parts of the Stobo estate.

Change quickened from around 1760 (Hassendean was divided in 1761–63; Eyemouth in 1764), and in 1761 James Dickson acquired the Ednam estate near Kelso. He drained the lands and rebuilt the village; he established a weaving mill, bleachfield and brewery, and commissioned the building of Ednam House and The Cross Keys in Kelso. Even though his plans for a canal from Kelso to the sea never materialised, he typified the new-found spirit of improvement and enterprise.

By the early 1790s, enclosure of the more kindly low-lying lands of the Merse and Teviotdale, as of Lothian, was almost complete and by the 1830s such as Smailholm and Kelso entirely so. Progress was slower, however, in the upland parishes of Roxburghshire, as more generally in Selkirkshire and Peeblesshire. Traditional methods continued longer in many places, and on the higher ground sheep were still left to fend for themselves summer and winter. Division of the commons also took longer. In Berwickshire 570 ha of Duns Common had only just been divided by 1794, whilst two large areas were still unenclosed – Chirnside Common and some 570 ha at Lauder (where there was still much to do in the 1830s).

Improvement took several forms. Once redivision was completed, longer leases were offered to progressive tenants. There followed improved drainage, levelling of the old rigs, new and improved seed and stock, crop rotations and use of fertilisers, improved implements and forms of traction, new roads, new farmhouses and steadings. The new farms were large – 160–240 ha arable in the Merse., 240–560 ha in the uplands (part arable, part permanent pasture), 400–1200 ha for hill farms. Where stone was scarce, fields of maybe 20 or even 25 ha on lighter drier soils, 6 ha on the heaviest clays, were enclosed mainly with quick-growing hawthorn, perhaps in association with ditches. Elsewhere the ubiquitous dry-stane dyke criss-crossed infield and high hills to create a landscape that would have been unrecognisable in the 1700s, but which has survived largely unchanged in modern times.

First recorded as a field crop in 1740 for Chirnside (and 1746 for the Lothians), potatoes had become general by the 1780s (c. 1765 around Edinburgh). By 1770, field turnips were widely cultivated in Roxburghshire and East Lothian, and by 1790 in Peeblesshire and Selkirkshire when Dawson of Frogden was producing some 40 ha. They were particularly valued as a pasture crop, planted in association with enclosed and regulated grazings for sheep and cattle – which led to mixed farming with a ewe stock in predominantly grain-growing areas, as well as to improved upland farming. Cheviot and Blackface, Galloway and Blue Black were the major livestock breeds – whether bred pure or cross-bred.

Along with new strains of sown grasses and clovers, fertilisers were critical for the continued health of land and crops, and in addition to traditional farmyard manure (and seaweed by the coast), clay and shell marl – or better still lime – helped improve sour, mossy land. Where found close to coalfields, as in Lothian, lime would be burnt locally in kilns; for the Merse, processed lime was imported by sea, through Eyemouth, from Northumberland – though imported coal allowed limestone to be burnt locally at Carham.

Creeping mechanisation, however, was the key to subsequent development. Rare remains of 18th century windmill stumps survive in Gordon and Eckford parishes; farm chimneys associated with mid-late 19th century steam engines survive more widely on the larger arable farms. The development of steam traction, moreover, led not only to steam ploughing but to the travelling mill, subsequently adapted to tractor power, which survived well into the mid 20th century in many parts of the Borders. It was the internal combustion engine that triggered more revolutionary change, however. On large lowland farms, tractors became more common after World War I; after World War Two they came into their own, and in the 1950s and 1960s the working Clydesdale disappeared quickly from the farms. In Peeblesshire, for instance:

1800	1562 horses
1864	1113 horses
1921	1274 horses
1964	fewer than 400 (including riding horses)

This led to a reduction in fodder crops (particularly oats) and in manpower. Multi-furrow reversible ploughs, combine harvesters and the need for noise-reducing ear muffs have made agriculture a much more isolated and lonely job than formerly!

Figure 10

The Borders and Lothians: Land Quality

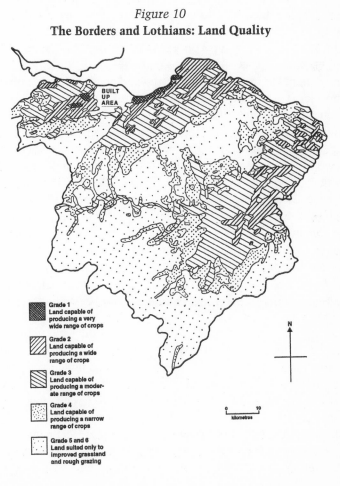

Grade 1
Land capable of producing a very wide range of crops

Grade 2
Land capable of producing a wide range of crops

Grade 3
Land capable of producing a moderate range of crops

Grade 4
Land capable of producing a narrow range of crops

Grade 5 and 6
Land suited only to improved grassland and rough grazing

In recent decades new varieties of grain have been developed to increase yields and to suit the combine, whilst the balance between grain, vegetables and stock-raising on low ground farms (and stock-raising and forestry on upland farms) has varied according to wartime requirements and the later targeting of UK government and European grants. Cattle and suckler cows have replaced breeding ewes on the low ground, often using such continental breeds as Charollais and Simmental; winter barley has been introduced with varying success to complement spring-grown barley; potatoes and turnips continue to be grown in some quantity; and from 1969 there have been attempts to diversify into vegetable and fruit production – particularly in Berwickshire and Roxburghshire (as in East Lothian and Northumberland). ELBA Growers Ltd was founded in 1971 (with a deep-freeze factory at Eyemouth, later taken over by the Salvesen Group) to grow and process peas, sprouts, cauliflowers, cabbage, strawberries and raspberries. Lucerne, field beans and chickory have been tried; bright yellow fields of oil seed rape have spread rapidly since 1967, particularly since the closure of Scotland's only sugar-beet factory at Cupar in Fife and more recently to replace other crops reckoned to be 'in surplus'.

Such attempts to intensify production and profits have not been without their problems – carryover of disease with winter barley or through processed animal feedstuffs; excessive levels of nitrates in drinking water; toxic residues clinging to crops. Furthermore, chemically-engineered production has weakened the reliance on well-tried rotations, resulting in a higher incidence of wrack (couch grass), wild oats and cereal root worm following 4, 5 or 6 successive cereal crops. The application of yet more chemicals to lessen the problem has further degraded the soil and helped fuel public concern over their effect on the reproductive and immune systems of humans as well as of other plants and wildlife.

Elsewhere, to accommodate larger machinery and to intensify cropping returns, hedges and dykes have been grubbed up to make larger fields (though less so than in many parts of southern and eastern England), ponds have been filled in, bits of policy woodland and shelter belts have been allowed to decay and die. Heavier machines, moreover, have impacted the soil and damaged long-established field drains, whilst intensive production has created surpluses of such proportions in European terms that quotas have been introduced for livestock and milk, and under 'set-aside' farmers are now paid not to farm substantial parts of their farms – a particularly negative policy which would have been better targeted at encouraging less intensive environmentally-friendly practices. In an attempt to come to terms with these varying pressures, over the ten years to 1993 land under oil seed rape showed a 428.2% increase in the Borders, with barley down 45.9%. Agricultural holdings, meantime, fell by 15.3% and agricultural labour by 30.2%.

WOODLAND AND FORESTRY

Whilst Roy's Military Survey shows the mid 18th century Borders to be rather bare, woodlands were recognised increasingly as a valuable asset. As short leases discouraged planting by improving tenants, however, it was left mainly to landowners to take the initiative. In south-east Scotland, hardwoods such as elm, alder, oak and birch were particularly popular, supplemented by Scots pine, beech, European (later Japanese) larch, limes and planes. Woodlands adorned the new mansions and policies, but they could also provide shelter for sheep and growing crops, cover for game and timber for buildings, fuel and fencing. Furthermore, they were a use for land otherwise seen as waste.

Long-established plantings were found on such estates as Ancrum, Dunglass and Dawyck where Sir John Nasmyth had planted 145 ha by 1834. The plantings at Dawyck (nowadays a favoured arboretum) began at least as early as the mid 17th century, and included some of the first horse chestnuts, European larches and Lombardy poplars in Scotland. Plantation in the Borders did not gather pace, however, until the late 18th century; and with the exception of such as Cademuir and Traquair, had all but ceased in Peeblesshire by the late 19th/early 20th century – when felling exceeded planting as the current owners sought to harvest their predecessors' investment.

Considerable felling of timber during World War One led to a growing shortage and to the establishment of the Forestry Commission in 1919, when an initial 405 ha at Glentress (Peeblesshire) were divided into small-holdings at Eshiels, a tree nursery established and the hill land afforested. By 1964, this had increased to 770 ha of trees with 161 ha of grazing. Further state forests followed at various locations along the Tweed (Cardrona, Elibank and Traquair, Yair, Tweedhopefoot, Badlieu and Glenbreck); also at Craik and Eskdalemuir, Wauchope and Newcastleton. There was private estate planting around eg Eddleston, Neidpath, Bowhill and Mellerstain.

By 1976 some 14% of the Borders was planted; in the 1970s and 1980s, tax incentives for private investors tempted some farmers/owners to sell their land for forestry; and between 1983 and 1993, whilst agricultural woodlands increased by 45.1% to 12,272 ha, conifers accounted for over 58,000 ha out of a total of 65,000 ha of commercial forestry plantations.

Blanket afforestation with Sitka spruce and similar species is not without its critics. In part this relates to scale and management; in part to ecological damage; in part to social and cultural impact. Recent trends towards contract labour squads, moreover, whose contribution to the local community is minimal, have hastened rural depopulation; and possible privatisation of all or parts of the Forestry Commission has caused concern amongst timber processors who fear a breakdown in overall strategic planning and in assured, regular and substantial supplies.

Elsewhere there is a growing realisation that better forest design follows natural contours and land form and keeps well clear of water courses, lochs, archaeological and historical sites; that greater diversification of species is to be preferred, with native hardwoods fringing and masking denser coniferous plantations; that clearings be left and allowed to regenerate as scrub; that felling and replanting should be staggered to create all-age forests. In this way, the forests would become visually more attractive and more receptive to colonisation by a richer cross-section of wildlife, whilst fulfilling their commercial purpose.

There is also a realisation that entire farms do not need to be sold off for afforestation, and that Scandinavian and other models of locally-owned, locally-worked farm-forestry are environmentally and culturally far more sympathetic. Indeed, a return to the woodland objectives of the late 18th century Border improvers would not be inappropriate – attractively designed and smaller blocks of trees planted as, say, 10% or so of the less suitable grazings and providing shelter for stock rotated regularly over a clearly-defined pattern of divided grazings. Historically, Borders hill sheep stocks and lambing percentages have suffered from lack of shelter in cold and wet weather (witness the stone-built, circular and now largely ruinous stells that characterise upland valleys and hillsides). Livestock potential could be increased, therefore, from less grazing; and the timber itself, once established and well-managed, would provide a regular and reliable crop.

FISHERIES

Sea Fisheries

Until well into the 19th century, Eyemouth had the only 'harbour', although small open inshore boats were stationed at a number of other places – notably at Bilsdean (just over the Dunglass Burn), Old Cambus, Redheugh and Lumsdaine (west of St. Abbs Head) as well as at Cove, Northfield (St. Abbs), Coldingham Sands, Burnmouth and Ross (a little north of Berwick). At Redheugh Shore, for instance, renowned for its smuggling as well as for its white herring and salmon fishery, a slipway was cleared up the beach and large boulders removed from the seaward approach.

By the 1830s, however, the need for greater protection was apparent. Cove finally had its harbour in 1831 (Plate 9) – after abortive attempts in the 1750s and 1820s. It was built by Sir John Hall of Dunglass and could accommodate boats of up to 60 tons burden. St. Abbs (1833, and later provided with outer breakwaters) served the fisher families who had previously lived at Coldingham; Burnmouth was built in 1831–2, and enlarged in 1877–9. At Eyemouth, early piers had been constructed in

1750; John Smeaton built the first real harbour 1768–70; there were further improvements between 1770 and 1841, 1885–7 and periodically during the 20th century. Whilst Eyemouth began as a small port serving the Berwickshire hinterland, therefore, it came to specialise in fisheries so that today its economy is based primarily on fishing and fish processing (and tourism).

Until well into the 18th century lobsters, white (salted) and red (cured) herrings caught off the Berwickshire coast were sent by sea to London, whilst fresh fish were sold locally at such inland markets as Kelso and Duns, and sent by carrier to Musselburgh, thence in creels on women's backs to Edinburgh. A little, mainly creel fishing, for lobsters and crabs continues (often on a part-time basis) out of St. Abbs and Burnmouth, as also at Cove where the access road – partly tunnelled through the cliff – subsided in the late 1980s. Otherwise, fisheries between Dunbar and Berwick are now centred on Eyemouth. Even at the beginning of the 20th century, the dozen and more 18 m (60 ft) sailing boats based at Burnmouth would fish mainly out of Eyemouth, Berwick or North Shields (May-August), before following the herring to Great Yarmouth in September.

Fishing technology has changed out of all recognition these past 100 and more years. Around the turn of the century, sailing Zulus and Fifies, successors to the earlier open boats, pursued a small-line fishery with hand-baited lines of up to 1000 hooks. They also drift-netted for herring March – early September. Steam drifters replaced sail, followed by paraffin-engined smaller boats from the 1910s and diesel engines from the 1940s. Great lining was introduced in the 1930s–40s, with the steam drifters, to complement the herring industry, but after World War Two line fishing died out, boats increased in length and pair trawling developed – two boats working a bigger area together.

Technological inventiveness has provided the means to catch larger numbers of fish more intensively and less selectively, so that in the 1980s and 1990s herring and traditional white fish stocks have declined dramatically. Meantime, species quotas, mesh restrictions and closed fisheries have reduced the potential for fishermen to generate sufficient income to pay off huge loans on their hi-tech and environmentally unfriendly boats and equipment. Encouraged by Government grants to replace older equipment and to upgrade, they are frequently now caught in a spiral caused in large part by the failure of both UK government and the European Union to undertake long-term, high quality research and strategic fisheries planning, and to recognise the critical social and economic value of sustainable fisheries to small coastal communities in northern countries on the periphery of Europe.

Ancillary facilities complemented the fisheries. At Redheugh, the establishment of a coastguard station in the 1820s effectively put paid to smuggling; and a sail and oar lifeboat was first stationed at Eyemouth in 1876 – replaced by a motor lifeboat in 1937 and by a fully up-to-date boat in 1974. Along the coast, lighthouses at St. Abbs Head (and Barns Ness and the Bass Rock to the north, and Longstone in the Farne Islands to the south) emphasise the treacherous nature of these cliff-girt shores and inshore waters. No lighthouse, lifeboat or coastguard, however, could prevent the October 1881 disaster when only 26 out of 45 sailing boats returned and 129 fishermen – half of the male fishing population – were drowned.

Freshwater Fisheries

There is little early reference to a sea fishery for salmon; alongside trout and sea trout, salmon formed part – the most prized part – of the river fishery.

In 1843, for instance, the Tweed comprised five sections – the river mouth to Berwick Bridge, Berwick Bridge to Norham, Norham to Coldstream Bridge, Coldstream to Kelso Bridge and upstream from Kelso. The first two reaches were tidal, fished only by net and coble (Ladykirk was once called the Kirk o' Steill, a deep pool where salmon nets were set). Up to Coldstream, net and coble could still be used, but so also were the methods employed in the upper reaches – including rod, leister, cairn net and straik net. These smaller-scale, fairly modest fisheries were probably quite numerous – Merton Parish alone had three in 1793, though there were suggestions that proprietors could greatly improve on the £20 – £25 per year income were they to adopt the long nets in use lower down the river.

Tensions between the commercial fisheries higher up river were as evident in the late 18th century, however, as they are today. At Innerleithen and Traquair, for instance, salmon were in such short supply (except after spates), that catching methods nearer the sea were blamed for depriving those higher up of a share in the profits. In the 19th century, the growing importance of the sporting fishery gave rise to complaints against what was said to be the indiscriminate use of rods and of large semi-circular pout or landing nets by the general population. There was a growing concern also at the amount of black fishing (poaching at night with a leister or waster), at the increasing number of mill dams and weirs obstructing the passage of fish, and at the increased frequency of faster-flowing spates brought about by improved agricultural drainage and faster run-off. These were concerns that applied equally to the Liddell Water in Roxburghshire, flowing down to the Esk and Solway Firth.

Whilst a few salmon might be sold locally, most caught in the lower parishes (and at least as far up as Maxton) were pickled, taken to Berwick and onwards to London. The subsequent introduction of ice, allowing the

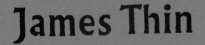
r increased their value and gave rise
nd to improved management.

es, both commercial and sporting,
th the Berwick Salmon Fishing Co.,
s. A remarkable number of fish were
catches were average, with several
ember. In the later 1980s and early
oor seasons, a growing number of
n fisheries (mainly on the more
bought out by the North Atlantic
to reduce the number of salmon
to conserve breeding stocks moving
opments strengthen the privately-
e of the less exclusive commercial
e employment for gillies and water
he river may be made available to

be less the result of shore and river
ent drift-netting offshore by boats
eep-sea interception of migrating
boats in the North Atlantic. These
ible changes in the food chain, the
erosion of spawning beds and river
upland afforestation and gang-
re instrumental in reducing and
e impact of traditional and long-
ries, however successful these may

r employment in the primary and manufacturing industries and below average for service industries. The 1991 Employment Census, however, shows a 27% increase in service industry employment since 1984, and 13.8% in construction, but a decline in the primary sector (47%) and in manufacturing (11%). Manufacturing (29.6%) is still above the Scottish average (19%), due to the strong presence of textiles, electronics, clothing, food and drink, printing and paper publishing; whilst the service industries (57.8%) are still under-represented on the national scale (70%).

With the exception of Hawick, which has relied overlong on its now depressed textile industry, the main Border towns have looked positively for new industry. Kelso has played host to electronics and plastics,

Jedburgh to plastics and precision tools, Gala to printed circuit boards and computerised printing (as well as the new settlement of Tweedbank), Selkirk to PCBs and industrial chemical cleaning. Eyemouth has its fish and vegetable processing; Chirnside its paper mill. Just as significant, however, is the expansion of forestry (along with tourism and other service industries).

The Borders never played any significant part in the heavy industrial development of central Scotland. There was no shale oil, no iron or steel works, no shipbuilding on any scale. Early attempts at mining coal near Cocksburnpath and around Whim, Lamancha and Macbiehill in the north of the area were abandoned, as were scattered limestone workings; otherwise there were occasional initiatives to extract sand, gravel, slate and stone. Recent applications for open-cast coal and gravel extraction in the region of Carlops and West Linton, by contrast, have brought strong objections on environmental grounds.

Traditionally, the principal manufacturing industries were textiles and paper, both of them originally dependant upon water power and located, therefore, alongside suitable rivers. Paper mills had been erected in both Ayton and Edrom Parishes by the 1790s. Subsequently at Ayton there was a mill at Millbank (burnt down 1866), whilst the Bleachfield Paper Mill (converted from a cloth waulk mill c. 1845) was the village's largest employer in the 1920s, albeit now long disused. In Edrom Parish, the original paper mill was established by John Pitcairn in 1786 at Broomhouse. In 1842 it was transferred three miles down the Whiteadder to its present site at Chirnside Bridge. By the early 1970s, the firm of Young Trotter and Sons, established in 1887 by Pitcairn's brother-in-law, had gone into liquidation. Only its acquisition in 1971 by C.H. Dexter Ltd., of Connecticut, USA saved it from permanent closure, since when it has expanded to produce such specialised paper products as tea bags, disposable surgical gowns and vacuum cleaner bags.

The most distinctive Border industry, the woollen industry, ultimately centred on Selkirk, Walkerburn, Innerleithen and Peebles (on the Tweed), Galashiels (the Gala Water), Hawick (the Teviot) and Jedburgh (the Jed). Mills could be grouped more closely on faster-flowing tributaries than on the Tweed itself.

Such a concentration was not always so, however. In the 17th and for much of the 18th century, the Border wool crop was exported to the Lothians, Aberdeen and Yorkshire and whilst the local linen industry, with its attendant bleachfields and lint mills, was essentially domestic. In the 1790s, Coldingham had 36 weavers, Earlston 40–50, whilst Melrose's linen weavers had been incorporated as early as 1668. By 1791–2, however, the Melrose industry was in decline, due partly to the increased cost of imported Dutch flax occasioned by the American war, and partly to the higher wages paid to spinners in the developing woollen manufactury of Galashiels.

Much of the earliest woollen yarn, spun at home and woven locally, was coarse and contaminated with the tar, butter and tobacco juice used by shepherds to smear their sheep. Quality improved, however, and by the 1790s mills had been established at Innerleithen, Ednam and Hawick, with others to follow at Duns and Peebles. Merchants and manufacturers were now more strongly involved, not simply landowners, and the Borders were already showing a shift of labour away from agriculture, which was affecting the balance of population within the area. As weaving expanded to become a part-time supplement to agricultural labouring, so a number of new villages were created – Newcastleton in 1793, Carlops in 1800 (albeit originally in 1784, for cotton-weaving). Denholm, with its stocking mill, is also late 18th century. By 1825, however, Hawick had 8 mills; Galashiels 10 by 1830; and Selkirk was emerging as an overflow for Galashiels.

In the 1850s, the newly-built railways brought coal from Lothian; steam power rapidly replaced water power, and power looms put an end to hand-loom weaving. Most surviving Border mills date from the mid-late 19th century when the industry reached its peak – looms in single-storey, north-lit sheds and spinning in 3–4 storey buildings; though sometimes vice-versa! Associated tanneries and skinworks were founded at eg Galashiels (1894) and Selkirk; and a silk works was established in Gala in 1932.

The Border mills produced a range of cloths and tweeds, hosiery and carpets, with knitwear developing on an increasingly large scale from the 1850s. Nowadays cashmere and mohair are at least as important as woollen knitwear, and such small items as ties, scarves, rugs and head squares have proliferated since the 1950s. Whilst much is sold to the home market, exports are critical to the survival of the industry – whether in eg Europe, America or Japan. Relatively few businesses are now family-owned, however. The financial implications of upgrading and difficult trading conditions have led to take-overs by national or multinational companies, and this tends, in turn, to lead to the absorption or closure of the 'small branch factory' – a well known syndrome elsewhere in Scotland.

COMMUNICATIONS

The main Border trade routes were with Edinburgh and the Lothians to the north. Peeblesshire would also trade with Lanarkshire through the Biggar Gap, whilst the more southerly parts of Berwickshire and Roxburghshire traded with Berwick and Northumberland, frequently using the sea routes through Eyemouth and Berwick to import lime and coal and to export grain, vegetables, livestock, fish and manufactured goods. Newcastleton, south of the watershed, found it equally difficult to trade through either Hawick or Langholm!

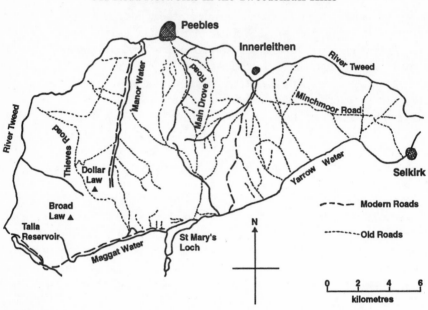

Figure 11
Old Road Networks in the Tweedsmuir Hills

Old trackways survive on the higher hills and moors, where they have not been destroyed by subsequent cultivation or development – Roman and medieval Dere Street, the Herring Road over the Lammermuirs, the Thieves' Road through the Tweedsmuir Hills, or fragments of the many mainly 16th – 19th century drove roads used for taking livestock south to the English markets.

The survival of such tracks does not presuppose the existence of a well-developed transport network by the 18th century. Hillier areas had no roads as such, and those in lowland areas were in a poor state, especially in winter. Local roads, in particular, were difficult, and packhorses and sleds were frequently of more use than carts. Agricultural improvement and the emergent textile industry hankered after better communications, but progress was slow until the Turnpike Trusts were formed to upgrade or build new roads, and tolls charged for their use. The Edinburgh-Berwick post-road was turnpiked in 1750. It was followed by routes from Edinburgh to Peebles, Moffat, Carlisle and Newcastle, and east-west routes from Glasgow and Hawick to Kelso and Berwick.

The turnpikes form the basis of the modern network of main roads. Though a number have been upgraded over the past 30 or so years, they now carry a burden of traffic far in excess of their design, and many would advocate a complete rebuilding of the Edinburgh-Hawick-Carlisle and the Edinburgh-Carter Bar roads, just as the Edinburgh-Berwick road is slowly emerging as a dual carriageway (though not yet as an east coast motorway). Whether the roads should be thus rebuilt, or course, with the many implications for the environment and public transport, is a further issue.

Bridges were vital to improved communications. A late 15th century (and subsequently widened) Tweed Bridge survives at Peebles; Jedburgh has its 16th century Canongate Bridge. Otherwise, bridges are mainly post-17th century. Single-span bridges at Innerleithen (1701) and Manor Water (1702) were followed by such as Smeaton's Coldstream Bridge and Toll House (1763–7), Kelso Bridge and Toll House (1800–3) and a more domestic, later, but equally fine bridge at Ashiestiel (1847). The invention of new materials, moreover, led to the graceful iron 'chain' or suspension bridges at Hutton (1820), Kalemouth (1820–30) and Melrose (1826) – the Union Bridge at Hutton being at that time the only bridge over the Tweed between Berwick and Coldstream. Toll houses, like milestones and signposts, survive in a number of places, frequently in association with bridges and turnpikes; when tolls were abolished by Act of Parliament in 1866, however, toll houses became redundant.

But what of the railways? In 1810 Telford was invited to design a cast-iron, horse-drawn railway as a measure of improving links between Berwick and Glasgow; in 1836 a Peeblesshire railway also came to nothing; but in 1846 the North British Railway Company's Edinburgh-Berwick line was opened, and in 1847 the Newcastle and Berwick Railway reached Tweedmouth. Between 1846 and 1849, trains carried 5792 passengers between Edinburgh and London, compared to 11584 by sea from Leith and Granton. In 1850, however, the Royal Border Bridge across the Tweed at Berwick was opened and in the autumn of that year 600 English visitors were brought north by rail to Edinburgh. Not only was fast, long-distance tourism born, but at 7.15 each morning a train arrived at Edinburgh's market, adjacent to Waverley Station, with fresh produce from the Borders.

Thereafter followed decades of expansion – including the Waverley line from Edinburgh to Hawick and Carlisle (1847–62), and ending with the line to Lauder (1901) (see Figure 12, overleaf). With the network complete, Galashiels and Newtown St Boswells emerged as main railway centres, and the railways enjoyed great popularity until the 1920s.

At that point the internal combustion engine took over; motor buses, cars and carriers' lorries eroded the railways' monopoly, and lines started closing from 1932 (Lauder). The storms and floods of August 1948 brought the permanent closure of lines to Jedburgh and between Duns and Earlston; the Duns and Selkirk lines closed in 1951; the Border Counties line in 1956; the Gala-Peebles and Eyemouth-Burnmouth lines in 1962. Finally, in 1969, the Waverley route closed. Whilst road transport had undoubtedly eroded rail transport, the railways could have striven more strenuously to integrate rail and road services, to identify needs and to market themselves more effectively. As it was, there was considerable unemployment, many alternative bus services (particularly where left to

Figure 12
The Development of the Railway Network

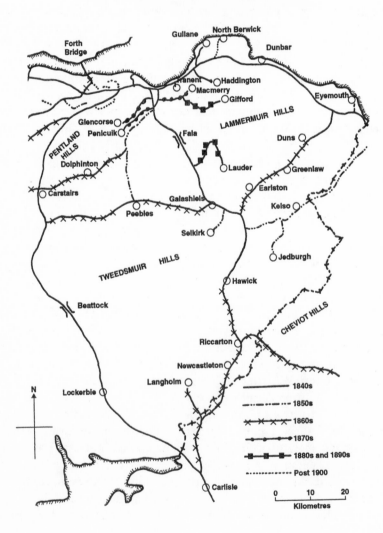

unsubsidised private operators) quickly faded away, and the subsequent growth in road transport has created a massive burden of congestion, structural damage and environmental pollution.

The railway map of the Borders, meantime, has returned to that of 1846, albeit the nearest functioning stations are Berwick, Dunbar and Edinburgh. While the east coast line has been electrified, with fully modernised track and signalling, it no longer serves the Borders. Travel over any distance is all but impossible for Borderers without access to a car, and it is not surprising that the Borders has higher car ownership figures (1991) than the Scottish average – 47.8% with 1 car (41.2%), 20.8% with 2 cars (16.2%), 31.4% with no car (42.6%).

The age of steam and diesel in the Borders is passed, tracks are long ago lifted, signal boxes demolished and such surviving stations as Melrose, Innerleithen, Roxburgh and Stobo converted to other uses. Whilst the trackways have generally reverted to nature, ironically one of the earliest viaducts, at Dunglass (1846), is still in use. Other fine surviving examples include curving Roxburgh (1850), skewed Lyne (1864) and Traquair (1866), and towering Leaderfoot (1865) – industrial dinosaurs in an otherwise pastoral landscape.

SOCIAL CONDITIONS

Comparative analysis of county population figures is hampered by the reorganisation of Local Government in 1975, when the new Ettrick and Lauderdale District gained nearly 3600 people from Berwickshire (mainly from Earlston and Lauder) and over 9500 from Roxburghshire (mainly from Hawick). The overall trend is fairly clear, however – a gradual rise during the 19th century to a peak of some 130,000 in the 1880s–1890s, followed by a falling away to 98,477 by 1971 and a modest recovery to 103,311 in 1991.

Overall totals, however, mask very considerable, more localised shifts. Historically, the more lowland and agricultural counties of Berwick and Roxburgh held the highest populations, peaking in 1861; and at its simplest the woollen towns of the middle Tweed gained considerably during the late 18th and 19th centuries, a gain reinforced by the coming of the railways and the modern road network. Indeed, Selkirkshire did not peak until 1911, though the woollen industry had begun to decline by 1891.

Ever since the disappearance of the old fermtouns, agricultural settlement has been based on individual farms – each with its farmhouse, steading and workers' cottages. From the initial improvement period, right through until the earlier-mid 20th century, a sizeable workforce was required for the seasonal round of tasks, complemented by tradesmen and craftsmen who inhabited the rural villages.

In some rural areas, even so, there was clear and early population loss. In

western Peeblesshire and the Lammermuirs, in the early 19th century if
not before, sheep farming replaced mixed marginal subsistence farming.
The highest, poorest upland farms around Bedshiel, for instance, in
Greenlaw Parish, were abandoned by the landowners and their populations
removed – a Borders precursor to the better-known Highland clearances.
Furthermore, there could be substantial and ongoing local migration. In
1839–42, 385 people moved into Greenlaw parish and 294 moved away
(sometimes the same people). These were mainly local movements of farm
servants – generally single people at Martinmas and families at Whit term.
On average, some 33% of moves were with neighbouring Eccles Parish,
and 50% with other Border parishes, notably in Berwickshire and
Roxburghshire. And in Maxton Parish, even as late as 1951, 10% moved
each year, though few going farther than 20 miles. It was part of normal
agricultural life, whereby discontented and ambitious farmers and farm
servants alike could seek a change at term.

Key factors influencing farm servants included pay, housing and the
farmer himself. By the late 18th century there were three types of farm
servant on the larger farms. The married hind – whose wife and children
were expected to help periodically on the farm – was provided with a
cottage and paid mainly in kind to the value of some £13–£20 a year. Hinds
were sometimes bound to maintain a female labourer or bondager. Single
farm servants, hired yearly or half-yearly, boarded with the farmer and
received £5–£10 a year (males) or £2–£5 (females). Day labourers, by
contrast, were generally fed by the farmer and received 1sh – 1sh 2d a day
in the summer, rising to 1sh 6d at harvest. Most farms employed a mix of
workers, although in the Merse the married hind was reckoned the most
reliable. Agricultural wages were said to be high on account of higher
wages paid in Northumberland; and craftsmen such as masons and
carpenters were frequently, but not necessarily, paid at higher rates.

Housing was not always satisfactory. By the 1830s, many farmers were
living in new spacious houses, modelled on those of the minor landowners
and the ministers – generally two-storey, symmetrical buildings of well-
dressed stone. For hinds, too, there was improved accommodation –
separate houses, often with sleeping apartments above, built in a row a
short distance from the farmhouse and steading. They were larger and
warmer than the 'wretched hovels' they replaced. Day labourers, however,
often paid by the piece or according to work completed, lived in the towns
or villages. They either walked several miles daily each way, with long
hours in the field, or lived away during the week in whatever
accommodation they could find – often bothies in the steading that also or
later accommodated seasonal Irish and other migrant workers.

In general, however, it would seem that agricultural workers were increasingly better housed, better fed and better clad than formerly. Their wages may not have been as high as for those working in the woollen mills, as long as the latter expanded and prospered; nor did they experience the degrading poverty, congested housing and growing crime of the mill towns.

Today's agricultural workers, like their industrial cousins, have regular hours of work, paid overtime and holidays. Since the 1940s, some have been drawn away by reports of attractive council housing or higher wages in industry, whilst girls have opted for shops and offices in the towns. Even though agricultural wages have risen over the past 30–40 years, they are still low. Some would argue that tied housing is cheaper than council or other rented houses, and that an open-air life supported by mechanisation can be attractive. However, others point to increased exposure to environmental hazards on the land, whilst tied housing leaves the problem of what happens on retirement or in the event of illness. Certainly, such improvements made steadily since the 1950s as the provision of electricity and piped water, indoor toilets and bathrooms, have allowed tenants to acquire facilities and equipment common in the towns – cooker, washing machine, vacuum cleaner and fridge(-freezer), and latterly a colour television, video recorder and maybe a computer. However, the standard of rural housing is still a problem, particularly damp, and though some industrial mill-town housing leaves much to be desired, there has been little new housing for working people in the countryside.

MIND, BODY AND SOUL

For much of the 20th century, government has overseen provision of health and education. In the 18th and 19th centuries, however, this was not so, and the church shouldered responsibilities for moral and social welfare, and mental improvement, well beyond its strictly religious obligations.

The Church of Scotland was far from being the only church, and by the 1790s seceders and dissenters may have comprised 15%–35% of the total population – almost 75% seemingly in Jedburgh. They include Burghers and Antiburghers, Cameronians and Relief Congregations, Methodists, Baptists and Quakers, alongside a number of Episcopalians and Roman Catholics. Kelso, indeed, would appear to have accommodated almost all of these groups.

The extent of true belief is unclear, except for dissenters' strong views on baptism and the registration of children. In any case, established church ministers considered them 'inferior ranks' – presumably meaning that they were neither landowners, merchants nor professional people, that they were poor rather than well-off, and that they sought social change rather than the status quo.

The poor, meantime (including large numbers of migrants returning home from England) were dependent upon charity – mainly collections taken at the (established) kirk door or, more effectively through a levy on heritors and tenants in proportion to the rental value of their lands. Established from the 1740s, this latter practice was largely confined to the Borders, albeit with the exception of much of Peeblesshire. In Selkirkshire in 1845, £70 was contributed from church collections, £24 from alms and legacies, and £490 6sh 7d from legal levies. Acceptance on to the poor roll required a person to sign away all rights to whatever property he/she might still own, to be sold on death to defray costs. Many commentators welcomed this early instance of formalised welfare (based on a targeted property tax!) as guaranteeing basic assistance to the needy and preserving family ties; others saw it as a dangerous recipe for sloth, fecklessness and dependency, leading to reduced family loyalties. As for the poor themselves, such was the indignity of assessment and admission procedures that many forewent such help.

The church's other supplementary responsibility was education. Parish schools emphasised the three 'Rs' and religious instruction, occasionally with such additional subjects as maths and surveying, book-keeping (Traquair, Bowden) and Latin (Hutton, St. Boswells). In the towns, there were parish 'English' schools which sometimes took boarders (Duns); there might also be 'Latin' or grammar schools (Kelso, Peebles) and specialist girls' boarding schools teaching sewing, embroidery, music and dancing (Duns). In Kelso, a 'School of Industry' for poor girls focused on reading and writing, sewing, knitting, 'tambouring' and 'moral doctrine'.

Up to one-third of children appear to have received a regular education in the 1790s. Many parents could not afford the fees, however, and even then attendance was irregular as children were kept back to help at home or on the land. Furthermore, education was disrupted when farm servants moved to new farms.

The schoolhouse and the schoolmaster's salary were provided by the heritors. The salary might be augmented from charitable funds (Hadden, Mellerstain) or by tenants clubbing together – particularly in remote areas too distant from the parish school (Lempitlaw). There might also be special funds for teaching the children of the enrolled poor (Earlston). However, teachers were not well paid, and unless they ran particularly large schools, their total annual income might be some £16–£20 – a sum that included extra payments for acting as session clerk, precentor and poor-rates collector. This was little more than a hind's wages, 'by far too small recompense for such a laborious job' (Newlands). Inevitably, 'every well-educated and virtuous man shrink(s) back from it as a place of hopeless penury'. Where direct cash comparisons can be made, teachers' income compared very badly with ministers' stipends:

	Minister's Stipend	Schoolmaster's Emoluments	[Salary	Fees]
Ednam Parish	£158	£70	[£34	£36]
Cavers Parish	£250	£120	[£57	£63]
Selkirkshire	£1034 0 5$^1/_4$	£341 6 6$^3/_4$	[£164 6 6$^3/_4$	£177]

In Ednam and Cavers it was less than half; over the whole of Selkirkshire, less than one-third.

There is less detail about health in the 18th and 19th centuries. Previously the Borders had suffered the same afflictions as other parts of the country – leprosy, malaria, plague, syphilis and smallpox were rife well into the 18th century; cholera, typhus, typhoid and tuberculosis well into the 19th and 20th centuries. The spread of these diseases was caused by polluted water supplies, overcrowding, poverty, vermin, lack of sanitation, filth and refuse. Whilst conditions were worse in Edinburgh, smaller towns and villages were equally affected.

In the Borders, smallpox inoculation was far from universal in the 1790s, due largely to surviving pockets of religious prejudice; and fevers, consumption and rheumatism were common. Agricultural drainage had much reduced the area of boggy marshy ground, reducing the amount of stagnant water and almost eliminating ague (malaria) so that ill-health in later life – primarily amongst the lower classes – was attributed to a harsh climate, poor housing, damp living conditions, poor diet and hygiene and 'low living'. In spite of the great advances in clinical and preventative medicine taking place in Edinburgh, medical provision in the Borders was embryonic. Records are patchy and incomplete, but the few doctors who were resident, were to be found only in such settlements as Coldstream, Swinton, Jedburgh, Smailholm and Lauder. Furthermore, only Kelso had a 'Dispensary' – established as early as 1775, supported by annual subscription and serving parishes on both sides of the border. Out-patient facilities were complemented by 12 surgical beds, and by 1792 8000–9000 of the 'lower orders' had been treated.

It took the best part of a further 100 years before public health and public education received the attention they deserved. Faced with patchy and ill-resourced provision under existing systems of private enterprise and charitable 'good works', Parliament eventually passed legislation requiring the setting up of well-designed, well-organised and high quality services for all sectors of the population. Acts of eg 1847, 1857 and 1862 covered sanitation, water supplies, drainage, cleansing, paving and lighting, along with the establishment of public health departments within local authorities. The Education Act (Scotland) of 1872 established a public system of 'elementary' education for all – though 'secondary' education was not funded until 1892.

The subsequent story of health and education follows the national pattern. Today there are 74 primary schools and 9 all-age comprehensive secondary schools in the Borders. Educational concerns are partly to do with quality and curricular relevance (as they always should be), but also with the continuing closure of small rural schools (themselves a community focus) and the possible break-up of a well-proven and well-organised, albeit under-resourced system under the impact of School Boards, Devolved School Management, Opting Out of Local Authority Control and Local Government Reorganisation.

Health services, too, have undergone change – one-doctor practices have virtually disappeared, replaced by group medical centres in the towns; and the new Borders General Hospital in Melrose (1988) replaced services previously available at Peel Hospital and many of those at smaller cottage hospitals that have subsequently closed.

The new arrangements provide a wide range of modern services – preventative as well as diagnostic and curative – and are easily accessible to urban-based and individually mobile patients. Once again it is the country dweller who is disadvantaged, particularly if dependent upon all but non-existent systems of public transport.

Furthermore, the spread of Hospital 'Trusts' and Budget-Holding GPs, linked to ever tighter central government controls on public spending and to ever-increasing numbers of health service administrators and managers, is seen by most as a particularly serious threat to the survival of high quality long-term as well as short-term provision for all, free at the point of delivery – given that this has already been paid for by the 'client' through decades of National Insurance contributions.

As for religion, it has a difficult furrow to hoe, and its impact on contemporary society is much reduced. Church of Scotland attendance is in serious decline; amalgamations and linkages are common in both urban and rural areas; congregations (and their ministers) are largely middle-aged and older; young people are generally conspicuous by their absence. The non-conformist churches, the Episcopalians and the Roman Catholics are maybe marginally less diminished, but all face an uncertain and uncomfortable future. Most people are well enough disposed towards the churches, but the churches are faced with a plethora of attractions competing for peoples' leisure time – in particular, sports and entertainment. They are also faced with secular and political leaders who understand the value of little albeit the cost of everything, and a popular press and wider media that all too often peddle personal gain, titillation and gratification as man's primary objectives, and whose subconscious influence is as enormous as it is vastly underrated.

Quite apart from failing to consider the 'joy of salvation' in these hedonistic times, people are largely apathetic about an institution that has yet to show its determination to challenge head on those politicians, media chiefs and captains of commerce and industry who have forgotten that man's primary role must be to protect his environment, to care for and support – not exploit – his fellow-man, and to work for a sustainable future for life on earth. Indeed, the staggeringly high salaries, share options and other perks awarded by company directors to themselves and to their senior management teams in recent years, at the same time as they have slashed workforces, lowered wages and created widespread job insecurity, simply exemplifies the moral bankruptcy that afflicts the country, and the lack of any recognisable or reasonable conscience amongst so many of its leaders. Any view on the late 20th century Borders, as on any other part of Scotland, cannot afford to ignore such issues.

POSTSCRIPT

To many, the present-day Borders may seem a douce place – a pleasing mosaic of rolling hills and moorland cut through by fertile valleys which lead gently downwards to prosperous agricultural lowlands and a rugged coastline. Industry is largely unobtrusive, apart from the impact of the textile industry, some modern industrial estates and expanses of dark coniferous plantation on much of the higher land. The Borders has few of the post-industrial and social problems of Scotland's central belt, its population appears to have stabilised, it has succeeded in attracting a reasonable share of new technology-based industry, and even if tourism is still a little slow to develop, it has its fair share of archaeological, architectural and environmental riches.

Nonetheless the Borders has undergone very substantial and far-reaching changes over the past half century – changes which include: intensive agricultural mechanisation, farm amalgamations, loss of hill farms to commercial forestry, closure of rural schools, shops, churches and hospitals, loss of public transport – particularly in rural areas, decline in full-time male employment, trends towards female and part-time employment, the advent of microtechnology, urban centralisation of services and entertainment, substantial rural depopulation, decaying villages and hamlets, inward migration; free market pressures and the planned destruction of public services. Their impact has been, and will continue to be, enormous.

Take inward migration as a final example. In recent decades, towns and villages such as Peebles, Broughton, Bowden, West Linton, Lauder, Earlston and Melrose in the north-west, and Coldstream, Eyemouth and the Yetholms in the south-east have tended to grow. In part this is due to continuing local migration away from the land; but many settlements in the north of the Borders have become preferred residential areas, popular with those retiring from the cities and with Edinburgh commuters seeking cheaper housing, lower Council taxes and a higher quality of life – and this goes some considerable way towards explaining overall population increase in the Borders these past twenty or so years. In 1986, for instance, over 31% of all immigrants to Tweeddale came from elsewhere in Scotland. Also in 1986, 30% of the population of Town and Kirk Yetholm were born outside Scotland, largely in north-east England, whilst in the year to April 1991, over 23% of inward migration to Berwickshire was from England and Wales.

Just as future historians will be better placed to judge the impact of present-day social mores and government policies on the Borders, so also only time will reveal the influence of such high concentrations of incomers on local life, attitudes, language and culture.

Meantime, the Borders is indeed pleasing and attractive. It has a remarkably varied history, it is managing to maintain a balanced economy and it offers a substantial range of interesting places to visit and explore. It is still much under-rated.

SECTION TWO

TEN

ABBEYS AND CHURCHES

How beautifully, how mellifluously the names of today's linked parish churches roll off the tongue! Ettrick with Yarrow, Bowden with Lilliesleaf, Ashkirk with Selkirk, Fogo and Swinton with Ladykirk with Leitholm with Whitsome, Gordon with Greenlaw with Legerwood with Westruther, Broughton, Glenholm, Kilbucho with Skirling with Stobo and Drumelzier with Tweedsmuir. They are a much loved heritage, as important for Borders folk as the remains of the medieval religious houses, Coldingham, Kelso, Melrose, Jedburgh, Dryburgh and Peebles, which do constitute the most visited and varied group in Scotland. The former are cherished locally but not, unfortunately, inspected by many outsiders. The latter became 'romantic ruins' to be preserved intact in accordance with the general canons of good taste laid down by William Gilpin and adopted by enlightened British landowners in the last two decades of the eighteenth century and at the beginning of the nineteenth century. Notably in the Borders the lead was taken by the Earl of Buchan at Dryburgh and by the Duke of Buccleuch at Melrose. At the same time most eighteenth century improvers would probably have shared Gibbon's view of monks as 'non-men' following a useless and irrational vocation.

This does raise a central problem, the difficulty of understanding and interpreting the past from the remains of buildings in use between eight hundred and three hundred years ago. Whether before or after the Reformation people then shared some basic beliefs not generally emphasised or even understood today: the essential importance of the life passage of the soul as a preparation for eternity and the assumption that God and his angels and the Devil or Anti-Christ and his agents intervened virtually on an everyday basis in the world and took possession of the souls of men and women. There is a danger of producing a safe, comfortable, nostalgic variety of history ignoring difficult or unpleasant realities, the intolerance and fanaticism, the formal cruelties of church and state, the brutality and slaughter inspired by religious enthusiasm, the support for crusades against pagans, infidels and heretics, the campaigns against deviance and the enforcement of alternate and mutually exclusive varieties of orthodoxy, or, more recently, the embarrassing predilection of evangelical Episcopalians and Presbyterians in seventeenth century Scotland for burning fellow Christians and others, women rather than men, as witches.

In twelfth century Scotland the kings, Alexander I (1107–24) and David I (1124–53), and their followers in the Borders, the new Anglo-Norman – French landed elite, de Morevilles, de Avenels, Lovels, Rules, Riddels, Somervilles, were by any standards rough, ruthless and hungry for power. But it was the same men who endowed the new churches, abbeys and priories with lands and revenues. No doubt their motives were a mixture of genuine piety, of concern for their own souls and of guilt for past misdeeds. They expected and got value for money in establishing religious houses for the new spiritual elites who collected holiness, monks, canons, friars and nuns who lived in large prayer factories, providing services and worship and intercession on a regular production line.

The religious orders, Benedictine, Cistercian and Tironensian monks, Augustinian and Premonstratensian canons, Franciscan, Dominican and Trinitarian friars, brought other benefits, political and economic. As supranational organisations coming originally from France and Italy they cut across national boundaries, and probably enhanced the position of the Scottish church and crown just because they had the special advantage of not being English. Their houses became something akin to modern development corporations and centres of enterprise and wealth generation staffed with men with special skills and experience in productive farming and land management, in architecture and craftsmanship, and in commerce and the accumulation of surplus capital for investment. They helped to bring order and stability defending, with armed force when required, their interest and properties against rivals and anarchic elements.

Inside the monasteries life was intensely communal and organised with abbots and priors controlling what were to an extent conscript armies (only some monks were recruited as adult volunteers) through a total control system of rigid discipline and detailed petty bureaucracy. Other complicated constitutional arrangements of management, supervision and inspection between houses in the same order provided an external element of quality assurance. In the same way the buildings were arranged in a formal, rigid, universal European pattern that applied whether in Burgundy or in Berwickshire with the church on the north side of the cloister (Melrose was one rare exception in this respect), with chapter house and dormitories in the east range, refectory and kitchen on the south, and the cellarer's rooms and abbot's chambers and guest accommodation in the west range.

In the Borders the old Benedictine tradition of balance between worship, scholarship, contemplation and labour was maintained at Coldingham Priory, founded c.1139 or earlier. Its special affiliation with Durham was terminated by Robert II in 1378 when it was linked to Dunfermline Abbey.

Coldingham was a rich house, but only the north and east walls of the choir of the church of *c.*1220 have survived as part of the post-Reformation parish church repaired and restored in 1662, 1854–55 and 1954. The Romanesque exterior pilaster style buttresses and arcading at the east end of the lancet windows and the carved capitals are very fine indeed. It is just about possible to imagine the sheer scale of the medieval church with its north and south transepts and a nave with north and south aisles.

The new orders based on the Benedictine Rule emphasised different aspects of the monastic tradition. The Cluniac houses in the eleventh and twelfth centuries developed a pattern of elaborate perfection in their church services and music allied to a new and highly centralised framework under which all the 1450 priories in Europe formed in theory a single congregation under Cluny. Cistercianism in the *Carta Caritatis* of 1119 marked a return to austerity, poverty and simplicity with a very different emphasis on manual labour, and a practical system of decentralised administration.

It is more convenient, however, in terms of architectural history to discuss the Tironensians at Kelso Abbey before Cistercian Melrose. The Order of Tiron, from Thiron – Gardais in the south-east of Normandy, was established *c.*1109 by Saint Bernard (1060–1117) from Poitiers. Like the Cistercians the Order of Tiron stressed the importance of simplicity and manual labour. The Cistercians were popular in Scotland where, with royal patronage, they had four abbeys and two priories.

The first group of Tironensians were settled at Lindean, near Selkirk in 1113 by the Earl David. In 1128 as David I he moved them to Kelso, probably to be closer to the great castle at Roxburgh. Kelso Abbey (Plate 10) was immensely wealthy, probably second only in Scotland in this respect to the Tironensian abbey at Arbroath. Kelso properties, farms, granges, mills, breweries, salt works, fisheries and the revenues of thirty four parish churches, extended across Scotland from Ayrshire to Aberdeenshire. The late twelfth century church, reminiscent of a Rhineland minster, looked from above like a double cross with transepts at both the east and west ends of the nave and two crossing towers. The massive, almost warlike remains of the west tower and north porch can only begin to suggest the exceptional size and magnificence of Kelso. Note the massive heavy Romanesque columns and arcaded galleries. Unfortunately, its location close to the Border and to Roxburgh Castle left it fatally vulnerable to damage and destruction in the wars between Scotland and England in the fourteenth, fifteenth and sixteenth centuries. The surviving fragments represent an even smaller proportion of the whole than at Coldingham, but the impact is nevertheless quite staggering. It captures the spirit of twelfth century monasticism, its directness and simplicity, its purity and piety, its brutality and naivety, better than anything anywhere else in Scotland.

Melrose Abbey (Plate 11) could scarcely be more different since it · represents fifteenth and sixteenth century degenerate Cistercianism at its best or worst. Stephen Harding, the abbot of Citeaux from 1110 to 1133, and the great St. Bernard of Clairvuax (1091–1153) would have been horrified at its luxurious architectural refinements, decorative embellishments and at the obvious wealth of the establishment. The whole ethos and wonderful appeal of twelfth century Cistercianism was in the return of conservative monastic principles, the veneration of poverty and devotion and hard work, preferably in remote and isolated places, the repudiation of irrelevant art and learning, pompous bell towers, stained glass, wall paintings and sculpture ('deformed beauty and beauty deformed'). The success of Citeaux can also be explained in terms of its efficient and adaptable constitutional framework with mother and daughter houses and a system of delegated administration and visitation, and in relation to the new and eminently sensible concept of recruiting lay brothers or *conversi* as an extra workforce for clearing land and running the granges. (A grange is a farm with an oratory and living accommodation attached).

The Cistercian order was immensely popular, with at its peak 742 monasteries and 900 nunneries in Europe. At Rievaulx in Yorkshire, for example, the great Ailred, the abbot from 1147 to 1167, had 140 monks and 500 conversi and another 250 laymen or *mercenarii* at the abbey and its sheep-walks or ranches. By the middle of the thirteenth century Rievaulx was the centre of a great commercial enterprise based on 14,000 sheep. It was no longer merely financially independent, but rather a highly profitable capitalist business operation.

Melrose Abbey was founded by David I in 1136 and was colonised from Rievaulx. In turn Melrose had daughter houses at Newbattle, Kinloss, Balmerino and Coupar Angus. Her endowments included tenements and tofts in Edinburgh, Roxburgh, Lanark and Berwick-on-Tweed as well as peat mosses, salt marshes and fisheries and holdings from Ayrshire to the Lothians and Aberdeenshire. Like Coldingham and Kelso, but on a much larger scale akin to Rievaulx, Melrose owned land, Eildon, Darnick, Gattonside, Newstead and other diverse units to some 5000 acres in all, and leased for pasture some 17,000 acres of upland in Ettrick Forest, Lauderdale, Teviotdale and in the Lammermuirs. The lay brothers on the granges ran vast flocks of sheep so that the abbey accumulated for export large quantities of wool on a scale well beyond the original spirit of Cistercianism. Penshiel (641632) grange north-west of Cranshaws is one identified example of these agricultural holdings.

The buildings at Melrose are all post the destruction by Edward II in

1322 and by Richard II in 1385. Perhaps the most striking initial impact from Melrose is the beautiful clarity of the monastic plan, the sheer size of the cloister laid out in the twelfth century and the scale of the engineering operations evident in the great drain lade system bringing water from the Tweed to the east and west ranges.

The church is a quite outstanding example of late medieval (c. 1385–1505) Scottish decorative work by Scottish, northern English and French masons and craftsmen, notably by John Morvo or Morow from Paris on the south transept. Note in particular the massive and magnificent east window, no doubt filled originally with richly coloured stained glass, and the wonderful bosses on the vaulted choir ceiling with Saints Matthew, Paul, James Greater and James the Less, Thomas, Peter, Bartholomew and Andrew and the Holy Trinity.

The south exterior of the nave and the south transept contain the richest, most exuberant, most extravagant, and also the most delightful and amusing medieval figure sculpture in Scotland. Note the exquisite Virgin and Child, saints, martyrs, angels with scrolls and musical instruments, dragons, demons and devils, faces smiling, sneering and scowling, a cook with his ladle, a mason with his chisel and mell, and a ludicrous little pig with bagpipes. Melrose is great fun!

Jedburgh Abbey (Plate 12), as the church of a community of canons regular or 'choir monks', is a more exclusively solemn experience. It exudes power, control, authority, crushing discipline.

The Augustinian and Premonstratensian canons were quite different from the Tironensian and Cistercian monks. As priests or regular clerks the Augustinians and Premonstratensians were actively engaged in preaching and evangelical and missionary work hopefully complementing the activities of parish clergy.

The Augustinians looked to the fifth century Rule of St. Augustine which had been adapted in 755 by Bishop Chrodegang of Metz and then revitalised and rewritten in the eleventh century for cathedral clergy and regular canons living in communities. In Scotland there were six Augustinian abbeys, including Holyrood and Jedburgh, and twelve priories, including Scone, Restenneth, St. Mary's Isle Kirkcudbright and Oronsay.

Jedburgh, founded as a priory by David I in 1138 and colonised from St. Quentin near Beauvais, became an abbey in 1154. The town and castle (occupied by the English from 1346 to 1409) was close to the frontier between Scotland and England and on a main invasion route from the south, so it is hardly surprising that the abbey suffered major war damage in 1297, 1410, 1416, 1464, 1523, 1544 and 1545. It is indeed faintly miraculous that so much of the church survived to become the Presbyterian kirk post 1642. The buildings round the cloister became simply, as at Melrose, a quarry for the town. The twelfth century church inevitably suffered from many repairs and changes, but the presbytery and choir and the east processional doorway and Romanesque west doorway are especially impressive. The fifteenth century rose window above the west door adds a touch of lightness and grace.

The Premonstratensian canons, founded by Archbishop Norbert of Magdeburg in 1121, followed the Rule of St. Augustine but adopted constitutional ideas from Cluniac and Cistercian practice, including the recruitment of lay brothers. Their six Scottish houses included Whithorn and Holywood Abbey near Dumfries. Dryburgh Abbey was founded in 1150 by Hugh de Moreville and his wife Beatrix. It was colonised from Alnwick in Northumberland.

In a sheltered wooded horseshoe bend of the Tweed, Dryburgh (Plate 13) has perhaps the most 'romantic' setting in the Borders – 'Oh what a beauty and perfection of a ruin' to echo the Honble. John Byng on Fountains. In spite of severe damage by the English in 1322, 1385, 1544 and 1545, enough has survived of the buildings round the cloister, the night stair, the library, the parlour, the chapter house, the warming house and the refectory with its rose window to leave some impression of the daily routine. A few fragments of wall painting, mainly geometric design patterns of black lines onto red, leave a tantalising memory of what has been lost.

In comparison, however, the four Cistercian nunneries in the Borders have been almost totally forgotten. The house at Berwick founded by David I in 1153 had been dissolved by 1390/91; the house at Coldstream was founded by Gospatric Earl of Dunbar before 1166; the nunnery at Eccles (763412) was founded by Gospatric and/or his wife Deidre in 1156. Some fragments of the buildings at Eccles survive at the west end of the churchyard and the parish church of 1774 may include some medieval stones. The nunnery at Abbey St. Bathans (758622) may have been founded c. 1184–1200 by Ada, the wife of the Earl of Dunbar, or by his second wife Christiana before 1214. The present parish kirk, which includes some fourteenth century stonework in its north and east walls, contains a staggeringly good recumbent effigy of a late fifteenth or sixteenth century Cistercian prioress. It was found during repairs to the church in 1857. It is well worthwhile visiting this beautiful and 'isolated' upland village on the Southern Upland Way to see her. It would make a good penance to walk the 'Way' from B6355 near Ellemford Bridge or even from Cockburnspath.

The new model preaching armies of the thirteenth century, the mendicant friars, with their fierce zeal to capture souls and eradicate ignorance and error, reached Scotland about 1230. Berwick-on-Tweed housed Franciscan (1231), Dominican (1240/41), Augustinian (1267) and Carmelite (1270) friars. In the Scottish Borders the Franciscans (Friars

Minor Conventual) were introduced to Roxburgh by Alexander II *c.* 1232–34. The Franciscans of the Observantine Reform had a small friary in Jedburgh. It was built about 1513 on the north-east side of the High Street at the Friarsgate end of land off Jerusalem Wynd. In 1984 excavations revealed the site of the cloister east range and the church.

The most unusual religious house in the Borders is the Holy Cross at Peebles belonging to the Trinitarians or Red Friars, the regular canons of the Order of the Holy Trinity for the Redemption of Captives. The order, founded at Cerfroy near Chateau-Thierry and recognised by Innocent III in 1198, existed to collect funds for the support of pilgrims in need and for the ransom of captives held by infidels. Their houses or 'ministries' included Berwick (1240/48), Fail near Tarbolton in Ayrshire (before 1335), and Houston (1270), Dirleton and Dunbar (1540/48) in East Lothian on the pilgrimage route to St. Andrews.

The Church of the Holy Cross at Peebles was endowed by Alexander III after the discovery of the (possibly Early Christian) cross of 'St. Nicholas the Bishop' in 1261. There may have been a Trinitarian presence as early as 1296, but the monastery was formally confirmed by James III in 1474. The site, west of and outside the medieval burgh, is on the plateau immediately above and north of the bridge over the A72 over the Eddleston Water. The buildings have no special architectural merit, but the little grassed over cloister is one of the sweetest and most peaceful corners in the Borders. The thirteenth century and later church with a five storey tower added *c.*1474 was rebuilt after destruction by the English in 1548–49. It was still attracting pilgrims as late as 1601. It was used as a parish kirk until 1784.

The destruction of the religious houses and hospitals in the Lothians and the Borders by the English armies between 1544 and 1549 was systematic, deliberate and comprehensive. It was perhaps seen as necessary just because of the vitality of the late medieval pre-Reformation church. That vitality is also suggested by the foundation of the collegiate churches at Peebles (1543) and Biggar (1545/46). St. Andrews at Peebles was established by the town magistrates and John Hay of Yester for a provost, twelve prebendaries and two choristers. It was burnt out by the English in 1548. The church tower was heavily restored by Dr Chambers *c.* 1882.

The religious orders and secular clergy also financed and controlled hospitals variously for the care of the ill and infirm, or for the relief of the poor, or for providing hospitality for pilgrims. Hospitals in the Borders with foundation dates from 1164 on to the early sixteenth century were located at Ancrum, Cockburnspath, Duns, Ednam, Fairnington, Hornden, Hutton, Jedburgh, Lauder, Legerwood, Nenthorn, Eshiels near Peebles,

Roxburgh (Mason Dieu, St. John, St. Peter), Rulemouth, Segden, Soutra and Wheel. Recent excavations at the Augustinian Holy Trinity Church and hospital at Soutra (452584) have established its importance as a large infirmary and medical research centre and burial place with plague pits and mass graves for victims of smallpox, anthrax, typhus and typhoid. The location, a hill site at 386m close to the Roman and medieval road north to Edinburgh is spectacular. The original church, drains and ditches, and miscellaneous structures lie under later medieval buildings.

BORDER CHURCHES

The Borders has some of the oldest churches still in use in Scotland. The architectural evidence of changes over the centuries remain as a barometer of the different needs of the pre and post Reformation religious establishments. In general in the medieval church the chancel or rectangular eastern part, with sometimes a circular or apsidal end, was reserved for the clergy, and the rectangular nave with altars and a pulpit, but probably without seating, was for the people.

The best evidence of organisation of the parishes and the boundaries of the dioceses of Glasgow and St. Andrews is in the 1274 lists prepared for a new papal tax on benefices. The huge Glasgow diocese included to the east and south Bowden, Maxton, Eckford, Linton, Roxburgh and Castleton, roughly Peebles, Selkirk and Roxburghshires. The Merse deanery in the St. Andrews diocese included Channelkirk, Lauder, Earlston, Mertoun, Ednam and Upsettlington (or Ladykirk), that is roughly Berwickshire.

There are good examples of the new Romanesque architectural fashions introduced in the twelfth century as part of a wider reorganisation of the Scottish church. Linton (773262), sitting on top of a sandy hillock, is one of the best small churches. Dating from c.1127 or 1160 the small nave and chancel was variously rebuilt, added to and altered in 1424–26, 1616, 1774, 1803, 1857 and 1912. The quite marvellous tympanum above the south doorway with two wild animals and bearded knight (St. George ?) is unique in Scotland.

Edrom churchyard (827558) has the roundheaded Romanesque doorway from the chancel of the church of c.1105 or 1139. Note also the arms (1499) of Archbishop Robert Blackadder of Glasgow on the south transept below the later church (1732). Bunkle (Bonkyl) churchyard (809597) has a small, primitive twelfth century chancel apse. The rectangular east end of Smailholm church (649364) is perhaps twelfth century. Chirnside church (870560) has a twelfth century south-west doorway. Legerwood church (594434) contains an outstandingly beautiful early twelfth century chancel arch with geometric and chequer pattern decoration.

Stobo church (182376), founded in 1127, has a twelfth century nave and chancel. The south porch and the north chapel off the nave were added in the fifteenth century and the spectacular west tower was rebuilt in the sixteenth century. Alterations and repairs in 1657, 1765, 1863, 1928–29 and 1947–48 give a complex history, but it is probably the most exciting parish church in the Borders.

The most complete medieval church is Ladykirk (888477), the church of the Blessed Virgin of the Steill, built for James IV *c*.1500-13. The only major external alteration of the cruciform plan with three sided apsidal choir and transept ends and the massive buttressing was the heightening of the west tower, possibly by William Adam *c*.1743. The classical cupola is odd, the Victorian (1882) clock face is horrid.

Churches 1560–1712

After the Reformation the church was essentially a single chamber with the emphasis very much on preaching and the importance of the minister: the pulpit was generally on the south centre wall with communion tables adjacent and the pews and the laird's loft at the east and/or west end focusing in towards the pulpit. A north aisle in a T plan was a frequent later addition.

In some ways the religious controversies and the alternating cycles through the seventeenth century between Episcopalianism and Presbyterianism brought out the worst in people. There was a vicious totalitarian brutality and a range of mutually competing intolerances at work which were not an obvious improvement on those they replaced. The statistics of 528 cases of witchcraft prosecutions in East Lothian and the eastern Borders from the 1590s to the 1690s are a stark reminder of realities. All the same, many of the more sane and sensible clergy switched loyalties from Catholicism to Protestantism and from Presbyterianism to Episcopalian-ism or vice versa to preserve their livelihoods.

Lauder church (Plate 14), completed in 1673 to plans by Sir William Bruce (1616–82), is an altogether splendid town church on a cruciform plan with four wings of equal length and a central octagonal tower with pulpit underneath. It was restored from 1969 to 1973 with pink harling as in the original. Greenlaw church was built from 1675 on pre-Reformation foundations. The church was lengthened in 1712 to join on to the tower which was built onto the adjacent courthouse and used as a prison. The east and west galleries were added in 1721 and the north aisle in 1855. The courthouse was removed in 1830. Cockburnspath church (774710) may be in part fourteenth century, but most of the church and the round west tower is sixteenth or early seventeenth century. The plain interior and galleries are nineteenth century.

In contrast Lyne church (191405) is very small and narrow. Rebuilt by Lord Hay of Yester 1640–45 it contains a rare contemporary oak pulpit and canopied pew. The first new church at Polwarth (750495) in 1242 was rebuilt in 1328, but much of the present kirk, including the tower, was built for Sir Patrick Hume, 1st Earl of Marchmont in 1703. The T plan, the external harling, the laird's loft and the clear glass and wood sashes are typical of the early eighteenth century. Eckford church (707270) was rebuilt 1665–58; the north aisle and laird's loft were added in 1772.

Churches 1712–1874

The final triumph of Presbyterianism in 1690 did not in itself bring tranquillity. From the restoration of patronage in 1712 until its abolition in 1874 the issue of who appointed parish ministers, landowners as patrons or kirk sessions and congregations, lead to a series of splits in 1733, 1761 and 1843 with reconciliations in 1900 and 1929. These were not, on the whole, disputes that affected church architecture or worship. In general by the end of the eighteenth century there was less fanatical evangelical zeal and more calm common sense, even the beginnings of a cautious and healthy scepticism.

The most interesting churches are those which retained something of their original austerity and simplicity and specific details such as the laird's loft with external stairs for access or some traditional seating arrangements. The most striking change in the later eighteenth and nineteenth century was the proliferation of manses that were almost country houses fit to express the almost local princely status of ministers of the kirk. Indeed the discrepancy between a huge manse with walled garden and a small kirk can be extraordinary. Note also in some rural parishes the location of the parish school close to the church (Newlands, Ashkirk).

The best country churchyards, which remind us of the fragility of life, the ever present imminence of death, also offer a comforting feeling of communion with the dead. A few had watch houses against pre-1832 resurrectionists or body snatchers supplying Edinburgh's medical schools.

Some parishes have church, manse and churchyard all worth visiting.

Fogo (772491) church 1243, 1570, 1670s, 1755, 1927; east and west lofts with external stairs; boxed pews c.1755; south transept; north wall pulpit; large former manse 1843; atmospheric churchyard with lychgate as War Memorial 1914–19.

Bowden (554301) church 15th century, 17th century, 1909; fine 17th century laird's loft; three external stairs; large manse; atmospheric churchyard.

Channelkirk (481545) church 1127, 1600s, 1817; hill site over Lauderdale; three galleries; sounding pulpit; red sandstone and pink harling; good churchyard with uprights and tablestones; large former manse.

Stobo (182376); exciting church plus large former manse; churchyard with good early 18th century sculpture including gamekeeper with flintlock.

Legerwood (594434) 12th century church repaired 1717, 1804, 1880, 1898; chancel arch; sundial south-west angle; former manse 1750, 1812, 1928; peaceful secluded site behind farm buildings.

Swinton (838476) church pre – 1209, 1593, 1729, 1782, 1800, 1837, 1910; late 16th century gallery with external stairs; south pulpit; large manse 1700, 1750, 1771, 1815, 1892.

Hownam (771193) church restored after 1906 fire; ootby location; large former manse.

Ashkirk (466220) 1790/1 church; gallery east end; former manse; old school; site of 'palace' of Bishops of Glasgow.

Kirkurd (127443) T Plan church 1766; former manse and school; watch house (1828) in churchyard; very peaceful location.

Yarrow (357278) church 1640, 1771, 1826, 1906, 1923; south-west (1640) sundial; large manse.

Drumelzier (134343) plain 1779 church; atmospheric site; large former manse.

Bunkle (809597); church 1820; 12th century chancel apse in yard; former manse 1840s.

Newlands (161465) 14th/16th century church in ruins; replaced by new church to north 1838; old manse 1740; old school and schoolhouse at bridge; medieval and 18th century churchyard stones.

Lyne (191405) church 1640-45; Adam and Eve stone 1712.

Polwarth (750495) historic church; huge former manse to north.

Maxton (610302) T plan church 1812; west and east galleries; south-west doorway from pre-Reformation church.

Mertoun (615318) T plan church on new site 1658, 1820, 1898 in grounds of Merton House; jougs, sundial.

Skirling (074390) church medieval, 1720, 1791, 1893; hill site with massive earth bank.

Makerston (668331) tiny church 1808 on new site; south belfry tower; vast wooded churchyard area to west.

Oxnam (701190) T plan mid 18th century church on new site; watch house; good uprights and tablestones.

Morebattle (772250) church 1757, 1899, 1903 beside site of 12th century church; former manse.

Bedrule (599179) T plan church 1803–4 on medieval site, 1876–77, 1914; hogback fragments in porch; birthplace of Bishop William Turnbull (c1400–54) founder of the University of Glasgow.

Eckford (707270) has fine crenellated 19th century watchhouse; Manor

(220380); Longformacus (694572), Cranshaws (692618) and Roxburgh (700306) are also worth visiting.

The large churches at Minto (566201) by William Playfair *c.* 1830, Hobkirk (587110) *c.* 1863, and Ayton (927609) *c.* 1864 are not in the Border tradition.

In the towns St. Mary's and Old Parish Church in Hawick on a 13th century site was rebuilt in 1764 with a six storey tower and further rebuilt in 1880; Kelso Old Parish Church is a superb octagonal town council church completed in 1773; and West Linton church, built in 1781 and reconstructed in 1871, is noted for exceptionally fine wood carving. Note also at West Linton the beeboles (shelters for beehives) in the churchyard wall.

All are worth examining and conserving.

ELEVEN

CASTLES AND COUNTRY HOUSES

The Borders has a complete range of Scottish country house types from later seventeenth century variations on the tower house to opulent early twentieth century Edwardian piles. It only requires a little ingenuity in crossing boundaries into East Lothian and Northumberland to study the evolution of the castle from twelfth century mottes to sixteenth century artillery forts, towers and bastels.

EARLY EARTHWORK CASTLES

In Galloway and Nithsdale and the Upper Ward of Lanarkshire early castles are so plentiful that motte-hunting can become a habit. In comparison the Borders have only a few examples of the twelfth century 'munitiones et castella', the ring works and mottes built by the same new ruling elites from Normandy, Britanny, Yorkshire, Cumbria and Somerset. There were the de Morevilles in Lauderdale, de Soulis in Liddesdale, Lovels and Riddells in Teviotdale, the Somervilles and Avenels being given land grants based on knight service by the Scottish kings, in particular by David I (1124–53) and also by Malcolm IV (1153–65) and William the Lion (1165–1214).

The traditional Christmas pudding shaped motte is a circular or oval or rectangular mound, artificial or partly natural, made up of a series of layers of earth and stone, and with a deep and wide ditch round the base. On the top of the mound, or built into it, was a wooden blockhouse or tower, possibly crenellated and perhaps with external fighting platforms, and round the edge of the mound was a timber stockade. Access to the top was by a flying bridge over the ditch from the counterscarp or by steps up the side of the motte from a bridge over the ditch at the base. Some may have had timber beams laid round the side of the mound so that the castle looked more like a massive tank than a grassy hillock. The motte as seen today may be much higher than the original as over 50 or 200 years of occupation the mound may have been improved and heightened on more than one occasion.

Some, probably most, mottes were inside or at the edge of an oval or rectangular or triangular or kidney-shaped bailey or courtyard, itself ditched and defended, with space inside for barns, stables, kitchens, a hall or chapel and retainers' huts or houses. They are usually found on sites with formidable natural defences, on promontories or on the bank of a river or on an 'island' surrounded by swamp or marshland. Some mottes are easily recognised today; in other cases identification is difficult or even essentially speculative without excavation.

There are no extant examples in the Borders to rival the huge 5 acre Motte of Urr in Galloway or the Bass of Inverurie in Aberdeenshire, although no doubt the twelfth century castles at Jedburgh, Roxburgh, Peebles and Berwick were comparable in strength. There is also nothing to parallel the intense concentration of mottes along the river valleys of the Nith, the Urr, the Dee and the Clyde, where the barons and knights had to deal with a series of local rebellions. Perhaps in the Borders the royal castle at Jedburgh and the establishment of sheriffdoms at Peebles, Selkirk, Roxburgh and Berwick provided a degree of central control and security absent in the south-west where many more castles were built.

The best and most easily located motte in the Borders is the Lovel caput in Hawick (499149) (Plate 15) above the town and also above and between the Teviot and the Slitrig Water. The steep-sided motte and the ditch was excavated in 1912 by A.O. Curle. The de Soulis motte at Liddel Castle (NY 510900) on the B 6357 north-east of Newcastleton is impressive. Other mottes include The Mount, Castle Law (814418) above the Leet Water near Coldstream, Riddell motte and bailey (520248), the 'Pele of Selkirk' at The Haining (470281), Howden (458268), Phenzhopehaugh or Rankilburn (318127) and Bedrule (595182). The motte and bailey in Peebles (249403) was at the obvious site between the Tweed and the Eddleston Water now overwhelmed by the Church of Scotland.

There is another and difficult to identify category of twelfth to sixteenth century earthworks, rectangular or oval with water filled ditches, homestead moats or moated manors or fortified farmhouses or granges. The best example is Muirhouselaw or Morhus (631284) near Ancrum which has two rectangular enclosures. Other examples, clearly recorded on the O.S. maps, include Florida (NY 517908) and Kirndean (NY 532909) off the B 6357, Dykehead (582073) and Bloomfield (588234).

STONE KEEPS AND COURTYARD CASTLES

The wars north and south of the frontier in the twelfth and early thirteenth century were not between 'Scotland' and 'England', but rather contests between competing warlords for power and authority over and across boundaries which might still be redefined. The invasions of England by Malcolm III (1057–93), by David I (1124–53) and by William the Lion (1165–1214) were unsuccessful attempts to seize hold of as much land as possible in Northumbria, Durham and Cumberland. The frontier as more or less finally defined in 1237, when Alexander II (1214–49) renounced any claim to the northern English counties, was essentially the same as that fixed in 1018 after the Battle of Carham in 1092 by William II at Carlisle and by Henry II in 1157. In comparison the Three Hundred Years War between Scotland and England after the death of Alexander III (1249–86) was not so much a dispute over frontiers as about wider questions of supremacy, and of international relations between a lesser and greater power set within a European context involving also Ireland and France.

Great castles in England by the 1150s or 1170s meant massive rectangular stone keeps, three or four storeys high, with immensely thick walls, and virtually impregnable without the use of powerful siege engines. The keeps at Newcastle-upon-Tyne (1167–70), Bamburgh, Wark, Norham and Carlisle constituted a very effective barrier to invading armies. Whether there were keeps in the castles above Berwick, Jedburgh and Roxburgh remains unknown in the absence of archaeological evidence; however, only a short distance away across the Tweed is Norham Castle (907476). Norham began in 1121 as Ranulf Flambard's motte and bailey castle. It was destroyed by the Scots in 1136 and 1138. The stone keep at the north-east corner of the inner ward was built between 1158 and 1174. Reconstructed and heightened between 1422 and 1425 it was taken and destroyed by James IV's army in 1513 before Flodden, but the castle had been rebuilt again by 1515.

By the 1290s modern military architecture in Scotland meant much more sophisticated, complex and costly castles having great curtain walls with round flanking towers, set behind concentric lines of defences, and sometimes with an aggressively sited frontal gatehouse keep. Tantallon Castle in East Lothian, north-west of Dunbar, and Caerlaverock Castle near Dumfries are the most spectacular examples in southern Scotland.

Roxburgh or Marchmount Castle (713337) (Plate 16) on its peninsular hill site between the Teviot and the Tweed near Kelso and above the medieval town of Roxburgh was more important than either Tantallon or Caerlaverock. Only Edinburgh and Stirling Castles were more vital to the medieval Scottish Kingdom. As a motte and bailey castle Roxburgh was a key fortress when it was surrendered by William the Lion to Henry II in 1157. Handed back by Richard I in 1189, it changed hands several times in the wars between 1296 and 1346, but was then held by England until 1460 when it was taken in the famous siege after James II had been killed when one of his own cannon blew up. 'Utterly broken' by 1416 'doung to the ground' in 1460, demolished in 1550 under the Treaty of Boulogne, little remains to be seen except the sheer scale of the site, a few fragments of buildings including an English artillery fort built by the Earl of Hertford in 1545, some remnants of the curtain wall above the Teviot and sections of the great ditch round the base of the hill.

The site of the important castle at Berwick is the track and goods yard and platform at the railway station. After 1333 it was permanently under English control except for brief periods 1355–56, 1378–82 and 1461–82. Hume Castle (704414), which probably was a thirteenth century enclosure castle with corner towers, is now an amazing folly, a 'sham antique' rebuilt between 1790 and 1796 by the Earl of Marchmont The hilltop site, dominating the Merse from the north, is impressive and the castle was besieged and taken as late as 1547, 1549, 1569 and 1651. Virtually nothing remains on the ground to locate the thirteenth century Comyn castle at Bedrule (598180).

Hermitage Castle (497960) on the invasion route through Liddesdale was another key fortress held variously by de Bolbeck and de Soulis, Dacre and Douglas and Bothwell. The site is probably thirteenth century, the core a compact mid fourteenth century hall house, the visible castle a central mass c.1358–65 with four great corner towers c.1400 submerged into the whole, which was then 'generously' restored in the early nineteenth century. It is almost impossible to make sense of it without seeing an aerial photograph. The complex pattern of ditches and mounds outside includes both sixteenth century artillery defences and platforms and earlier defensive lines.

TOWER HOUSES AND BASTELS

The standard fortified dwelling in the Borders from the fourteenth to the seventeenth century was the tower house. Only the largest were really castles in the sense of being able to withstand a prolonged attack by a force of any size. Most were small and solid three or four storeys high rectangular towers with thick walls which concealed a labyrinth of passages, stairways and latrine closets. The wing in the L plan variation provided more space for a stairway, at least up to the first floor, and additional rooms. In early towers the entrance might be at first floor level; in most the entrance was on the ground floor. By the later sixteenth century the parapet walk sometimes featured ornamental corner turrets and embellishments such as pepper pot stone cannon to run off drainwater. Clustered round the tower were various barns, stables and outhouses, the whole inside a barmkin wall. Some had a strategic role as watch towers against the English, but most were designed for security against attack by neighbours, friends, relatives and miscellaneous reivers or raiding parties. There were many tower houses, over a hundred in Roxburghshire, over twenty buildings or sites in Liddesdale alone.

The Borders remained a frontier province, suffering from wars and violence generated by disputes between Scotland and England, worst of all perhaps during the English invasions and 'Protestant crusade' to sack and destroy Scottish Catholic churches, abbeys and towns between 1544 and 1550. Castles on the invasion routes through Liddesdale and Lauderdale and the Merse suffered most of all.

However, it is too easy to explain problems too exclusively in terms of international relations. Some cross Border disputes were settled by the Wardens at the 'Days of Truce' in the East, Middle and West Marches. The reality was that the Scottish Borders, like the Highlands, remained outside the effective control of Scottish central Government until well into the seventeenth century, in spite of the some eighty punitive expeditions between 1513 and 1603 by James IV, James V and James VI. It was impossible to control the mobile raiding parties intent to 'rob, burn, spoil, slay, murder and destroy', 'Scottish when they will and English at their pleasure', difficult to bring them into a proper 'feare of Justice'. Until reivers were hunted down and hung or departed to Ireland in sufficient numbers internal security was a mirage. Only 'a thread, a sheet of glass' separated 'civilisation from barbarism'. The constant thieving of cattle, the robberies and kidnappings and blackmail, the abduction of heiresses, the fire-raising, the overall lawlessness and banditry, riot, rape, ransom, rampage and reprisal, was not remotely romantic. Most of it originated from feuds and rivalries between Scotts and Kerrs, Maxwells and Johnstones, Armstrongs, Grahams, Douglases, Humes,Pringles, Nixons, Elliots, the 'surnames' or extended families. The hanging of Johnnie and Thomas Armstrong and some thirty followers in 1530 was a rough but a necessary justice.

At least three tower houses were major castles. The Kerr stronghold, Cessford Castle (738238) (Plate 17) in the hills south of the Kale Water, is of national importance. The L plan Tower of *c.*1446 is massive. Outer defences included a deep moat. It was dismantled after a siege in 1523 by the Earl of Surrey and again in 1545. Newark Castle (421294) on the Buccleuch estate above the Yarrow Water is another massive five storey high tower house with two late sixteenth century caphouses and battlements. It is set inside a well-preserved barmkin with gunports. Neidpath Castle (236404), the late fourteenth/fifteenth century L plan tower house of the Hays of Yester, has the most wonderfully spectacular site above the Tweed. It was heightened in 1654 by the Earl of Tweeddale, who also added the fine entrance doorway and terraced gardens ('hanging gardens' or 'a sloping parterre') above the river.

Amongst the many smaller towers Smailholm (637346) (Plate 4) is outstanding. The stark rock outcrop site is immensely dramatic; the history is ferocious as the Pringles who built it *c.*1500 had as devious and complex a record as most Border families. The upper floor was added *c.*1590/1600, but the tower is still amazingly austere and plain; by the middle of the seventeenth century it belonged to the Scotts of Harden. Cranshaws (680619) above the Whiteadder Water may be the least altered and most perfect tower. Held by the Swintons from c.1400 to 1702 it stands five storeys high with a fine parapet walk including projecting gargoyles setting off the rounded wall angles below. It is enhanced by its setting within a complex of nineteenth century farm buildings. Barns (215391) was built for the Burnets of Burnetland c.1576. The small three storey tower was extensively modernised in the late eighteenth century. Greenknowe (639428) built for James Seton c.1581 and held in the seventeenth century by the Pringles of Stichel, is on a strong site protected by marshy swampland on all sides. The L plan tower has many pleasing decorative features including a turret staircase over the re-entrant angle, three corner turrets and crowsteps. Dryhope (267247) on a plateau site above the Yarrow Water looks early, but may have been rebuilt for Philip Scott c.1613. Kirkhope (379250) above the Ettrick Water was probably built c.1600 for the Scotts of Harden. The four storey and cap house plan is very typical of many later towers. Darnick (523343) now sheltered behind a high garden wall in the village of the same name, belonged to the Heiton family. The later additions blend successfully with the tower which was built in the 1560s and 1590s.

Small tower houses can be readily converted into prestigious and comfortable vertical residences. Hillslap (513394) which has been restored by a London architect post 1982, was with Colmslie and Langshaw one of a cluster of ruined towers on the moorland plateau country above the Allan Water. Aikwood (420260), or Oakwood, is a compact late sixteenth century three storey rectangular tower which belonged to the Scotts of Harden. Although uninhabited for over 200 years it had been used as a storage area for the adjacent farm. It has been restored between 1990 and 1992 by the local M.P., Sir David Steel, with the adjoining byre made over into an exhibition area. Also of interest is the recreated fifteenth or sixteenth century walled garden. In the centre of Hawick the sixteenth century 'L plan Black Tower of Drumlanrig', formerly part of the Tower Hotel, is currently (1994/95) undergoing restoration.

Dovecots or pigeon houses, which provided fresh meat in the winter months, are amongst the most attractive buildings associated with Lowland lairds. They were usually conveniently located to enable the pigeons to feed off their tenants' fields. There are splendid, well-preserved round beehive type dovecots at Chirnside (870562) which has two string courses, and the larger and later (?1576 or seventeenth century) and exotic example with three string courses in the garden behind Mertoun House (620319).

The Most Ingenious Places

There are two unique tower houses in the Borders. Littledean (633313) sits at the top of a steep bank on the north side of the Tweed with the Broomhouse Burn to the east. It belonged to the Kerrs of Cessford and may date from the second quarter of the sixteenth century. It is extraordinary: from the west a round tower of high quality masonry with behind an almost apologetic, self-effacing east end. The quasi-circular front has a terrifying barrage of five great gun ports, opened wide on the outside, with two other gun ports at the splayed base and a third facing south behind. Was this an exercise in ingenuity commissioned from the fine scholarly hand of Sir James Hamilton of Finnart, who in building Craignethan Castle between 1532 and 1540 was showing off the latest architectural fashions from France and Italy? Or was it an archaic imitation of Ravenscraig Castle in Fife? Excavation of the area surrounding the tower is needed to understand the strategic plan of its architect.

Drochil Castle (162434) (Plate 18) above the Tarth and Lyne Waters was built for the Earl of Morton, the Regent of Scotland from 1572 to 1578. It may not have been completed when he was executed in 1581. It was built on the Z plan, with two round towers at the opposite corners of a massive central block with a central barrel-vaulted corridor running underneath through the middle of the castle. The overall concept, the quality of the stonework, and the rich decorative corbelling and gun ports are fascinating.

Recommendation

Cessford, Littledean and Drochil are in a poor state of repair and desperately need major conservation measures. They merit the early attention of national and local authorities.

Bastel Houses

Recent work on seventeenth wills and testaments and archaeological fieldwork in the Upper Ward of Lanarkshire and in the Borders has produced a new picture of the farming economy in the hill country. Tenant farmers and bonnet lairds still needed defensible, rather than 'fortified', farmhouses for security against wandering marauders and bands of robbers. This was especially the case in the more isolated areas near Elvanfoot, Crawfordjohn and Abington in the west and in the Roxburghshire and Northumberland ootby hill and moorland country twenty miles north and south of the Border.

Bastels or pele (pyle) houses (in England 'bastles') were typically compact two storey farmhouses with the family occupying the upper floor, which was reached by a moveable ladder. The ground floor was used for storage space or for accommodation for cattle or sheep. There were probably several hundred such houses in northern England and southern Scotland. Black Middens (NY 774900) and Hole (NY 867846) respectively north-west and north-east of Bellingham and Mervinslaw (671117) and Slacks (644098) above the Jed Water are good examples.

WALLED TOWNS AND ARTILLERY FORTS

The strains and tensions of international relations from the 1530s to the 1570s involving England, France, Scotland and Spain had drastic consequences for townsfolk in the Borders. The old town of Duns, for example, was burnt out in 1544, 1545, and 1548: the site, in the grounds of the modern Duns Castle, was subsequently abandoned. In Peebles, which was sacked in 1549, earlier defences were improved with the building of a new town wall c.1569–74. A small section with a corner tower by the mason Thomas Lauder survives close to a modern supermarket and car park on the old railway station precinct. In Lauder the town wall survives only in the names such as the East Port and West Port: the last remnants were removed c.1800.

In the south of England Henry VIII had erected new round, squat artillery castles with tiers of gun ports c. 1538–40 at Deal, Walmer, St. Mawes and Pendennis. On the northern frontier the massive investment of capital in modernising the defences of Berwick begun by Henry VIII and Mary Tudor was completed by Sir Richard Lee for Elizabeth I between 1558 and 1570 at a cost of £128,648. Vast open ditches and lines of defence with bastions in the new fashion with two outer faces and two flanks were built to plans by the Italian military engineers Contio and Portinari. Old curtain walls were lowered and reinforced with earthworks. Further earthwork platforms and parapets were added between 1639 and 1653 and the Ravenswood Barracks were built in two phases in 1717–21 and 1739–41. Most of the town defences are still intact.

Between 1544 and 1549 English armies controlled for some of the time most of the Borders and the Lothians from the Merse to the Firth of Forth to the Solway.

English garrisons variously held Roxburgh, Eyemouth, Hume, Lauder, Haddington, Dunglass, Dumfries, Lochwood, Castlemilk, Lochmaben and Threave. Under legislation reminiscent of English policies in Ireland all Scots within 'the pale', 'the King's dominions in Scotland', were required to recognise Edward VI as their king and to abandon the Catholic Church. In turn French armies assisting the Scots held Leith for twelve years and garrisoned Hume, Dunglass, Blackness, Dunbar, and Eyemouth. New forts were built by the English or the French or each in turn at Roxburgh, Lauder, Haddington, Dunglass and Eyemouth. The artillery fort on Fort Point promontory (943648) at Eyemouth was developed by the English army in 1547 and then extended and improved by the French from 1557 to 1559. Farther west the Corn Fort (940650) and the 'French Camp' at Dunglass belong to the same period.

The square fort with four corner bastions on Duns Law (786547), set inside prehistoric oval defences and above cultivation terraces, was the work of General Leslie's army in 1639–40.

THE FIRST 'GREAT HOUSES'

The transition from fortified residence to undefended country house is often a complex story. Commonly until the 1660s, and sometimes much later, buildings were almost heterogeneously added on to existing tower houses. By the end of the seventeenth century new houses appear, some admittedly archaic in style, but others following classical plans introduced by Edinburgh based professional architects and consultants of whom the most famous were James Smith (c.1646–1731) and then Sir William Bruce of Blairhall near Culross (1625/1630–1710), architect, politician, and Member of the Scottish Parliament 1669–74, 1681–82 and 1685–86.

Traquair House (330353) (Plate 19), simply the best country house in the south of Scotland, has a complex architectural history. The oldest part is the c.1492 three storey tower house at the north-east end: the south wing was added in 1559, with another extension to the south again in 1599: James Stuart, the 1st Earl of Traquair, in raising the height of the building by an extra storey in 1642 might perhaps be said to have turned it into a country house: the service wings, the two garden pavilions and terraces, the forecourt and entrance gateway and the new overall external appearance was the work of James Smith in 1695. The Bear Gates (1737–38) (Plate 20) with George Jamesone's bears (1745) were closed after the funeral of the last Countess in 1796. The grounds include a rare survivor, the wonderful 'moss house' or Summer House built in 1834 and made of hazel twigs and heather and reed. It was restored in 1990 and still has its original fittings including a curved arcade bench. The interior of the house and its contents, including sixteenth century carved wooden panels, sixteenth/seventeenth century painted ceiling beams, the Tom Scott painting of *Traquair and River* (1902) and a vast collection of muniments, is superb.

The older part of Thirlestane Castle (532479) (Plate 21) is the long oblong sixteenth century block with four round corner towers. The greater mansion house was built between 1670 and 1682 by Robert Mylne under the direction of Sir William Bruce for the Duke of Lauderdale, who managed and controlled Scotland for Charles II from 1660 to 1680. Two west pavilions flank the now massive and heightened six storey western end, the whole given a dramatic flavour by the flight of steps up to the terrace. The three small semi-circular towers on the north and south of the older block are very unusual. The north and south wings at the front were added by David Bryce in 1841. The great state room has a remarkable display of Restoration panache, the elaborate large plaster work fruits and flowers by Dutch craftsmen between 1675 and 1680.

The Black Barony Hotel (236472), or Darnhall, sits above the Fairydean Burn at the end of a long lime tree avenue. The central block of the Murrays' house dates back to 1536: the east facing towers on each side belong to the refurbishment of 1700–1715: later additions, including work in 1855 and 1877, give it a complex history. The grounds include a fine egg-shaped ice house dating to 1753.

The Kerr stronghold above the Jed Water, Ferniehurst Castle (652179), was severely damaged in attacks and sieges in 1523, 1549 and 1570. It was demolished on the orders of James VI in 1593. The new castle, a large central block with wings at the west end and a south-east corner tower, was rebuilt in 1598. It has remained largely unchanged externally, apart from some remodelling in the seventeenth century.

There are many more examples, however, of a tower house evolving into a country house. Branxholme Castle (464116), which was developed as a Z plan tower house for Sir Walter Scott c.1570–74, had extensive eighteenth century additions; Bemersyde tower (592333), which was completed in 1581 for Andrew Haig, and has a wing built in 1860, was redesigned by Ian G. Lindsay in 1960; Houndwood House (853630) near Reston incorporates an earlier tower house in the seventeenth century house with additions in 1900; Lessuden House (598314) near St. Boswells has a central sixteenth century L plan rectangular block with additions in 1666 and 1685 and an eighteenth century wing; Nisbet House (795512) near Duns consists of a seventeenth century rectangular block with two round towers at the south-east and south-west angles, and with a large crenellated tower added in 1774. The Hirsel (828408) near Coldstream consists of a sixteenth century tower house, next to an early eighteenth century block with two wings, which is adjacent to an early nineteenth century extension: it stands splendidly above an ornamental lake created out of swamp land in the late 1700s.

Old Gala House in the older town above the present Galashiels town centre incorporates a two storey tower house of 1583, a south-east extension of 1611 built for Sir James Pringle, a south-west wing of c.1760, with further additions and alterations in the 1830s. The top floor of what is now a museum and gallery has a fine painted ceiling with rich fruits and cherubs completed for Hugh Scott and Jean Pringle in 1635.

COUNTRY HOUSES: ELEGANCE AND EQUIPOISE

The eighteenth century country house is the most visible evidence of major changes for the better in rural areas. Recent research has shown the extent to which there were significant improvements in agricultural productivity and profitability in the Lothians and the eastern Borders from 1660s onwards. Although much depended on the imagination and enthusiasm of individual landowners, the Scottish Parliament did pass a series of acts in 1661, 1669, 1686 and 1695 enabling and encouraging landed proprietors to introduce new ideas, enclosures and the consolidation of holdings, drainage and reclamation schemes to extend the area under cultivation, and marling and liming to improve yields. Of course, having said that, the 'Agricultural Revolution' was still a slow process with a series of changes accelerating in the 1730s and again from the 1760s to the 1820s.

The scale of the surpluses generated, or optimistic expectations of profitability, was reflected in the new classical country houses built at the turn of the century, and more generally in the 1720s and 1730s by William Adam (1689–1748), as well as in the more exuberant work of Robert Adam (1728–92) in the 1770s and 1780s. 'A place in the country' for 'the great and the good' was not, however, merely a great house: it had also to be located in an environment of ordered calm and enlightened tranquillity, a landscape laid out with avenues and vistas, with bridges, gardens, orchards, orangeries, deer parks, heronries, ice houses, artificial lakes, fish ponds and waterfalls, arbours and wildernesses, delights and follies.

The finest early classical house in the Borders is Mertoun (618318) built in 1702–3 for Sir William Scott of Harden to plans by Sir William Bruce and recently restored to its original size by the Duke of Sutherland. Mellerstain (Plate 22) (647390) was a commission given to William Adam by George and Lady Grisell Baillie in 1725: what makes it a key house is the superb interior including wondrous plaster work ceilings and friezes in the most delicate greens and pinks by Robert Adam between 1770 and 1778: the contents include paintings by Van Dyck, Raeburn, Ramsay and Gainsborough: the terrace garden looking over a lake to the hills was laid out by Sir Reginald Blomfield in 1909. Marchmont (742484) was built for the 3rd Earl of Marchmont in 1750: some embellishments by Sir Robert Lorimer were added in 1913: the interior has some spectacular French and Italian plaster work. Enough survives to suggest the scale of the original avenues and vistas. Paxton House (931520) was built for Patrick Home between 1756 and 1772 by John and James Adam: the exquisite plaster work ceilings may be by Robert Adam. There is a fine collection of mahogany furniture by Thomas Chippendale: the Picture Gallery by

Robert Reid c.1811, now restored to its condition as it had been reconstructed in 1876, is a National Gallery of Scotland outstation whose collection may include work by Opie, Bough, Morland and Cotman.

Bowhill (425278), set in an estate so carefully landscaped it seems almost natural, began in 1708 as a small house: the present house is William Atkinson's Georgian mansion of c.1812–19, with enlargements and additions mainly between 1831 and 1833 by William Burn, and with further additions and alterations including the east wing by David Bryce 1874–76. It contains room after room devoted to accommodating the best private art collection in Scotland, with at least seven Van Dycks in the gallery hall by Burn, the Wilkie painting of George IV in 1822, a stunning Raeburn of a youthful Walter Scott in 1808 with his dog Camp, *Bran*, a Scottish deer hound by Thomas Duncan, *Busy, Minette, Spy, Oscar, Grog, Caro* (six dogs at Dalkeith House) by Alexander Naesmyth, a show stopping Canaletto of London Whitehall to St.Pauls, Claud Lorrain, Thomas Gainsborough, Kneller, Reynolds and so on!

Important 'lost houses' include Pirn House (c.1700 and 1730) near Innerleithen demolished in 1950; Minto House near Ancrum built by William Adam 1738–43 with additions by Archibald Elliot in 1810 and W.H. Playfair in 1837; and Ladykirk House near Norham, built in 1797 and demolished in 1966.

The many good smaller houses include Ednam or Havannah House in Kelso by James Nisbet of London in 1761 with plaster work ceilings, Aurora and her chariot, Europa and the Bull, of major importance; Castle Craig (136442) c.1798; Barns (216392) by Michael Naesmyth of Edinburgh 1773–80; Kilbucho Place (093351); Scotston (141454) 1770; Netherurd (116447) 1791–94; Chisholme (418122); The Yair (453329) 1788; Allerly (547352) 1810; Hunthill (666190); Hobsburn (581119); Crailing (688243) 1803; Bughtrig (796447) c. 1790; Renton (822652); Edrington (941550); Bogangreen House, Coldingham; and James Adam's Gunsgree House (the Customs House) of 1753 in Eyemouth.

Dawyck (168351), Kailzie (282385) and Monteviot (650245) Gardens, the last with the sublime and restored folly, the Waterloo Monument or Wellington's Pillar 1815–14 on Peniel Heugh (Plate 5), all deserve detailed study and exploration. Dawyck arboretum in particular is quite outstanding.

Opulence and even Excess
Fashions in architectural styles and concepts of good taste come and go and some landowners inevitably preferred to indulge in exuberant Gothic fantasies or pseudo-baronial excesses. Wedderburn Castle (809528) was built for Patrick Home of Billy between 1770 and 1775 to plans by Robert

and James Adam executed by James Nisbet. The plan, with three octagonal corner towers on the main fronts, is that of a mock castle, but as at Culzean and Oxenfoord and even Mellerstain there are both classical and 'battlemented' motifs. Some early nineteenth century alterations were perhaps by James Gillespie Graham (1776–1855), who was building Duns Castle (778544) between 1818 and 1822 in the Regency Gothic style for William Hay.

Jedburgh Castle Gaol (647202), which was built to plans by Archibald Elliot between 1820 and 1823 on the site of the medieval castle, has a central core, the gaoler's house, which is like a miniature Inveraray, and three blocks set around it separated by large healthy exercise yards, all surrounded by a battlemented curtain wall.

Stobo Castle (173366) was built by Archibald and James Elliot for James Montgomery between 1805 and 1811; here again the Georgian Gothic is very reminiscent of Inveraray. The lake and water garden add more visual delights.

Floors Castle (711346) (Plate 23) cannot be neatly pigeonholed as one thing or the other: as built by William Adam after 1721 it was a large plain house, but the castle as remodelled by William H. Playfair (1789–1857) between 1838 and 1849 was almost incredibly fussily ornate, over-embellished with pinnacles and turrets and crenellations that turn it into a child's dream of what a castle should be.

Abbotsford (508342) (Plate 24) is another, even more remarkable, 'romance in stone', a Tudor Gothic Scottish Jacobean house in a style suitable for a squire. 'Cartlethole' purchased by Scott in 1811 became 'Abbotsford', an essay like the house into self-conscious romanticism. The new house was almost built by a committee. It emerged out of Scott's own antiquarian tastes and the designs and ideas of two architects, William Atkinson and Edward Blore, and of another antiquarian, James Skene of Rubislaw. Between 1816 and 1824 they created instant history, but they also employed some very novel ideas including polychromatic stonework, gas lighting and a sort of 'rescue' archaeology programme through which carved stones and woodwork from much older buildings throughout Scotland ended up in Abbotsford.

Ashiestiel (430351), which Scott rented from General Russell between 1804 and 1812, and where he wrote some of his best work was a very different smaller, more sedate, multi-period Scottish country house with a central block and west wing. The east wing was added in 1830.

Victorian Baronial architecture in the Borders is seen at its richest in Ayton Castle (929614), a massive red Chirnside sandstone pile above the Eye Water built to plans by James Gillespie Graham in 1846. Hutton Castle (889549) above the Whiteadder Water became the country residence of Sir William Burrell. His gifts over two decades until his death in 1958 gave Berwick Town Museum and Art Gallery a sufficient accumulation of 'excess baggage' and marginalia to form a second Burrell Collection. It includes some more than merely useful items, five Crawhalls, a Degas, examples of works by Daubigny, Fantin Latour and Lavery, and two charming Boudins.

The swan song of great houses in the Borders is extraordinary. Manderston (810543) is one of the great British Edwardian country houses: between 1903 and 1905 Sir James Miller had the 1790s Georgian house extended and deepened. The still severely classical exterior conceals an interior of extreme opulence, a staircase with a silver balustrade, baths coated with silver leaf, domestic quarters to impress even the most snobbish servants. The other buildings include stables (1895) with teak stalls and marble floors, a vaulted marble dairy arranged round a fountain, and a tower house folly for tea parties and picnics with a hidden staircase for the maids.

Leithen Lodge (320427), an older house redesigned by Sydney Mitchell in 1887–88 in the Arts and Crafts style, has recently been restored with the addition in the courtyard of the Lochend Archway built to plans by James Smith in 1684 for Sir John Sinclair's house at Dunbar.

Peebles Hydropathic Hotel, built in 1905 to plans by the architect James Miller (1860–1947) replace the earlier Hydropathic Institute (1878) destroyed in a fire in the same year, can scarcely be bettered as an example of the sort of country hotel patronised by the genteel citizens of Edinburgh and Glasgow who travelled there by railway.

Skirling House (076389) built between 1905 and 1908 to plans by Ramsay Traquair for Lord Carmichael, the Governor of Bengal, sits at the edge of the village green. The contents include a 1590 Florentine wood panelled ceiling and a remarkable collection of wrought iron work, birds, reptiles, tulips, lilies and lanterns by Thomas Harper of Edinburgh.

Broughton Place (115372) looks as if it ought to be a seventeenth laird's house. There is even a barmkin beyond the rectangular block with one large and one small corner tower. In fact it was a commission received by Basil Spence (1907–76) completed in 1937–38.

TWELVE

THE SELKIRK PAPERS

At the start of World War II, there was a general panic throughout Britain that the German Luftwaffe would bomb and burn the whole country into oblivion. A 1940 War Office directive ordered that no quantities of paper or any other combustible material should be kept in attics where there was a greater incendiary risk. In Selkirk, the manager of the Commercial Bank, knowing that he had a lot of paper in the upper storeys of his bank on the High Street, ordered the odd-job man to carry it down to the back garden and burn it.

Next door to the bank was the bakery of Mason's Tearoom where the brothers Bruce and Walter Mason worked as bakers. Seeing the smoke, they went to investigate and were aghast to find over four hundred years of Selkirk's history going up in flames. They asked permission from the Bank Manager to be allowed to look through the mass of paper but this was refused owing to the 'confidentiality' of some of them. With the help of a spare half-crown, they persuaded the odd-job man to carry the sackloads of documents slowly down the stairs. By this ploy, they managed to save about five per cent of the documents being destroyed. In weight about half a ton, the rescued papers were dismissed as 'jist some dirty auld bits o paper' but this has recently been described by Donald Galbraith, the Keeper of the Historical Records of Scotland, as 'the most valuable collection of medieval documents to have come to light in this country in my experience'.

Being interested in the history and archaeology of the Borders, the Writer was shown the collection in the late 1950s. In 'the bakehoose loft' was an Aladdin's cave, amongst the flints and Roman pottery which were the result of the Mason brothers' years of field-walking, were boxes, flour barrels and tea-chests holding literally thousands of documents. Bruce Mason died in 1963 and the Writer became a joint keeper of the collection and the secret of its acquisition. Walter Mason was a shy, quiet and gentle man in every sense, whose unassuming nature concealed a vast knowledge. It became a matter of deduction for us to work out how such a wide range of documents from the pre-Reformation to the late Victorian days became jumbled together in the attic of a Selkirk bank. The early documents and books had been written by the priests and notaries of the town before 1560. After the Reformation, the same men carried on as notaries and clerks to the burgh. The shared occupation of lawyers and town clerks did not change much until about the middle 1700s when they started to dabble in banking and as insurance agents. Gradually the banking interest strengthened and eventually the Commercial Bank took over this sphere of activity. Through these four centuries, an enormous amount of paperwork had accrued; with five per cent saved, what must have been burned? At the beginning of his last illness, Walter Mason asked me to take the documents, especially the protocol books, for safekeeping. With no immediate family, he was frightened that they might be returned to the bonfire from whence he and his brother had rescued them. He asked only that I 'put them to the best possible use' and opined that I would have a lot of fun with them. He died in January 1988 and I lost a good friend whose intellectual stimulus I had enjoyed for many years.

As the new owner of half a ton of documents, some written when James the Fourth was King of Scots, what was I going to do? Some of the material was dry, brittle and unhandleable; some was damp and growing varieties of fungi. I asked advice from Dr John Imrie who had recently retired as Keeper of the Scottish Records. He inspected the documents for two days and said the protocol books in particular were of national interest. It would have been easy to have given the collection to the care of the Scottish Records Office. However, being a thrawn and stubborn Borderer, I was determined that they should stay in Selkirk where they were written and that the collection would bear the name of Walter Mason. Accordingly, I enlisted a few friends and formed the Walter Mason Trust with the sole purpose of raising money to conserve and transcribe the papers. This would preserve the unique collection and make them available to all for study and interest – this was 'the best possible use' to my mind. A short time previously by reason of a fractured skull, I had given up working as an agricultural fencing contractor and had joined the Ettrick and Lauderdale Museum Service. I donated the collected to them rather than to the Archives Section of the Borders Regional Library which should have been their home. The reason for this was purely selfish – I wanted to work on the transcription and translations myself.

Many of the 17th/19th century papers contain fascinating details of national and social history of the period but the most historically exciting part of the Mason Collection is contained within the protocol books. These were the legal notebooks kept by the priests and notaries from pre-Reformation to post-Reformation times; importantly they recorded the customs, deeds and disputes of the common people of the town and country far more than the land transfers of the great and good/bad which are the usual surviving documentation of this period. That they were written in medieval Latin, medieval Scots in a form of shorthand to save paper and with many of the papers frayed at the edges by damp, nibbled by mice and partly burned by the English, the Bank Manager and probably my own ancestors, only made the task somewhat harder than normal. I could read the medieval forms of Latin and Scots although the shortened writing posed some problems. There were sixteen protocol books covering the period 1511–1667: some in scattered folio and one, in itself containing eighteen hundred and forty two pages. A formidable task! However, help was at hand when Teresa Maley came to the district. She is a Cambridge History graduate specialising in medieval Latin and Anglo-Saxon with additional medieval Welsh from Bangor and is a trained archivist – manna from Heaven! Her knowledge of palaeography and Latin exceed mine whereas my reading of Scots and knowledge of local place names and customs, meant that I can add a contribution. Our individual spheres of knowledge were and are complementary. After three years working together Teresa's Scots has improved immensely although my Latin is still a bit sluggish!

PRESERVATION

The first task was to get the books user-friendly because to turn over a page in their original condition, meant that you were usually left with a scrap of paper containing two or three letters between your fingers. Each handling of the page could result in destroying the meaning of a sentence. When the Trust had raised sufficient funds, Tom Valentine, the paper conservator and bookbinder, was given the task of unpicking the bindings, washing the pages, sealing each page between two layers of fine paper or Chinese silk and re-binding the whole. This done, we proceeded with the transcription and translation of over five thousand pages which contained new insights into the history of the Borders and Scotland.

For the next two years, we struggled through the often atrocious writing, puzzled over the word contractions used, wondered about the Scots legal system, debated the varied legal instruments involved and in general had a great time. Working from original sources has an excitement which is not there while using someone-else's work. In two years of part-time work, we transcribed and translated the first four early protocol books. These were John Chepman 1511–36 and 1545–47, John Chepman 1536–43, John and Ninian Brydin 1526–36 and John Brydin 1530–37. The Latin sections we translated into English quoting the original only when it was deemed important or when we weren't quite sure what it meant; the Scots we left as it was as examples of the Border Scots of the period. Sometimes the Latin was Scoticised and sometimes the Scots was Latinised. After going through each book four or five times and letter by letter, we were determined to publish. Since the books were from roughly the same period, we decided to publish the four together with an introduction and one index.

When it came to publication, we received a very interesting offer from the Stair Society. The Stair Society was founded to 'encourage the study and advance the knowledge of the History of Scots Law' and, as our protocol books were all legal documents, could they publish them for us? Indeed they could, especially as the Glenfiddich Trust put up the money for our share of the publication costs. Since Teresa is an English archivist and palaeographer and I am a Border fencer and generally interested person, neither of us is a specialist in Scots Medieval law. Help was required to ensure that our work conformed with the exacting standards of the Stair Society. We asked Professor Bill Gordon and Dr John Durkan of Glasgow and Dr. John Imrie, the former Keeper of the Scottish Records for advice on the Scots legal terms and instruments of the period. This was willingly given and these gentlemen picked up some of the points we had missed. I think that they were surprised on how much we had managed to get right. So, the four books were published under the auspices of the Stair Society with the title of *The Selkirk Protocol Books 1511–1547*. Additional work for the publication was undertaken by two members of the Walter Mason Trust. The introduction was written by Dr Peter Symms and Dr Donald Galbraith took on the awesome responsibility of doing the index (Plate 25).

The texts are so wide and varied in nature that it is not easy to choose typical examples. There are land transactions, feuds and feus, wills and some new concepts of customs and ways of life in that period. But did the Kers and Scots of Selkirk really apologise to the Moffat traders and return the goods and gear which they had taken 'by mistake'? And why were stress stools placed at house doors to signify that the inhabitants were being forced to flit? Who was Troilus Maguu who signed one of the legal instructions as a witness? Was George Brown really given the choice of wife in Janet or Margaret Hoppringill of Galashiels, 'as he pleases'? There is a great deal of social and economic history to be gleaned from the pages. Wills and lists of goods show the standard of living of the people. Property deals and land transfers show who owned the land and houses within the burgh. Selkirk families sent one of their members to become a burgess of Edinburgh to give them trading rights within the capital. The list is practically endless.

The transcription team have already produced two rough drafts of the next protocol book, that of Ninian Brydin 1536–64. It contains some 569 legal instruments and will probably be the star of the collection. Ninian started his life in Selkirk as a priest and notary in the late 1520s, moved to Edinburgh in middle age and returned to the Borders in 1560. It covers one of the most interesting periods of Scottish history and with luck should be published in 1995. Following on after that is the one thousand, eight hundred and forty two page Protocol Book of William Brydin. Despite its size it only covers the period 1579 to 1587. There is still a long way to go.

THIRTEEN

THE DISCOVERY OF THE BORDERS: SIR WALTER SCOTT

We are used to the merging of geography and literature that occurs when a part of the country is given an imaginative identity by a poet or novelist. Well-known examples are the moors of West Yorkshire known as Bronte country, and Thomas Hardy's Wessex. This literary enhancement of geographical identity itself has a history: it is a feature of romanticism, and cannot be traced much before the late eighteenth century. The creation of a literary identity for a region offers an alternative to both a metropolitan and a national culture; it expresses an interest in the indigenous and local. It flourished in a society of readers willing to be enchanted by poetry and novels, and to respond to the varieties of human experience generated by unfamiliar landscapes. Such readers might even be moved to visit the area, and a growth in the number of visitors is usually a consequence of a region's heightened identity, as if readers wish to experience for themselves that coming together of geography and the imagination. This chapter is concerned with the way in which the Borders were given an imaginative identity by a writer, Walter Scott. It is an attempt to describe the 'discovery' of the Borders. Of course the Borders as a geographical area were known before, both to those who lived there and to others who had occasion to consider the regions of Scotland. The discovery explored in this chapter is the creation of an imaginative identity from geographical and social features which had been there before, a creation both for those outside the region and ultimately also for those living within it. In this project it might be questioned whether it is appropriate to give so much attention to Walter Scott. After all there were other writers who wrote about the Borders, several of them his contemporaries of whom the most distinguished were John Leyden and James Hogg (see Chapter 18). It was Scott, however, who because of the popularity of the works he published in the first decade of the nineteenth century established an idea of the Borders which other writers from their different vantage points extended and amplified. It was the works of Scott which gave the valleys of the Border rivers of Teviot and Tweed the alternative name 'Scott country'.

Historians commonly point out that in studying a border territory one should give equal emphasis to both sides, as one side of a border is a mirror image of the other. In cultural history this is not so. This is illustrated by considering the term which gives this book its title, the Borders. That term does not equally describe both sides of the Anglo-Scottish Border. It is a specifically Scottish term, and it describes a substantial part of southern Scotland adjacent to the Border. The term describes, roughly, the area covered by a triangle drawn through Berwick, Carlisle and Peebles. Except for the English towns on the Border itself the term does not include England, and certainly not an equivalent geographical area south of the Border itself. (The northern English, in so far as they have a comparable phrase for the areas of Cumbria and Northumberland adjacent to the Border, call it 'the Border country'). In Scott's day the counties included in the Borders were Roxburgh, Selkirk, Peebles, and parts of Berwickshire and Dumfriesshire. Since the local government reorganisation of 1974 much of this area has been called The Borders Region. The term is now so accepted in Scotland that we need to be reminded that it was not a term widely current in the eighteenth century. The Border, meaning the Anglo-Scottish Border, and Borderers, meaning those who live near the Border, are terms several centuries old[1]. But the phrase the Borders in our sense of a region seems to date from the late eighteenth century; the growing currency of the phrase indicates a shift from identity being claimed through the inhabitants, the borderers, to its association with place, the Borders.

I have suggested that the literary creation of regional identities was a feature of romanticism. This can be illustrated by the situation in Scotland. The culture of the Gaelic-speaking Highlands had been brought into the consciousness of Lowland and English readers by the works of 'Ossian', translations of Gaelic epic poetry published by James Macpherson in the 1760s. The other Scottish poet to bring an area of Scotland to a wider readership was Robert Burns, who gave voice not simply to the rural labourers of Lowland Scotland but specifically to the culture of his native Ayrshire. In the north of England the late eighteenth century saw the discovery of the English Lakes. The writer most associated with this discovery is William Wordsworth, but it is apparent that he had several predecessors and contemporaries who contributed to the creation of its imaginative identity[2]. The pattern of the discovery of the Borders seems to have been similar: an interest was growing throughout the eighteenth century; there was a cluster of important writers in the area in the early nineteenth century; and one writer, because of his stature and reputation outside the area itself, seems to stand forth as the creative inspiration. In the Lake District that man was Wordsworth, and in the Borders, Scott.

Walter Scott (Plate 26) was a Borderer by birth on both sides of his family. He was descended from a doughty Borderer 'Auld Wat', Walter Scott of Harden, a kinsman of the family of Buccleuch, who married Mary Scott 'the Flower of Yarrow' in 1567. Scott remarked that it was 'No bad

Plate 1

The folded greywacke at St Abbs Head (Pettigo Wick).
Source: Dr C. Gillen

Plate 2

James Hutton's geological unconformity at Siccar Point.
Source: Dr C. Gillen

Plate 3

Eildon Hills – Trimontium of the Romans.

Plate 4

Smailholm Tower. This superb tower house, associated with Sir Walter Scott, dominates the skyline from its stark location.

Source: Gordon Lockie

Plate 5

Peniel Heugh: a monument to the Duke of Wellington.
Source: Dr C. Gillen

Plate 6

The three bridges at Leaderfoot.
Source: Southern Reporter

Plate 7

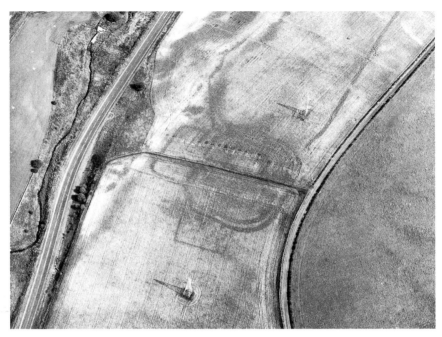

The Roman fortlet at Oxton.
Source: RCAHMS

Plate 8

The medieval village of Midlem showing early medieval Anglian field systems.
Source: RCAHMS

Plate 9

Cove harbour.
Source: Dr C. Gillen

Plate 10

Kelso Abbey was the first monastery of the reformed Benedictine order (Tironensian). The abbey was founded by King David I in 1128.
Source: Scottish Borders Tourist Board

Plate 11

Melrose Abbey. This is one of the most beautiful of our abbeys, founded in 1136 by King David I.

Source: Walter Brydon

Plate 12

Jedburgh Abbey was built on an earlier ecclesiastical site. It was founded in 1139 by Kind David I.

Source: Scottish Borders Tourist Board

Plate 13

Dryburgh Abbey. The abbey is located in a lovely setting on a secluded promontory by the River Tweed. It is a 12th century foundation of the Constable of Scotland, Hugh de Moreville.

Source: Dr C. Gillen

Plate 14

Lauder Kirk

Source: Gordon Lockie

Plate 15

The early medieval motte at Hawick – probably constructed by Richard Lovell.

Source: From the Walter Brydon Collection in care of Ettrick & Lauderdale Museums Service

Plate 16

Roxburgh Castle. Originally known as Marchmount, Roxburgh Castle became the strongest fortress in the Borders.

Source: Ettrick & Lauderdale Museums Service

Plate 17

Cessford Castle. This is an L-plan Kerr castle construced *c.* 1446
Source: Gordon Lockie

Plate 18

Drochil Castle. This is a Z-plan castle with rich, decorative corbelling and gun ports. It was built in the latter part of the 16th century.
Source: Walter Brydon

Plate 19

Plate 20

Traquair House, reputedly the oldest inhabited house in Scotland.

Source: Scottish Borders Tourist Board

The Bear Gates at Traquair House.

Source: Dr C. Gillen

Plate 21

Thirlestane Castle. To the north east of historic Lauder lies the imposing structure of Thirlestane Castle built c. 1590 for the first Baron Maitland of Thirlestane.

Source: Dr C. Gillen

Plate 22

Mellerstain House. This is one of Scotland's grandest Georgian houses with outstanding interior decor and a superb collection of paintings.

Source: Scottish Borders Tourist Board

Plate 23

Located on the outskirts of Kelso is the magnificently ornate 18th century Floors Castle.

Source: Lee Leaven

Plate 24

Abbotsford House. On this site stood the farmhouse of Cartlehole which was bought by Sir Walter Scott in 1811. It was demolished in 1822 and replaced in 1824 by the present mansion in which many of Scott's famous works were written.

Source: Scottish Borders Tourist Board

Plate 25

The Selkirk Papers. Dr Donald Galbraith, Teresa Maley and Walter Elliot examine the conserved protocol book of Sir Ninian Brydin (1536–1564).

Source: Gordon Lockie

Plate 26

Sir Walter Scott, by Chantrey.
Source: Ettrick & Lauderdale Museums Service

Plate 27

Kelso Square. This is one of the most elegant and picturesque of any town squares in Scotland.
Source: Gordon Lockie

Plate 28

Plate 29

Mosstroopers.

James Hogg.
Source: Ettrick & Lauderdale Museums Service

Plate 30

The River Tweed at Coldstream Bridge, which connects Scotland and England.
Source: Walter Brydon

Plate 31

Pipes and Drums of the King's Own Scottish Borderers.
Commanding Officer 1st BN KOSB. Source L/Cpl Laird KOSB

Plate 32

The King's Own Scottish Borderers excercise their right to march through the streets of Edinburgh with their bayonets fixed and colours flying on 1st August 1989 in their 300th year.
Source: Scotsman Publications

Plate 33

The Melrose Sevens in 1983, at the Greenyards home of the Melrose Rugby Football Club.

Source: Southern Reporter

Plate 34

Casting the Colours, Selkirk.

Source: Gordon Lockie

genealogy for a Border minstrel'[3]. Scott was born in 1771 in Edinburgh where his father was a lawyer. As a young child he suffered from what is thought to have been polio, and was sent to stay with his paternal grandparents at their farm at Sandyknowe, under the sixteenth century tower at Smailholm, near Kelso. This was the beginning of his experience of Border life. He heard Border tales from his grandmother and aunt, and from the cow-bailie Sandy Ormistoun[4]. In 1779 he was sent to the High School in Edinburgh. For some months in 1783 Scott again lived in the Borders, and attended the grammar school in Kelso; it was there that he met his future printer and business partner, James Ballantyne. He returned to Edinburgh and enrolled at the University with a view to entering his father's profession of the law. He became an advocate (barrister) in 1792, but he did not practise for long. In 1799 he was appointed Sheriff-Depute of the county of Selkirk. The need to live in the county he served led to his renting a house at Ashestiel near Selkirk in 1804. In 1806 he was appointed one of the Clerks of the Court of Session in Edinburgh. In 1811 he bought a farm on the banks of the Tweed near Melrose, which he took delight in turning into a house in the Gothic style, Abbotsford (Plate 24). He moved into Abbotsford in 1812 and lived there until his death in 1832. Scott was a Borderer by birth and by choice; but he also had experience of the city, and education at its University, at a time when both were centres of that flowering of learning and culture known as 'the Scottish enlightenment'.

The most important of Scott's early works concern the Borders. In 1802 he brought out a collection of Border ballads entitled *The Minstrelsy of the Scottish Border*, published by James Ballantyne in Kelso. The work which made Scott famous, however, was *The Lay of the Last Minstrel*, a verse romance set in the Borders, which appeared in 1805. In the poem the Last Minstrel tells his tale in the late seventeenth century to Anne, Duchess of Buccleuch, in Newark Castle. The tale itself is set in the sixteenth century and recounts the love between a daughter of Buccleuch and a kinsman of their enemies the Kerrs of Cessford; it involves the supernatural and the grave of the wizard Michael Scott in Melrose Abbey. Three years later Scott published another verse romance entitled *Marmion* (1808). *Marmion* is set in 1513 and ends with the battle of Flodden. The story starts with a description of Norham and ranges between Edinburgh Castle and the Northumbrian coast of Lindisfarne; but the cantos have autobiographical introductions which contain descriptions of the Borders. The next of Scott's poems, *The Lady of the Lake*, published in 1810, is set in the Trossachs, and so leaves the Borders for the Highlands of West Perthshire.

Scott was well known as a poet for almost a decade before the first of his novels appeared. *Waverley*, which gave its name to the series, was published in 1814; its setting is, again, the Perthshire Highlands. Some of the later novels have settings in the Borders: *Guy Mannering* (1815), the second of them, which is set mainly west of the Borders in Galloway, has the famous character of Dandy Dinmont, a Liddesdale farmer. The short novel *The Black Dwarf* (1816) is set in Liddesdale; [5] *The Monastery* and *The Abbot* (both 1820) share a fictitious monastery based on Melrose; *St. Ronan's Well* (1824) is set in Innerleithen. Scott also published scholarly work on the Borders. *The Minstrelsy of the Scottish Border* contained a long historical introduction, and he published an account of *The Border Antiquities of England and Scotland* in 1814. If the discovery of the Borders is to be attributed chiefly to Scott it should be in virtue of his early works: *The Minstrelsy of the Scottish Border, The Lay of the Last Minstrel* and *Marmion*, published between 1802 and 1808. The most important of these for the discovery of the Borders were the two poems; collections of ballads, however significant, always tend to have a narrower appeal. Scott's verse romances did not always enjoy the approval of the critic but they were immensely popular with readers in both Britain and America and in succeeding decades in the rest of the English-speaking world. In his later poems and novels Scott chose settings from many different parts of Scotland; he became in them a Scottish writer rather than a Border writer. Curiously, although it appears that his first attempt at prose fiction was to have been set in the Borders[6] (and there are Border scenes and characters in the later novels) none of the first-ranking Waverley novels is centrally set in the Borders. So, in what follows I shall draw on Scott's writing on the Borders early in his literary career. This is the period when his discovery of the Borders started. After about 1808 one has to reckon with other influences, for instance, the growing reputation of James Hogg, 'The Ettrick Shepherd', and the work of artists who, drawn there by Scott's poems, started to paint scenes from the Borders.

To justify the claim that Scott inaugurated a shift in the perception of the Borders it is necessary to consider in what respects the area was known before. There were places where the general reader could read about the history and social organisation of the Borders, for instance in Camden's *Britannia* from which many other writers quote. In the enlarged edition of *Britannia* produced by Edmund Gibson in 1695 the author, dividing the inhabitants of Scotland into Highlanders and Lowlanders added this:

> Out of this division I exclude the *Borderers*, because they by the blessed and happy Union (of 1603) enjoying the *Sun-shine* of peace on every side, are to be lookt upon as living in the very midst of the British Empire; and begin (being sufficiently tir'd with war) to grow acquainted with, and to have an inclination for peace.[7]

The eighteenth century Welsh traveller Thomas Pennant described the clans and surnames of the Borders, including *noms de guerre* such as *Tom*

Trotter of the hill, the *Goodman Dickson of Bucktrig, Ralph Burn of the Coit, George Hall,* called *Pat's Geordie* there...these and many more, merry men all, of *Robin Hood's* fraternity, superior to the little distinctions of *meum* and *tuum*[8]

Pennant knew, however, that the society he described had been radically altered since the cessation of warfare across the Border brought about by James VI's accession to the English throne in 1603. He rejoiced that no longer did the mistress of a castle have to present her men folk with their spurs 'to remind them that her larder was empty'[9] as Scott's forbear the Flower of Yarrow had done.

As the Border reivers were relegated to the past the Border valleys started to have a different, softer reputation. In the eighteenth century Scottish songs became popular. Although drawing on Scottish rural life they were popular in drawing-rooms and concert halls in Edinburgh and London, and several collections were published, the most famous of which is Allan Ramsay's *Tea-Table Miscellany* (1723–26). Some of these songs were old ballads rewritten and others were new compositions. Among such songs were many set beside the Tweed, and together they gave an impression of a wooded pastoral landscape. In 1778 the Aberdeenshire poet James Beattie made this comment:

> Several of the old Scotch songs take their names from the rivulets, villages and hills, adjoining to the Tweed near Melrose; a region distinguished by many charming varieties of rural scenery, and which, whether we consider the face of the country, or the genius of the people, may properly enough be termed the Arcadia of Scotland. And all these songs are sweetly and powerfully expressive of love and tenderness and other emotions suited to the tranquillity of pastoral life.[10]

Sometimes in history absence is as important as presence. The eighteenth century saw a growth in travel. One of the things which attracted travellers to northern England and Scotland was an interest in Roman antiquities. In the twentieth century the successful tracing of the route of the Roman Dere Street over the Border, and the discovery of the archaeological remains at Newstead mean that there are important Roman sites in the heart of the Borders. In the eighteenth century this was not so. Eighteenth-century archaeological maps of the Borders show it to be an area with almost nothing to offer, and the visitor in search of Roman antiquities would have been deflected to the Roman walls to the north and south. Astonishing though it may seem to anyone who has stood on the ridge above Chew Green looking into Scotland in the eighteenth century there was no agreement among archaeologists as to the site of Trimontium. Attempts were made to locate it in Annandale before William Roy in his *Military Antiquities of the Romans in Britain* (1793) placed Trimontium near the Eildon Hills above Melrose.[11] This archaeological absence should be borne in mind in considering Scott's imaginative creation of the Borders. For Scott the triple hills of the Eildons were noteworthy not as Ptolemy's Trimontium, but for the tale of their being cleft in three at the behest of Michael Scott.

Scott is a historian, but his interest did not extend so far back as Roman history. (He treated an enthusiast for Roman remains with affectionate satire in his novel *The Antiquary*). Scott was interested in medieval and more recent history, and in both documented history and oral traditions; it was drawing on these that he created his imaginative picture of the Borders.

The richness of the Anglo-Scottish border in ballad texts had been noted by Thomas Percy in the introduction of his pioneering collection of *Reliques of Ancient English Poetry* published in 1765. After noting how many English songs came from the north of the country he added that 'the scene of the finest Scottish ballads is laid in the South of Scotland'.[12] In publishing *The Minstrelsy of the Scottish Border* (1802–3) Scott followed Percy's lead and produced the first volume of orally transmitted ballads to be devoted to one area. Scott divided his book into three sections: historical ballads, romantic ballads, and ballad imitations. Of these he preferred the historical ballads. Scott liked a ballad which could be placed geographically and historically, and these he supplied with full annotation. The historical ballads of the Borders are often called 'riding ballads', in reference to the mounted expeditions and raids described in them. Although the texts are known only in much later versions they seem to describe society in the Borders before the Union of the Crowns of England and Scotland in 1603. The inhabitants are presented in kinship groups and live a life in which their chief economic activity, keeping cattle, is interspersed with raids and fighting on both across the border and between rival named groups on the same side of the border. What was the appeal for Scott of these wild narratives? They describe courage and resourcefulness, loyalty to the kinship ground and a sense of identity. The activity of these Border reivers is precisely the sort of thing that Scott, trained in law in Enlightenment Edinburgh, was professionally committed to curbing. Scott's enthusiasm may have been a romantic yearning for qualities his modern rationalistic urban world was eliminating. The Border reivers whom Scott celebrated were in the past. Thomas Pennant had been glad to inform his readers that the days of the Border reivers were over. Pennant was a Whiggish commentator. Scott was never a Whig, nor a straight-forward Tory. The whole debate between gain and loss in the historical process was the basic subject matter of all his writing.

The Lay of the Last Minstrel tells a tale set in the sixteenth century, in the world of the riding ballads. It differs from them, however, in that the characters illustrate the higher levels of Border feudal society. They are not for the most part robbers and cattle-rustlers, but Wardens of the Marches and defenders of the Scottish border, 'Kinsmen to the bold Buccleuch'. The men are warriors; the women, either the young whose role is defined by love and marriage, or the older woman who has power through strength of will, are like the women in the ballad world. The plot has two strands, one telling of lovers separated by family feud, and the other telling of the abduction of the young heir of Buccleuch by a goblin page, and his restoration through the valour of the hero. The activities of the goblin page are assisted by a spell found in the magic book taken from the grave of the wizard Michael Scott in Melrose Abbey. Scott creates not only a Border world but a medieval world and dwells on the details of social hierarchy, armour, hunting, a tournament, a monastery, pilgrimage, clothing, feasts, and minstrels. It is all conveyed in a fluent, accessible verse in which the only things the reader might find difficult are the terms describing medieval life and Border names. William of Deloraine's ride from Branksome to Melrose is an opportunity to trace the route, through place names, each evoking some identifying description, and the rallying of the Border clans against an English incursion is a roll-call of family names. The theme of the love story is the conquest of dynastic pride by love, 'For Love shall still be lord of all!' The hero's love for Margaret of Buccleuch manifests itself in his standing in for his feudal enemy, Deloraine, whom he had injured, against an English champion. Such a plot, in uniting love and chivalry, invites imaginative entry into the ideals of an earlier society, one apparently less compromised than the post-Union, commercial society of Scott's day. The upper-class world of the *Lay* allowed freedom for the description of life lived according to ultimate values of love and honour, and there was always one value left to enoble the retainers and lower classes, namely loyalty. The world of the *Lay* also confronted the supernatural, the evil supernatural of the goblin and the good supernatural of the church shown as healing social and spiritual wounds in the last canto.

Scott brought to a world-wide audience the names of the well-known Border families and tales and legends associated with them. He conveyed something of the pride of family and strength of beliefs which held late medieval society together through romantic historical reconstruction. Border society was an important aspect of Scott's creation of the Borders, so too was its setting both manmade and natural. Scott drew to his reader's attention types of architecture which were strange to the eighteenth century classical taste: peel towers, fortified houses, Gothic ruins. Buildings of these sorts were plainly visible in the Border landscape, but alienated from their original use. An aspect of Scott's creative imagination was his capacity for describing ruined buildings as they were when serving their original function. His first exercise of this capacity seems to have taken place when he was a very young child at Sandyknowe. The invalid child explored Smailholm Tower with tales of the Borders in his ears

> Methought that still with trump and clang
> The gateway's broken arches rang;
> Methought grim features, seam'd with scars,
> Glar'd through the window's rusty bars...[13]

There is a double vision in Scott's description of the Border architecture: the vital life of the buildings in their heyday is seen by the imagination, while the eye sees the ruins of today.

An example of the role of architecture in the imaginative idea of the Borders is the treatment of Melrose Abbey. In the eighteenth century the Border Abbeys belonged to private landowners; Melrose Abbey belonged to the Duke of Buccleuch. They had all been neglected since their destruction in the sixteenth century by English invaders and protestant reformers; and their stones had been repeatedly plundered for local building. Daniel Defoe in his *Tour Thro' the Whole Island of Great Britain* (1727) gave his opinion of Melrose:

> Here we saw the ruins of the once famous Abbey of *Mailross,* the greatness of which may be a little judg'd of by its vastly extended Remains... But the Reformation has triumph's over all these Things ...nor can any Protestant mourn the Loss of these Seminaries of Superstition.[14]

The mid-eighteenth century saw the beginning of the rehabilitation of the Border Abbeys. The first to receive attention was Melrose because its architecture was Gothic, which was starting to be fashionable, in contrast to the Norman architecture prominent in Kelso and Jedburgh. Visitors started to come to admire the architecture. One of them was the poet Thomas Gray, who wrote in 1764 of the 'noble ruins of the Abbey-Church.... exquisitely adorn'd'.[15] Another was Robert Burns who went to Melrose in 1787 and noted in his diary: 'dine there and visit that far-fam'd glorious ruins'.[16] The end of the eighteenth century saw the beginning of care being taken of the fabric of the ruins. The Earl of Buchan had ambitious plans for Dryburgh, which he bought in 1786. At Melrose in 1822 Scott and his kinsman the Duke of Buccleuch undertook repair of the buildings, saving the East Window.

Scott did more for Melrose Abbey than institute physical restoration. Some of the most famous lines in The Lay of the Minstrel are about Melrose Abbey:

> If thou would'st view fair Melrose aright,
> Go visit it by the pale moonlight;
> For the gay beams of lightsome day
> Gild, but to flout, the ruins grey.[17]

Scott's description of the Abbey, with its stone tracery, and carvings of flowers and foliage rendered 'ebon and ivory' by the moonlight, had enormous impact. More people came to visit the Abbey and painters painted it.[18] His description of the East Window was in Keats's mind when he wrote of the 'casement high and triple-arched' in Madeline's bedchamber in *The Eve of St. Agnes* (1820). The famous lines in the *Lay* are an invitation to melancholy reflection in the precincts of the ruined Abbey. But Scott had a more astringent side to his mind than that. He confessed in a letter to being 'guilty of sending persons a bat-hunting to see the ruins of Melrose by moonlight which I never saw myself'.[19] Scott had more in common with his moss-trooper Sir William Deloraine 'good at need', who was sent on an urgent errand to Melrose by the Lady of Buccleuch:

> Short halt did Deloraine make there;
> Little reck'd he of the scene so fair:
> With dagger's hilt, on the wicket strong
> He struck full loud, and struck full long.

The ruins of Melrose, whether by moonlight or not, are not what the main part of *The Lay of the Last Minstrel* presents. The tale is set in pre-Reformation Scotland; the Abbey is functioning as a sacred place. It represents a system of authority to check that of the Border warriors, and spiritual power to check that of 'dark magic'. Scott's evocation of Melrose Abbey suggests that his representation of the Borders involved giving back the spiritual and non-rational to an age of suffering from its own self-conscious rationality.

I have suggested that others before Scott had been charmed by the attractive scenery of the Border, by the wooded river banks presenting a picture of a northern Arcadia. Scott shared their enthusiasm – he was a keen tree-planter on the Abbotsford Estate – but he was also the celebrator of the Border landscape in its less benign aspect. He frequently wrote of autumn and winter, of bare, brown hills and raging torrents. His flower is the 'wild heath-bell'. This was a liberation in a way, from the picturesque in landscape. And it has its special compensations: 'Caledonia! stern and wild/Meet nurse for a poetic child!' Scott had the romantic poet's association of place with the human mind. Two famous examples are in the Introduction to the second canto of *Marmion*. There Scott displays two contrasting temperaments, contentment and rebellion, in terms of two Borders lochs. The mood 'Twixt resignation and content' is matched by St. Mary's Loch from which flows the Yarrow river:

> nor fen, nor sedge,
> Pollute the pure lake's crystal edge;
> Abrupt and sheer, the mountains sink
> At once upon the level brink;
> And just a trace of silver sand
> Marks where the water meets the land.
> Far in the mirror, bright and blue,
> Each hill's huge outline you may view;
> Shaggy with heath, but lonely bare,
> Nor tree, nor bush, nor brake is there...[21]

The person whose heart is 'ill at ease' will prefer Loch Skene from which flows the waterfall known as the Grey Mare's Tail:

> There eagles scream from isle to shore;
> Down all the rocks the torrents roar;
> O'er the black waves incessant driven,
> Dark mists infect the summer heaven;
> Through the rude barriers of the lake,
> Away its hurrying waters break,
> Faster and whiter dash and curl,
> Till down yon dark abyss they hurl.[22]

Earlier tourists had visited the Grey Mare's Tail, but it was Scott who used its source, the dark Loch Skene, as a metaphor for a mood of the human mind.

This way of looking at landscape as offering analogues of human experience Scott shared with other romantic poets. What other poets saw in the Lake District or the Alps Scott saw in the varied terrain of hills, lochs and rivers of the Borders. The intervention of time and history complicates the metaphorical relationship between landscape and human feeling. This is clear from the address to the river Teviot in *The Lay of the Last Minstrel:*

> Sweet Teviot! on thy silver tide
>   The glaring bale-fires blaze no more;
> No longer steel-clad warriors ride
>   Along thy wild and willow'd shore;
> Where'er thou wind'st, by dale or hill,
>   All, all is peaceful, all is still,
> As if thy waves, since Time was born,
>   Since first they roll'd upon the Tweed,
> Had only heard the shepherd's reed,
>   Nor started at the bugle-horn.
>
> Unlike the tide of human time, –
>   Which, though it change in ceaseless flow,
> Retains each grief, retains each crime
>   Its earliest course was doom'd to know;
> And, darker as it downward bears,
>   Is stain'd with past and present tears.[23]

The Teviot, whose banks were once ridden by steel-clad warriers, now flows peacefully as if they had always been the contented retreat of the shepherd. But, Scott is saying, human history is not like that; it 'Retains each grief, retains each crime/Its earliest course was deemed to know'. In human affairs the past will not be forgotten. This is not romantic melancholy, but the grief that was for Scott the burden of history. Writers on the Borders before Scott had rejoiced in the progress which had civilised them, and admired in landscape what met their picture of what was beautiful. Scott inspires the same double vision in the countryside as he had with architecture: the eye sees the Teviot flowing in pastoral tranquillity; the imagination supplies the bale-fires which announced invasion and war.

Scott created in his early works a romantic terrain in the Borders which involved a juxtaposition of the present and the past, the human and natural world. It looks like romance, and can be defended as romance usually is by reference to those ideals which are always under threat from realism and cynicism. But Scott is also a historian. He did not simply take Border history and turn it into romance; his work has a historical foundation, visible in the teller of *The Lay of the Last Minstrel*. The Minstrel, a feudal figure of a poet, has called at Newark Castle in the late seventeenth century. Scott himself, despite having to use commercial publishing instead of the feudal setting in which to woo his audience, invites identification with the Last Minstrel. If the Minstrel, performing before Anne Duchess of Buccleuch, told of days long gone, how much more so is Scott. Since the sixteenth century Border society had been turned from one of warring families whose chief means of livelihood were cattle, into a society of landlords and tenants rearing sheep. In that process the late seventeenth century was significant. In a letter to the Earl of Dalkeith (heir of the Duke of Buccleuch) in 1806 Scott attributed the diminishing of patriarchal ideas among the Scott clan to Anne Duchess of Buccleuch's marrying and going to live in England. In the late seventeenth century there started the depopulation of the Borders to make way for extensive sheep runs. In 1688 there had been 'an hundred landed proprietors of the name of Scott living on the Borders'; in Scott's day it was hard to find ten. The process was still going on. 'I could name many farms where the old people remember twenty *smoking chimneys* and where there are now not two'.[24] *The Lay of the Last Minstrel*, Scott's first long poem, is an evocation of the older Border society. His first novel, *Waverley*, is an evocation of earlier Highland society. Both works were immensely popular, and perhaps for the same reason. It was an implicit criticism of the ideology of progress to find the imagination kindled by systems of value and manners represented by a society that had irrevocably gone.

Scott's early writings gave imaginative identity to the Borders in a series of images which were in opposition to eighteenth century ideas; his Borders are nationalist and feudal; the landscape is bare and often hostile; human life confronts the supernatural at several levels. If that seems backward-looking one should remember also what was new: his presentation of the Borders as a setting in which to reflect on the mysterious interaction between the human mind and the natural world, and human societies and history.

References

1. *The Oxford English Dictionary*, 2nd ed., Oxford, 1989 Border 3a; Borderer 1.

2. Norman Nicholson, *The Lakers; The First Tourists*, London 1955; *The Discovery of the Lake District*, catalogue of an exhibition at the Victoria and Albert Museum, London, 1984.

3. J.G. Lockhart, *Memoirs of the Life of Sir Walter Scott*, Bart., Edinburgh and London, 7 vols, 1837–8, 1, 3, 66.

4. Arthur Melville Clark, *Sir Walter Scott: the Formative Years*, Edinburgh and London, 1969, 49–50.

5. Walter Scott, *The Black Dwarf* ed. P.D. Garside, *The Edinburgh Edition of the Waverley Novels*, Edinburgh, 1993, 131.

6. A fragment of an early attempt by Scott to write a 'tale of chivalry' set in the Borders was published the 'Magnum Opus' edition of *Waverley*, Edinburgh, 1829, I, xli–liv.

7. William Camden, *A Second Edition of Camden's Description of Scotland*, London, 1695, col. 885.

8. Thomas Pennant, *A Tour in Scotland, and Voyage to the Hebrides: MDCCLXXII* Chester, 1774, 90.

9. Thomas Pennant, *A Tour in Scotland MDCCLXXII*, Part II, London, 1776, 276.

10. James Beattie, *Essays: on Poetry and Music*, Edinburgh, 1778, 186–7.

11. William Roy, *The Military Antiquities of the Romans in Britain*, London, 1793, 79 and plate xxi.

12. Thomas Percy, *Reliques of Ancient English Poetry*, London, 1765, quoted from the edition of 1812, I, liii.

13. *Marmion*, Introduction to Canto 3, Walter Scott, *Poetical Works*, ed. J. Logie Robertson, London 1904, 115.

14. Daniel Defoe, *A Tour thro' the Whole Island of Great Britain*, London, 1724–27, ed. G.D.H. Cole, London, 1927, II, 763.

15. Duncan Tovey, *Gray and his Friends*, London, 1890, 263.

16. *Robert Burns's Tour of the Borders*, ed. Raymond Lamont Brown, London, 1972, 21.

17. *The Lay of the Last Minstrel*, Canto 2, *ed. cit.* 8.

18. James Holloway and Lindsay Errington, *The Discovery of Scotland: The Appreciation of Scottish Scenery through Two Centuries of Painting*, National Gallery of Scotland, Edinburgh, 1978, 89–95.

19. Letter to Bernard Barton, 4 October, 1824. *The Letters of Sir Walter Scott* ed. H.J.C. Grierson, London, 12 vols. 1932–37 *Letters 1823-1825*, 387.

20. *The Lay of the Last Minstrel*, Canto 6, *ed. cit.* 39.

21. *Marmion*, Introduction to Canto 2, *ed. cit.* 102.

22. *Ibid*, 103.

23. *The Lay of the Last Minstrel*, Canto 4, *ed. cit.* 21.

24. Letter to the Earl of Dalkeith, 23 November, 1806. *The Letters of Sir Walter Scott* *ed. cit.Letters 1787–1807*, 332–333.

FOURTEEN

THE BURGHS, TOWNS AND VILLAGES

With nearly a hundred burghs, towns and villages in the Borders, there is not space in one chapter to consider each one and tell why and how it grew where it did; consequently, this chapter will be a shortened version of the history and forces shaping the communities of the Borders. The story cannot be told without encroaching into spheres already covered in greater depth in other chapters of this book.

There were places where people gathered to live in communities throughout the area from the earliest times. They would start as extended family units and expand into what we would now think of as villages. In the Dark Ages and early medieval times (see Chapters 5 and 6) the flatter and more productive lands of the lower Tweed were dotted with Anglian villages. These were largely self-sufficient communities dependent on the produce of their fields with part-time craftsmen like smiths, weavers, wood turners, carpenters and perhaps potters selling their work within the immediate area.

It used to be thought that a community grew up because of the security afforded by being near a castle or fortified place but this idea must be questioned in the Borders. Certainly there have been castles located beside several Border burghs but these were held quite independently from the burghs and there was always a space between the two.

Another theory is that towns grew up round a market place; this could be at a busy cross-roads, at a port or river crossing. Where there was a place where people gathered, there was the opportunity to buy and sell (Plate 27). The place might be near an abbey or royal castle and administrative centre which required supplies and services. This might have been a combination of trading opportunity and security to the inhabitants.

Several Border burghs have grown up in such circumstances but most of the towns and villages have different reasons for development. Thus Birgham grew because of the bridge; Yetholm was beside an ancient road while St. Boswells and Broughton were at cross-roads; Peebles and Selkirk because they were near a king's castle which was the administrative centre of the shire; Kelso and Melrose to serve the needs of the abbey; Eccles for a nunnery; Coldstream for a priory; Galashiels because the Gala Water flowed strongly in its final two miles and Newcastleton because an improving landowner wished it to be there. There are as many reasons why the Border towns grew up where and why they did as there are towns.

THE BURGHS

There were two communities which may have been big enough to be called towns before the reign of David I. Berwick was important because of its port which had been there in Roman times. Roxburgh dominated the middle lands of the productive lower Tweed and was situated at a place where both Tweed and Teviot could be forded. Perhaps Jedburgh should be added to the list of important centres of population since Anglo-Saxon coins of the tenth and eleventh centuries have been found in the vicinity. This could suggest a more sophisticated trading centre than has yet been located in the Borders region. Jedburgh was close by the Roman road called Dere Street which provided the main line of road transport into Scotland until the seventeenth century.

The Kings' or Royal Burghs

It was in the reign of David I that small communities were given the incentive to expand. David ruled the south of Scotland and much of northern England as David the Earl from 1113 to 1124 and as David I, King of Scots from 1124 to 1153. In this time he encouraged the development of burgh communities by granting land and special trading rights. During his reign, David granted the status of 'King's or Royal burgh' to Roxburgh, Berwick, Jedburgh, Peebles and probably Selkirk where an immense common land of 22,000 acres was still being claimed by the burgesses there in the seventeenth century. Lauder was granted King's burgh status by his grandson William I but would be a well-established burgh long before that.

The King did not give the land to the burgh but rather gave the use of it. The community might be permitted to till a stated acreage but in the main the use was confined to grazing and certain rights of woodland; hunting rights were usually retained by the monarch and forest laws strictly enforced. Through the centuries, the land held in common with the king was looked on as belonging to the burgh and burgesses who used it. This led to the burgesses having to ride and defend their common lands against neighbouring lairds; this duty became the annual Common Riding as is described in Chapter 19.

The eleventh and early twelfth centuries were times of growing population in Europe and the King and community of Scotland could benefit in creating an environment which made trading possible. In creating burghs with favoured trading concessions, the king was able to divert some of the profits to the crown by means of tolls and harbour dues. Again, there was the added incentive that it gave him a reservoir of free men ie, men who did not have any feudal commitment to other than the king himself.

This was to prove very important in later years as a counterbalance to the growing power of great landowners.

A King's burgh was a privileged community to which the crown had given common lands to be held by the community and a measure of self-rule, the burgh law, with the right to hold a weekly market and annual fair. The importance of the monopoly market can be illustrated by an example in the reign of William I. The inhabitants of the nearby abbot's regality village of Kelso were allowed to buy fuel and corn for those carting it and could sell the food made from the commodities in their booths. However, this concession was cancelled on Roxburgh market days as the king's burgesses took precedence over all others.

For the privileges conferred, the burgesses of the royal burgh paid in watch and ward service and in rents paid directly to the king. Even if the rents were paid in kind they could easily be turned into money, providing an income for the king which he seldom received from his estates. To be a king's burgess was a privilege not to be bought by simply paying a rent, for the burgh laws had to be obeyed. These were established in the twelfth century 'Leges Burgorum' which set out the regulations for the burgesses of Berwick, Roxburgh, Edinburgh and Stirling, the four most important burghs in Scotland. They were largely market and behavioural regulations, eg, who was allowed to be a burgess and the conditions; setting standards for the goods sold and penalties involved if these were broken; how disputes were to be settled between burgesses. In short, they were the rules of a civilised urban society. The Leges Burgorum were taken as the standard for all the burghs within the kingdom and maintained even in the sixteenth century Court Books of Selkirk and Peebles.

Many Kings of Scotland were particularly anxious to encourage settlers from the Low Countries into the burghs. By the early thirteenth century Flemish merchants were being offered tofts within some burghs for rent-free periods of up to ten years. At Berwick, the rent-free settling-in period was only for one year and this in itself shows the importance of Berwick as the main trading port of the country. The foreign market for Cheviot wool was expanding faster than the Border monasteries could get their flocks to produce it.

Flemish merchants seem to appear in many of the surviving documents of the early medieval times. This might be because the important Flemings needed the assurance of written title deeds to keep them in the country. They brought their commercial expertise into their adopted country and became Scottish citizens. There are references to Flemings settling in several parts of the Borders: the parish of Ayton in Berwickshire has farms called Flemington and Redhall, Redhall being the name given to a Flemish market.

Certainly the grants they received were repaid in loyalty; thirty Flemish merchants were slaughtered in Berwick when they defied Edward I in

1296. Even in the inland burgh of Selkirk, there were burgesses with Low Country names in the sixteenth century rolls.

The Burghs of Barony and Regality

The king was not the only person with power and land. Many landowners had an equal interest in increasing their money rents with the consequent power opportunities and influence which could be gained by development. There was the church which was itself a great landowner and its officers commanded respect and yielded much power.

These factors led to the foundation of the Burghs of Barony and Burghs of Regality in the Borders. There are so many of this type of burgh within the Borders Region that in this chapter if must be sufficient to note them for a future inquiring mind; nor should this list necessarily be deemed complete.

The Burghs of Barony or Regality	When created	By whom
Duns	1489	Home of Ayton
Earlston	1489	Home of Whitrig
Langton	1509	Cockburn of Langton
Hawick	1511	Douglas of Drumlanrig
Dryburgh	1526	Abbot of Dryburgh
Old Greenlaw	1596	Home of Sprott
New Greenlaw	1598	Home of Sprott
Eyemouth	1598	Home of Wedderburn
Galashiels	1599	Pringle of Gala
Preston	1602	Earl of Angus
Melrose	1609	Earl of Haddington
Eddleston	1607	Murray of Darnhall
Cockburnspath	1612	Arnot of Cockburnspath
Kelso	1614	Earl of Roxburgh
Coldstream	1621	Hamilton of Trabroun
Linton	1631	Stewart of Traquair
Longnewton	1634	Earl of Lothian
Hyndlawhill	1635	Hoe of Hyndlawhill
Coldingham	1638	Stewart of Coldingham
Ancrum	1638	Earl of Roxburgh
Kilbucho	1650	Dickson of Harttree
Thirlstane	1661	Lady Mary Maitland
Town Yetholm	1655	Wauchope of Niddrie
Rutherford	1666	Lord Rutherford
Smailholm	1687	Don of Smailholm
Minto	1695	Scott of Haychester

The Burgh of Barony was rather like the Royal Burgh in that it was established by Royal Charter. In this case, the Crown gave the landowner the right to erect a Burgh of Barony on his land and gave the royal approval some time later. For the landowner the establishment of such a burgh on his land meant greater power and a boost to his cash income by way of increased rents as the land became more valuable. As the burgh grew, so did the power and influence of the laird. The Burghs of Barony were rules by the Baron's Court ie, the laird who had created the burgh and his representative there was the Baron's Baillie.

There was some time between the granting of the Charter and the Royal Charter of Confirmation. In the case of Galashiels, the Charter founding the burgh of barony was given in December, 1599 while it was confirmed by Royal Charter in 1617. For the Crown, the creating of the Burghs of Barony with additional trade and wealth, meant an increase in the tax revenues for the Exchequer.

The Burgh of Barony had the right to hold a weekly market and one or more yearly fairs but could not do so if it infringed the rights of a Royal Burgh. The monopoly of trade and manufacture in the area was one of the most jealously guarded privileges of the Royal Burghs. To take an example of the rivalry between the Ancient and Royal Burghs and the Burghs of Barony, we can do no better than to examine the case of Selkirk and Galashiels, six miles apart.

Selkirk was an ancient King's Burgh from the time of David I, an administrative centre for the area, the county town of Selkirkshire and possessor of a common of some 22,000 acres which was the envy of the neighbouring lairds.

Galashiels was a village which only became a Burgh of Barony in 1559 when Sir James Pringle, a favourite of James VI, decided to enhance his prestige at Court by having his own burgh; the financial aspect may have come into the equation as he eventually was to lose his large estates in payment of debts incurred. Galashiels had no common land to benefit the burgesses unless the lands known as The Cuddie Green were held by the community.

Before the early 1600s, Selkirk craftsmen and traders had never felt the need to form themselves into trades guilds because they were secure in the burgess rights of a Royal Burgh which protected their monopoly trading in the area. Galashiels was a village of about two hundred inhabitants before being granted its charter. Galashiels did have one valuable commodity in the fast-flowing Gala Water. A document in the Walter Mason Papers, mentions thirteen mills in the lower few miles of the Gala Water, three of these being waulk mills; so we can surmise that weaving was an important business in the area.

The Selkirk trades began to become alarmed at this growing threat to their livelihood. The Selkirk Weavers formed themselves into an incorporation in 1608; the Shoemakers in 1609; The Tailors in 1610. The Fleshers were formed much later in 1679; the Hammermen in 1681.

Despite the best Selkirk efforts, Galashiels continued to grow with about eight hundred inhabitants in the middle sixteen hundreds. Meanwhile, Selkirk stayed around seven hundred people which was the same approximate number as at the time of Flodden. In the early seventeenth century, the Anglo-Scottish wars were a thing of the immediate past and the threats of destruction no longer hovered over the burghs. This was a time for economic expansion and most of the larger burghs formed trades guilds similar to those of Selkirk.

The Burghs of Regality were very similar to the Royal Burghs and the Burghs of Barony in practical terms. The main difference was that they had a religious organisation or a secular lord from that organisation as their superior rather than the king in the case of a Royal Burgh or a landowner in a Burgh of Barony.

A regality is a state within a state where the lord of the regality had the same powers of jurisdiction as could be found in the king's law. Otherwise, the inhabitants of a Burgh of Regality enjoyed the same privileges of marketing as the Burghs of Barony. There are villages in the Borders which could have been Burghs of Regality; in the case of Stow, there is a document dated 21st January 1604, where Mark Lord Borthwick conveys the 'office of justiciarie and bailliarie of the whole regality of Stow' to James Pringle of Galashiels.

The regality of Sprouston was given to Eustace de Vesci when he married one of the many illegitimate daughters of William the Lion in 1193. It is suspected that many Border villages which have an ancient pedigree fell into the same category but their superior or lord never took the trouble and expense of making them a legal Burgh of Regality.

It was possible for a Burgh of Barony to become a Burgh of Regality as Melrose did in 1621 and Hawick did in 1669. Melrose has a rather peculiar history with a barony of regality under the Abbots of Melrose which then became a legal Burgh of Barony under the Earl of Haddington in 1609 and resumed the status of a Burgh of Regality twelve years later. Burghs of Regality were abolished in 1747.

The Anomalies

Not everything goes smoothly in Borders history, even in the well documented sphere of burgh rights. Nor were the communities fussy from whom they accepted rights; For instance, Coldingham was given the right to establish a weekly market and hold an annual fair by Edward I of England.

It is recorded that in 1602, the Earl of Douglas erected Selkirk into a Burgh of Barony despite the fact that it was already a Royal Burgh. This deed seems to have been quietly ignored then as now.

In September 1639, the Earl of Roxburgh proposed that Nether Ancrum be the head Burgh of Baronies for Ancrum, Lilliesleaf and Ashkirk with the rights of proclamations at the cross. However, after two years dispute, the proposal was dropped in September 1641.

There are other villages in the Borders which should have been erected to the status of Burghs of Barony with market and other rights. For example, the Berwickshire village of Gordon has an ancient history, stands on a defensible site with a castle near, lies in the centre of good arable land and stands at a busy cross-roads. This should have been an ideal place to create a burgh and site a market. However, no documentation has survived to this effect although it may have existed at one time. The indwellers of Gordon had, and still have, certain rights of fail and fuel on Gordon Common. Perhaps the rights had been unwritten but long-established and the phrase 'It's aye been' is usually sufficient to pass as law with the average Borderer.

The same criteria might be applied to several other villages in the Borders region. Denholm has as strong qualifications as Gordon. Fieldwalkers and metal detectors have located a number of late thirteenth/ fifteenth century coins and pottery at Sprouston which suggests that there was an active market there at that period. Coin and pottery finds at Lilliesleaf and Midlem make it fairly certain that trading took place there in the fourteenth century.

THE VILLAGES

There are reckoned to be some 70 villages in the Borders. A few are planned while some have grown in a pattern set by land availability and suitability. Most were originally based on land use with a few specialist craftsmen working within the community. Some villages grew up around a cornmill, a tower, a religious establishment or a cross-roads. Some thriving communities have disappeared entirely or are mere shadows of their former glory; others have survived and grown.

The villages in the flatter lands of the Merse tend to be based on the Anglian pattern as described in Chapter 6. This type of 'town planning' can be seen in many of the Border villages to this day, notably in Berwickshire where the ground tillage has remained the most important aspect of life. Evidence of land formerly under the plough is preserved in some of the Roxburghshire villages like Bowden, Lilliesleaf, Maxton and Midlem where the field patterns of the Anglian plough system can be traced on air photographs and early maps.

In the upper valleys of the Tweed basin, the picture is different. Here, there were few villages in medieval times and the people lived in the sparse houses which nestled near the many small towers. These could best be called tower hamlets, although that might be an aggrandisement for them since there would seldom be more than five houses in use at any one time. Only the laird's immediate followers would live near his tower. Theirs was a pastoral, grazing economy with a few small fields in the haughs near the settlement. Until the end of the sixteenth century, reiving had been an acceptable means of supplementing their sparse living.

With a more peaceable time in the seventeenth century, the towers gradually became less desirable as residences and the tower hamlets disappeared in the early nineteenth century with the Agricultural Revolution. Towers only survived in a few cases where there was sufficient agricultural land to sustain the population. The tower could finish its life as a storehouse or a cattle court in modern times; more often it was a convenient source of building stone for the new farmhouse.

The coastal villages of Berwickshire had their economies based on the sea. Eyemouth had grown into a fishing town; Cove, St. Abbs and Burnmouth remained as small fishing communities. Only Eyemouth could have had the possibility of becoming a medieval port like Berwick.

AGRICULTURAL DEVELOPMENT AND CHANGES

The dominant role of agriculture in the landscape of the Borders and the shaping of communities cannot be underestimated, for until the early twentieth century the area remained a rurally based economy with some concentrated pockets of industry in the towns. Even in the centre of Hawick, which was the most industrialised of all the Border towns, there was a thriving sheep and cattle market until a few years ago.

The eighteenth century saw agriculture shift from a basically barter system to a money economy. In the early part of the century, money accumulated from distant sources was being spent on land acquisition and capital investment was channelled into building and improvements.

In 1763, a sweeping change took place in the agricultural methods of the Borders with the advent of the smaller plough. This was the invention of James Small of Blackadder Mount in Berwickshire and was marketed under the title of 'Small's Chain or Swing Plough'; it was to revolutionise agriculture in the Borders and indeed throughout the world.

The old oak plough which had been in use since Anglian times, needed a large ox team and required a long narrow field to operate efficiently. The fields had been unenclosed and operated a one year crop, one year fallow, rotation system.

Agriculture was changing with new ideas and methods. The new plough was made of iron, was much shorter and was pulled by one, two or three horses. It had greater manoeuvrability and this meant that ground which had previously been pastoral could be tilled. Fields were enclosed and a five year rotation of crops was common. In the flatter lands of the Merse and eastern Roxburghshire the fermtoun started to appear. Some of the fermtouns had originally been Anglian settlements where the land was farmed by husbandmen and cottars on a communal basis. However, as the farming methods improved, the ground was gradually amalgamated into bigger and better holdings and farms as we would recognise them began to emerge.

The displaced cottars became the work force available to farms and estates, depending on this work for their daily bread. As a farm grew bigger and needed more labour, what was, in effect, a village was laid out to house the workers; this 'ferm raw' then expanded into a double raw and evolved into a village. As it grew, not all the workers would be employed on the one farm but became a reservoir of labour for times when extra manpower was needed.

The nineteenth century was the era of the Border farm worker with male and female workers, the bondagers, having a culture of their own. Some Berwickshire villages housing this work force had a population running into two or three hundred. With a population of this size, there was the need for back up services both for the people and for agricultural requirements. For the inhabitants there had to be provision shops, weavers, and tailors, a school and kirk and sometimes a doctor. For the new large farms, there were seedsmen, dykers, ditchers, hedgers, smiths, masons, carters and the numerous casual labourers for hay and harvest times. The late eighteenth and nineteenth centuries were the times of expansion for villages like Earlston, Greenlaw, Gordon and Reston which were in the centre of fine agricultural land. As well as providing a market for produce, they were the focal points of the immediate area for entertainment, hiring fairs and simply places to meet people.

The town of Duns could come into the above category except that it became the county town of Berwickshire from 1661 to 1696 and from 1882 to the present day. Berwick had been held by the English since the fifteenth century and Greenlaw had held the honour from 1696 to 1882. As well as being market towns, both were the administrative centres of the county with their share of sheriffs, lawyers and other civil servants.

The Estate Toun

With the fermtoun, there was a similar type of establishment – the estate toun. This was a service village for the large estates which now dotted the countryside. It was for the convenience of 'the big hoose' where servants of many kinds were needed thus giving employment to the wives and daughters of the men who worked on the estate.

The paternalistic attitudes of the Border estate owners was not something to be derided, for their extended family of workers was cared for in a manner which was an extension of the reiving days. Then the laird depended on his men as much as they depended on him. In the days of the large estates like Buccleuch it was possible to be born on the estate, be educated in the estate school free of charge, spend all your working life working there and be guaranteed a house and sustenance until you died. Ability was recognised and many young people could thank the estate for their university education. Throughout the nineteenth century, this type of caring paternalism provided a secure standard of living.

In the hill regions, the sheep farm had taken the place of the tower hamlet. Sheep farming, not being labour intensive (and with no need for the laird to have armed followers) the former inhabitants drifted away; some went into the towns where the Industrial Revolution was starting to be felt, some emigrated and some started agricultural service villages as at Yarrow feus where there were several dyking families, three smiths and a cartwright. However, in the hill country, these service villages were few and far between, so that the general population declined. About the only noticeable change in the hill country, was the number of dykes which divided one sheep farm from the next. It is amazing to think that the muscle power of man and horse took the many thousands of tons of stone up the rugged Border hills.

The Improving Lairds

In the late nineteenth century Borders, there were a few 'planned villages' built. These were largely the inspiration of the third Duke of Buccleuch who was one of the improving lairds.

At Copshawholm, he built a weavers' village for the estate workers and its symmetrical plan is typical of similar planned villages throughout Scotland. The village was renamed Newcastleton although it is still called its original name by the native inhabitants.

At other places on his estates as at Yarrow feus mentioned above, he broke down a large area of land into smaller pockets of a few acres each and leased or feud them to his tenants. Although they were not big enough to be classed as farms, these cottar holdings provided enough land for a family to live and this encouraged tradesmen and craftsmen to stay within the community. It is interesting to note that the inhabitants of Yarrowfeus were dykers, joiners and smiths with a row of weavers' cottages being the only craft not directly related to agricultural supply. A similar pattern of labour could be observed at Ettrickbridgend in the neighbouring valley.

The improving lairds did add a measure of industrial development to the countryside. Before the coming of the railway, when bricks were required, the laird would have a brickworks built near a suitable clay dub on his estate and produced enough for the estate's use. Tiles were the main production as vast quantities were used in the drainage of fields during the Agricultural Revolution. This activity sometimes expanded into a commercial venture with bricks and tiles being sold in the immediate area.

In the case of the Stirches brickworks near Hawick, the laird ventured into the tableware market, making teapots and some plates. This was not commercially viable and the local brickworks was closed with the coming of the railway. With easy transport, it was cheaper to bring the bricks and tiles from the Lothians than to try to make them in the Borders.

THE INDUSTRIAL REVOLUTION

The Industrial Revolution in the Borders coincided with the Agricultural Revolution; it is questionable which sparked off the other. This was the time when Border towns grew to near their present size. Despite the industrialisation, they were still oriented towards the production of fish, cattle, sheep or grain until the start of the twentieth century; the most industrialised of all, Hawick, retained its cattle/sheep market until a few years ago.

By the late seventeen hundreds there were fewer opportunities for employment on the land especially in the hill lands. For many, the choice was either to find work in the local towns or to emigrate to the New World or the new industries of England. Many chose to look for work in the Border towns among their ain folk; this was not an easy choice since any manufacturing there was still a family cottage industry employing few outsiders. Many of the hill folk drifted into their nearest town.

It has been observed that the older forms of a language are best preserved in the hill country where there are few incomers and it is noticeable that the broadest Border Scots is spoken in Hawick, Selkirk and Langholm, the towns nearest the hill areas.

In the burghs, manufacturing had always been encouraged. Here they used the produce of the land – linen from the flax, wool from the sheep and hides from the cattle. The sixteenth century Selkirk Court and Protocol Books are full of references to weavers, tailors, shoemakers and fleshers.

The Cordwainer Trade

The working of leather was carried on in all the burghs and villages. Raw hides were tanned in tan pits and 'the tannage' can still be found as a name in most burghs. The dressed leather became the shoes, jerkins, harness, buckets and other goods required for daily life.

Selkirk was famous for its shoemakers and 'Souter' is the name still given to an inhabitant of that burgh. The shoemaker connection is remembered when some notable is being made a Freeman of the burgh. The recipient has to 'lick the birse', the birse being the boar's bristles with which the shoemaker pointed his lingles or thread. The birse is dipped in wine to make the duty more palatable to the new Freeman! In 1715, the Selkirk shoemakers provided two hundred and twenty pairs of shoes for the Jacobite army then camped at Kelso. In 1745, a repeat order for two thousand, four hundred pairs was supplied to the Young Pretender's forces. The Souters of Selkirk are still awaiting payment!

The Textile Trade

> Tarry woo, tarry woo,
> Tarry woo is ill tae spin;
> Caird it weel, caird it weel,
> Caird it weel ere ye begin.
> When it's cairded, row'd an spun
> The wark is haflins dun;
> But when it's woven, drest and clean
> It's cleadin for a queen.

Wool has always been the staple product of the area and the textile trade has long been the cornerstone of urban expansion in the Border burghs. Galashiels, Selkirk, Hawick, Peebles, Jedburgh, Lauder, Earlston and Innerleithen have grown on the textile trade; Walkerburn was founded on it too. So, it is worth while to take a closer look at the links between wool production and wool manufacturing in the Border burghs.

In medieval times, wool was the principal export of the kingdom benefiting, the Border monasteries who were the main producers of it, the people of the area who collected and packed it and the port of Berwick which received the harbour dues. The importance of the wool trade seemed to transcend national barriers and wars for when Berwick was in English hands, the wool crop of the Scottish Border was still being exported to the Continent from that port. The only difference was that the harbour dues went to the English Crown.

Henry III of England gave leave for the Abbot of Melrose to send a ship to Flanders loaded with his wool. This cargo was in charge of William of Leith and Friar Thomas of Bowden. From 1370 to 1394, the Abbot of Melrose was allowed to export his wool free from the king's tolls.

The soldiers of Richard II of England had caused damage to Melrose Abbey and its outlying granges in 1385 and in recompense, he remitted two shillings on each of the one thousand sacks of wool which the abbey should have sent to Berwick for export.

James I, King of Scots, knowing a good business proposition when he saw it, decided to get into the export business himself. In 1428, he added £900 to his revenues by directly exporting the wool from the Crown lands.

Each king of Scots recognised the commercial benefit of having wool production from his own flocks grazing in the Ettrick Forest (under the supervision of his flockmasters) and of exporting it directly. James IV ran a flock of 10,000 on his forest lands. James V had a Great Hall in Selkirk where his forest wool crop was graded and packed into suitable packloads before being sent to Leith. His activities did not go unnoticed as he was given a postal reprimand by his uncle Henry VIII of England for his participation in this trade. Henry pointed out that being a wool trader was not commensurate with the nobility of kingship.

Although wool was exported in bulk, cloth was on the export list too. In 1492, a superior cloth called 'Peebles White' was sent to Antwerp where it was dyed red and presumably became known as 'Antwerp Red'.

The Kings of Scots constantly suffered financial embarrassment and frequently tried to boost their income by inducing Flemish craftsmen to settle in Scottish burghs. (Some examples of the incentive have been given above.) The reason why Flemings were so popular has a simple explanation. Although coarse cloth was made all over the Borders in burgh and countryside, the technique of weaving fine fabric was concentrated in Flanders and some cities in Northern Italy. With the raw material coming from the Borders, it made economic sense to bring the craftsmen to it rather than the other way round. Which is why in 1587, the Scots Parliament passed an Act to encourage the settlement of Flemish craftsmen with the condition that they employ Scottish apprentices. At this time three waulk mills were operated on the lower Gala Water. The waulk mills felted or milled the webs of rough cloth woven from the wool of the surrounding district. They must have produced a superior type of cloth because the reivers of Liddesdale, the Armstrongs, Elliots, Nixons and Crosiers would take it in preference to any other.

> 'Thair is ane callet Clement's Hob
> Fra ilk puir wyffe reiffis the wob'

(A discriminating reiver or a fashion-conscious one?)

During the seventeenth century there were many acts passed by king or commonwealth to aid the production of woollen goods in Scotland. In the period of the Civil War, any person setting up a factory was allowed to import wool or oil and export cloth free from customs dues. In every shire, a manufactory school was set up to which each parish was required to send one or more boys for instruction in the art of cloth making.

In 1645, the year of the Battle of Philiphaugh, no manufacturing master or workman was required to serve in the army, or to have troops quartered on him or to pay taxes. This Act was to be read out at every market cross and at each kirk door after the service. No records exist to say whether this Act caused a sudden increase in textile production.

Charles II went one better in the years after the Restoration. Not only did he renew and extend the privileges given to founders of any kind of industry but he also empowered them to 'seize beggars, vagabonds and idle persons and employ them in their works'. Several Border burghs had Weavers Incorporations at this time but there was a request from a native of Bruges, one Philip Van der Straten, to become a naturalised Scot. Stratten was willing to spend a considerable amount of money to establish a manufactory in Kelso 'for the dressing and refining of wool'.

The 1707 Union of Parliaments threatened the Border wool trade for Scots wool was considered much superior to the English variety and it was the export market which kept up the price. Scots wool producers were afraid that the cheaper English product would ruin their trade while the English producers feared that their wool would be taken into Scotland and re-exported to the Continent for a much higher price. At one period, Scots were prohibited from selling their wool in England under pain of death. The last boost that the Scots Parliament gave to the trade was in passing an act rescinding compulsory burial in a Scots linen shroud and decreeing that all bodies be buried in a woollen one instead. Perhaps their pre-Union fears had been justified for the Border wool producers found that the price of wool halved in the years after 1707.

To attempt to detail all the Acts encouraging the woollen and linen trades in the Border towns would require a book on its own. So, we will have to limit our observations by looking at a few of the innovators and benefactors to the trade.

Flax had been grown for the production of linen in the Borders from early times. With names like Linthill and the Bleachfield which can be found in most burghs, it appears that this was an important and widespread textile trade. In 1750, the Rev. James Brown of Melrose was instrumental in setting up a bleachfield on a flat piece of ground near the river Tweed; this was at a time when the Melrose linen weavers were producing over 33,000 yards of linen cloth a year and Melrose Linen was famed through the land. Then, Melrose was the textile capital of the Borders; in 1776, there were a hundred and forty looms mainly employed in the woollen trade; add to that the two hundred or so spinners required to service the looms. To compare the woollen towns: Hawick had 65 looms, Jedburgh 55, Kelso 40, Yetholm 35, Gala 30, Earlston 20, Lauder, 17 and Lilliesleaf 14.

In 1771, James Rodger of Selkirk was given £30 a year for three years to establish a woollen and linen factory in the town. A report of 1778 notes that this inkle factory employs 'many young girls and boys'. (Inkle is a linen cloth approximately a metre wide.)

In the 1780s an Innerleithen blacksmith called Alex Brodie who had made a fortune in the Shropshire iron trade returned to his native village where he built a five storey woollen mill.

In Galashiels, the Rev. Dr. Robert Douglas organised and encouraged over forty weavers and sixty spinners to band together in marketing their goods. He often placed his own fortune at their disposal for funding improvements and tiding them over in times of trade depression. It was thanks to Dr. Douglas and Sir Walter Scott (who was a fine PR man) that 'Galashiels Grey' was the fashion for most of the early nineteenth century. When the Gala Water could take no more mills, the Gala manufacturers spread out into the neighbouring burghs, wherever a fall of water was available to drive the new machinery.

Dr. Douglas was a founder member and had a quarter share in the new Buckholmside Brewery in 1811 so that 'the people of Gala could have decent ale'. It should be stated that this was not due to any intemperance on behalf of the good doctor. Every Border burgh had one or more brewery and most households brewed their own ale. It should also be noted that the quality of water supply in the most burghs verged on the lethal!

If Gala was the tweed town of the Borders, Hawick was the hosiery capital. This industry was started in 1771 by Baillie Hardie. It began as stocking-making with batches of linen and worsted being given out to women in the town to card and spin; lambs wool was a later addition. This was the beginning of a trade which saw 1200 stocking makers in Hawick in 1890 working only on hand frames. Statistically, the population of Hawick increased fourfold between 1801 and 1860. Add in the knitwear division and Hawick has much to thank Baillie Hardie for in his small hosiery industry.

A paper making factory was established near Duns in 1786 and one near Ayton shortly afterwards. In Edrom parish there were fifty five people employed in paper making around 1799 and the value of the paper produced was £5000 sterling per annum.

The Chrinside Bridgemill was established in 1842. It was so successful that female labour had to be brought from as far away as Dalkeith.

The peak industrial times for the Border towns coincided with the textile boom periods of 1865 to 1893 and from 1902 to the start of the First World War. Demand for tweed was great; profits were high which meant that the millowners could commission big new houses for themselves and small ones for their workers. Blacksmiths' workshops became machine factories and shops multiplied.

Textile mills had to look overseas for their raw material, buying wool from Australia and New Zealand and often investing in sheep stations there.

Gradually demand for woollen goods fell and mechanisation took the place of workers.

TRANSPORT

In a widespread area like the Borders, the need to get yourself and your goods from one place to another becomes a matter of importance. Where you can stop and sell is another, for these factors determine the siting and size of a community. When the goods produced are bulky or weighty, an effective means of transport is necessary. The reasons why communities have sprung up around cross-roads and bridges is apparent as here was a place where people congregated to rest for the night, perhaps to trade. If conditions were good, they might even settle.

Early Roads

The Romans were the first to build a definite road system through the Borders. Dere Street, the main north/south road entered the region near Chew Green on the border, headed for the place of the three hills, Trimontium, and went on up the valley of the Leader. There were east/west roads joining Dere Street at various places along its route. One crossed the river Tweed near Trimontium and went along the north bank towards the Lynne complex of camps; another came from Craik Cross, travelled down the Borthwick Water and crossed the present Selkirk/Hawick road at Grundistone Heights before joining and crossing Dere Street near St. Boswells. It then passed near Roxburgh Castle and Kelso while making for the conjectured harbour at Tweedmouth.

It is a fallacy to suggest that no roads were constructed in the Borders between the Roman period and the eighteenth century. Dark Age roads may have only been rough tracks and medieval roads did not have the same metalled construction as the Roman ones, but they did exist. The difference between the Roman roads and the later ones was that Roman roads were designed primarily for military use while the later roads were required for trade and communication.

Examples of medieval roads abound throughout the Borders. The engineered Roman roads were, however, still the main arteries of movement, with Dere Street providing the principal north/south line. This was in such fine condition that in the War of Independence, the English Edwards I and II could have a wagon train which measured twenty miles in length moving along it. Edward I transported stone, iron and timber by wagon, cart and packhorse from Berwick to his New Pele at Selkirk; he could not do this if there had been no semblance of a track. After Edward's carts, there was no wheeled transport in Selkirk until 1715.

The monasteries needed a road system to transport their wool to Berwick and fetch coal and other supplies from the Lothians. With monastic settlements dotted in many parts of the Borders, a new road system evolved; this one was devoted to communication and trade. When Alexander II gave Kelso Abbey a certain piece of land for the perpetual maintenance of a bridge over the Ettrick in 1234, he was subsidising a necessary road link. The ground is still called The Briglands.

Abbey records show roads were also used as a convenient means of marking land boundaries. Dere Street is frequently mentioned and the Via Regis or King's Way which goes from Annandale to Roxburgh is based on a minor Roman road which had become a major thoroughfare in medieval times.

The Turnpike Acts of 1750 and after, gave a push to build or improve the roads although it was 1764 before the first signs appeared in the Borders with a twelve mile stretch from Crosslee near Bowland to Haremoss outside Selkirk.

On the rougher hilly ground, the Dark Age Ridge Ways remained in use until the eighteenth century. Herring roads crossed the Lammermoors into Berwickshire. Salt roads criss-crossed the region bringing salt from the pans of Salt Preston. Drove roads were in use in the seventeenth century, driving cattle from the Falkirk Trysts into the growing towns in the north of England. These roads were mainly in the western half of the region where the hill land was unenclosed until the early nineteenth century. For the drovers, it was essential to have a 'stand' where the herds could lie for a night. When Hawick common was split up in 1777, it deprived the drovers of resting and grazing facilities.

The coming of the railway to the Borders killed off the droving trade but provided a fresh impetus to agriculture and industry.

The Railway

Andrew Scott, the Bowden Poet, has a poem written in 1825 entitled 'Railroads' in which he has two rustic labourers discussing the strong rumour that a railroad was about to be built through the Borders. One thought that it would put all honest farm labourers out of a job while the other pointed out what benefits it could provide by bringing in coal and lime and taking out people and produce. Both were right, for when the first railway track from Edinburgh to Berwick was opened in 1844, it was the start of a new era of opportunity. The Waverley Line from Edinburgh to Hawick followed in 1849 and the Edinburgh to Peebles Line in 1855. Soon the Borders was covered in a spider's web of branch lines with a station at nearly every town or village and at places like Belses and Lynne which had no pre-railway housing. Riccarton became a village solely for railway workers. Newton St. Boswells was a railway development village with stock sales being held regularly, the railway having taken the place of drovers to bring in the animals.

Not only did the railway encourage growth within the burghs but it was in itself an industrial development. The manpower required to dig the cuttings, lay track and build bridges was vast. With famine in Ireland and clearances in the Highlands, the greatest percentage of the railway navvies had Irish or Highland names, leavening the basic Anglo-Saxon stock of the Borders with fresh Celtic strains. War memorials of the First World War tell that they settled here in numbers.

Rail transport made it possible to move the agricultural and industrial products of the Borders quickly to outside markets and without this it is questionable if the Border tweeds and knitwear would have made such an impact on the national and international market. Transport has now been taken over by the lorry and the older industries are largely superseded by the new ones of electronics, chemicals and tourism.

Despite the changes, or because of them, folk still come to the Borders simply because it is an attractive place to live and work.

FIFTEEN
BORDERS PLACE-NAMES

INTRODUCTION

The place-names of any part of Scotland give us a very special insight into its historical and linguistic development. The Borders, lying as they do in close proximity to Northumberland, can be said to have much in common with it as far as place-names are concerned, and the two areas share a stock of place-name terms, especially those relating to the landscape, which immediately tell us of a common heritage of language, such as *burn, fell, law, pike, garth* and so on. In some respects, the line which we regard as the England-Scotland border can be disregarded for the purpose of place-name study although in terms of dialect, it has become significant since the sixteenth century, if not earlier.

If the Borders are regarded as the most 'English' part of Scotland, it is not entirely surprising. Those areas closest to the present borderline, such as the Lower Tweed valley, have a pattern of place-names which have counterparts or parallels on the English side, and a study of the distribution of the more important Anglian place-names must be seen in a cross-border context. For example, English names ending in *-ham* 'farmstead', 'hamlet' are most profitably studied by considering not only the Scottish examples, but those in the area between Berwick and Alnwick. For the purposes of this chapter, however, we must limit our study to the Scottish names.

It must not be thought, however, that the stock of place-names currently in use in the Borders are entirely of Anglian origin. We have to remember that there was a substantial Celtic-speaking population here right up to medieval times, and important place-names survive which have easily-identified Cumbric/Welsh elements such as *Melrose, Eccles, Traquair,* and *Peebles*.

Similarly, we have to be aware of the large number of place-names which have emerged in the modern period, that reflect the development of agriculture in a large variety of forms, and which are generally simple to understand, such as *Whitehill, Northfield, Mount Pleasant, Birkhill* and many others.

The earliest names to be found in the Borders are those of the major rivers. This is generally true not only of our area of study but of most other parts of Britain. It might seem unusual that river names should be in this category, but the major rivers of Europe have the most durable names for a variety of reasons. The river in time has acted as a vital part of human activity. It provides water for drinking and is a food source which is usually reliable. It can serve as a medium for communications, either by boat or by foot. At the same time, large rivers were often zones of conflict, acting as a protective border between peoples, or as a place of meeting in times of peace. This ancient role has survived into the modern period in many ways. Many of the sixteenth-century Border wardens' meetings on days of truce were held beside fords on major rivers, and to this day there are innumerable administrative boundaries which use rivers at some point. It is therefore not surprising that rivers have ancient names which have stood the test of time, and the many political and linguistic changes that have taken place since early peoples coined them.

Surprisingly, the name *Tweed*, which is by far the most important geographical feature in the Borders has never been satisfactorily explained, since we have no real clue as to its origin. Bede refers to is as *Tuidus* or *Twidus*, in a Latinised form, and it is mentioned in a Chronicle of 970 AD. as *Tweoda*, but it may well be pre-Indo-European, and reflect a coinage by a people whose very identity is unknown. Other important river-names are equally obscure as to derivation: both *Tyne* and *Teviot* may contain a common Indo-European root *ta*, 'to melt, flow or dissolve'. It is significant that the Northumbrian *Tyne* is not far to the south and must be considered in the same group, which according to Nicolaisen (1976, 190) includes the name *Thames* as well as the *Glentanner Water* SLK. It is instructive to consult Nicolaisen's discussion (1976, 184–186) on the *River Adder*, where he analyses the complex nature of what he regards as a pre-Celtic Indo-European stream-name, together with its secondary developments, *Blackadder* and *Whiteadder*, as well as the various settlement names which are associated with this system, such as *Edrington* and *Edrom*. The formation of such prefixes as black- and white- simply serve to distinguish the two branches of the river from one another, and do not necessarily imply a difference in colour. However, black/white pairs are common in Scotland, and are found in such name pairs as Deveron and Findhorn, Black Glen and White Glen in Morvern, and Black Esk and White Esk in Dumfriesshire.

River names in the early Celtic group which are found in the Borders include the *Leithen Water* PEB, containing the root *leg-* 'to drip, ooze or dissolve'; The *Caddon Water* SLK and *Kale Water* ROX, which may contain the Welsh *caled* 'hard'; and possibly the *Lyne Water* PEB. Some, however, are in the same obscure category as the Tweed, such as the name *Ettrick*, for which no satisfactory root has ever been established.

THE CELTIC STRATUM

During the Roman occupation, the whole of our study area was inhabited by folk who spoke some form of p-Celtic, considered by most scholars to be similar in many ways to Welsh, and which will be referred to here as Cumbric. Again, the present boundary with England may be seen as an artificial one, since at least one of the Celtic kingdoms, Rheged, on the shores of the Solway, contained part of present-day Cumbria. The Cheviot Hills in the east, however, formed a natural boundary with neighbouring tribes in what is today Northumberland.

Two significant place-name generics, probably dating from *c.*400–*c.*1100 are perhaps the best indicators of this Cumbric settlement. These are cair, 'fort' and tref 'homestead', 'village'. Both are found in modern Wales (in cases such as Caerphilly and Tredegar) while tref is also to be seen in Cornish names like *Trevescan* and *Tregony*.

As a rule, *cair-* in Wales is a defensive site, often with a military fortification, but the Scottish examples are not nearly so impressive, simply being farms or manors, originally surrounded by a palisade, more to protect livestock than to act as a defence against human attack. Few of the surviving *cair-* names are found in the Borders region, with the exception of *Caerlaverock* ROX, *caer-lanerch*, 'hamlet in the glade', and *Carfrae* BWK which contains bre 'hill'. It is significant that several *cair-* names survive in Cumberland, notably *Cardew, Cardurnock* and *Carlisle*, the last of which owes it second element to Latin *Luguvalium* (Rivet & Smith, 1979, 402). The problem with *cair-*names is that we can identify a number of place-names in *Keir* and *Kier* which may very well be from similar Cumbric origins, but for which no early documentation is available. There is a similar position with names containing Gaelic *cathair* 'seat, 'fort', which may be in the same category.

Names in *tref*, however, clearly mark a farm settlement, and date from roughly the same period as those in *cair*. To be more precise, the exact meaning is 'homestead' or 'village', since there is some evidence that these settlements were small nucleated villages, perhaps the centres of important estates. This element is unusual in that it can appear as a prefix or as a suffix, where it is found in endings like *-try* or *-trie*. Examples in the Borders include *Traquair* PEB 'village on the River Quair' and *Trabrown* BWK, 'hill village', for which we have an early spelling, Treuerbrun, *c.*1170.

Apart from names in *cair-* and *tref* there are several Cumbric generics that are represented in the Borders. These are also topographic terms which have survived in the old area of Cumbric speech. Cumbric *pen*, is cognate with Welsh *pen* 'head'; 'end' has a similar distribution to *cair*, and occurs in names like *Pennygant Hill* ROX and *Penmanshiel* BWK, but it is the element *pren* 'tree' which we find most commonly in the Borders, usually in metathesised form as *Prin* near Innerleithen PEB, *Pirnie* ROX, near Maxton, *Primrose* ROX, from *pren ros* 'tree on the moor' and *Primside* ROX for which we have an early spelling 'Prenwensete', giving 'white tree' with an Anglian ending (OE *sete*, 'seat'). The significance of such 'tree-'names is obscure, but the presence of an important tree, even in forested landscape, may have had local importance, as a meeting place, or as a place of worship. To this day in Scotland, ancient trees are regarded as historically important and are frequently named.

It is of interest to note that one of the most prolific p-Celtic topographic names, *aber* 'confluence', so common north of the Forth is absent in the Borders, and is present in only a few instances west of the watershed. In an area where confluences are plentiful, one might have expected *aber* to survive in the area, but its absence suggests a real distinction between the language of Southern Scotland and that of the Picts beyond the Forth, despite the stock of generics which they share (Nicolaisen 1975, 164–5).

Nevertheless, an examination of the 1:50,000 Ordnance Survey map reveals a surprising number of p-Celtic survivals in the Borders, especially in the northern counties. Names like *Drumelzier* PEB, *Melrose* ROX (maol ros 'bare moor'), *Mossfennon* PEB, 'fountain moss', *Mosspeeble* 'tent-field' and *Peebles* itself are typical. Peebles is on a strategic site at or near the junction of several streams including the Eddleston Water, which affords relatively easy access from the Lothian plains, and must have been the site of an important meeting place from the earliest times. The derivation is Cumbric *pebyll* 'booths', 'tents', or 'place of tents', an indication of the function of this site as a place where conventions of various kinds took place, necessitating the erection of temporary booths as accommodation. Flat land at the confluence of the Eddleston Water and the River Tweed was used for the usual jousting and sporting activities which invariably accompanied these meetings. However, the earliest reference which we have for the place is one referring to the church in 'Pobles' accompanied by a ploughgate of land, in 1116 (Renwick, 1903, 140).

To the north of Peebles, *Eddleston* appears on record first as *Penteiacob* 'headland of James's house' before undergoing a change to *Gillemorestun* in the twelfth century. But before 1189, it was in the hands of an Anglian, Edulf son of Utred, and was thereafter called *Edulfstun*, and finally *Eddleston*. This uniquely shows the transformation from Cumbric to Gaelic and eventually to Anglian, as the ownership changes over a very brief period (in historical terms) of approximately eighty years (Watson, 1926, 35).

Watson assessed the number of surviving British names in our area of study as 159, in a 'rough provisional list' which he compiled from the one-inch Ordnance Survey map, although he does not differentiate between settlement names and topographic names. The resurgence of Gaelic in the period from *c.* 960 AD onwards seems to have had relatively little impact on the overall picture of Border place-names, although a number of Gaelic personal names are evident in Lothian settlement names, and a few examples such as *Bedrule* ROX, and *Abbotrule* ROX testify to Gaelic influence in the area, while we have a useful list of names of men living near Peebles about 1200 which contains Gaelic, Welsh and English personal names, (Watson, 1926, 134).

A number of Borders place-names nevertheless show signs of this Gaelic overlordship. *Bonjedward* ROX, for example, contains the Gaelic *bun* 'river-mouth', and such Gaelic topographic terms as ceap 'lump' 'block', is found in names in *Kip(p)*, while *creag* 'rock is common in its Scots variant *craig*, and in isolated settlement names like *Craigover* ROX, perhaps *creag odhar* 'dun craig'. *Gleann* 'valley' is another term which may originate in this period, but its Scots form *glen* may well be of more recent coinage, although *Glengaber* SLK, on the Megget Water, is 'goats' glen', *Glenrath* PEB may be 'fortress glen' from *rath* 'fortress', and Glenlude PEB is a few miles north of Yarrow on the boundary between Yarrow parish SLK and Traquair parish PEB.

With so many valley sites which contain the term *haugh* 'water meadow', 'riverside meadow', it is not surprising that the Gaelic equivalent *dail* is found in one or two instances. This term in fact has its origins in the Cumbric *dol*, 'meadow', 'dale', 'valley', and is widely found throughout Scotland, not only in the Gaelic north, but in Strathclyde and Galloway. The most obvious example in the Borders is *Deloraine* SLK, on the Ettrick Water. This appears on record in the Exchequer Rolls of 1486, where it is spelt 'Doloraine'. There is uncertainty about the second part of the name, but it is clearly a 'haugh' site (see Watson, 1926, 417). *Dalgleish* 'green haugh' and Dalziel 'white haugh', both SLK are in the same category. The term *allt* 'burn' in Gaelic was originally applied to a steep cliff, and there is often doubt as to which of these derivations applies when we examine such names in south east Scotland. However, *Cramalt* in Meggat SLK is likely to be *crom alt* 'bent precipice', while *Garvald* PEB is 'rough burn'. *Glack* PEB, on Manor Water is obviously from G. glac, 'dell', 'ravine'.

All this evidence strongly suggests an important role for Gaelic speech in the Borders, especially in the north west part of our area. Clearly Anglian power was always liable to be less concentrated in these marginal areas, and the fact is that Cumbric survivals are present here also. Watson suggests that the situation in Peebles *c.*1200 did not exclude men of both Celtic origins – Gaelic and Cumbric – from holding a certain amount of social standing, and the presence of these Gaelic place-names certainly confirms this.

ANGLIAN PLACE-NAMES

Dark Age historical and literary sources can be notoriously inaccurate, especially for this frontier area between Celt and Northumbrian Angle. The founding, according to Bede, of the kingdom of Bernicia by King Ida in 547 AD was one of the more significant events in the development of Anglian power in Scotland, and heralded a great movement of English speaking folk into what had long been a Celtic heartland, albeit one that had been part of the Roman world for several centuries. The conquest of this part of Scotland by Anglians was initially characterised by the establishment of defensive settlements in the major river valleys of Tweed and Tyne, and it is in the eastern parts of these valleys that we find the earliest Anglian names, mostly at no very great distance from the coast. However, as consultation took place, Anglian names appear in the interior, so that by c.800 AD, they become numerous as far west as Peebles and the borders with Lothian.

One of the major problems with many of these early Anglian names lies in the lack of much contemporary documentary evidence. For many of the key names, we find that the earliest available forms do not occur until after the eleventh century, although there are a few notable exceptions. This is partly due to the fact that much of Scotland's documentation for the Dark Age period is absent, and there are few sources to compare with the large bodies of manuscripts in England, such as the Anglo-Saxon Chronicles. Nevertheless, Anglian names from the period 650–850 AD are fairly well represented in our area, especially in the south east section.

Names containing -ingas originally meaning 'descendants of', 'followers of' when attached to a personal name are among the earliest of English names. Later this comes to mean 'the settlement at', or 'settlers at'. Although *Crailing* ROX and *Simprim* BWK (which has early forms Simprinc 1153–65, Simprig 1159 and Simpring c.1280) ostensibly come into this category, they are probably not genuine -ingas names, or at least cannot be proven to be such. Crailing, in any case, is too far inland to be a candidate. The earliest example of Anglian nomenclature in the border is probably *Coldingham* BWK, 'the settlement of the followers of Colud', which is found as Coludesburh, in the Anglo-Saxon Chronicle of 679 AD and is mentioned in the Anonymous Life of St. Cuthbert as Colodesbyrig 699–705. In Bede, it appears as Coludi urbem, c.730. We later find it in an altered form, Collingaham, 1095–1100, and Coldingaham, 1097–1107. Originally this applied to the Celtic fortress at St. Abb's Head which was called *Caer Golud* by the Cumbric folk, but which the Anglians renamed *Coludesburh*, using their familiar OE burh 'fortress' as generic. When the settlement developed near the fortress, it came to be called *Coldingaham*, 'the settlement near Colud'. This is the sole -ingham name in the Borders, although two others, *Whittingham* and *Tyningham* are in East Lothian, both close to the coast.

The loss of the medial *-ing* in Anglian place-names must have taken place fairly early on in the Scottish settlements, although it is seldom possible to be precise with dating. The next generic which appears chronologically is OE *ham*, 'estate', 'manor', 'village', and this probably represents consolidation of Anglian settlement. These include *Ednam* ROX 'the ham on the River Eden', *Midlem* ROX 'the middle village', *Oxnam* ROX, 'oxen village', *Smailholm* ROX, 'small village', *Yetholm* ROX 'village on the gate or pass' (where the Bowmont Water cuts through a gap in the hills), *Birgham* BWK, 'bridge village', *Edrom* BWK, 'village on the River Adder', *Kimmerghame* BWK, 'village at the cows' bridge', and *Leitholm* BWK, in Eccles parish, 'village on the Leet Water'. It is significant that Ednam, Smailholm, Oxnam, Yetham and Edrom have all become names of parishes, indicating not only antiquity in terms of place-names but also commercial significance. These became the centres of manorial lands, primarily because of their sites and the quality in terms of land value, situation and natural resources.

Of similar age, although we cannot be absolutely certain, is a group of names in *-ingtun*, many of which have a personal name as specific. These are *Edington* BWK (obscure, but possibly a personal name Eadda, giving 'farm associated with *Eadda*'), *Edrington* BWK, 'farm of the settlers by the River Adder' (*cf. Edrom* above), *Hassington* BWK 'Hadsing's farm', *Mersington* BWK, 'Mersige's farm', *Renton* BWK (spelt Regninton in 1095), 'Regna's farm' and *Upsettlington* BWK, in Ladykirk, 'farm on a seat, ledge or bench'. None of these, either in ham or ingtun are on record before *c*.1050.

By far the most common generic in the area, however is OE *tun*, 'enclosed homestead, dwelling, village, farm'. Normally these end in *-ton*, and although some clearly originate in the early period of Anglian settlement, and can be identified by the OE topographical terms or OE personal names of their specific, others are much later, as *-ton* – names continued to be coined right down to the modern period. To complicate the situation even further, incoming Scandinavian-speaking settlers used *-ton* as the generic for their farms, as did Norman incomers in the eleventh and twelfth centuries.

Some of these *-ton* names are documented in the eleventh century. *Clifton* ROX in Morebattle is Cliftun 1050, 'dwelling by a cliff' and *Whitton* in the same parish, 'white homestead', is first recorded as Waquirtun at the same time. *Wilton* ROX, perhaps 'farm by the willows' is Wiltuna *c*.1050, and *Ayton* BWK as Eitun 1095–1100 is thought to be 'the farm on an island of land in marshland'. *Hilton Bay* BWK first appears as

Hilton, 1095, and is 'hill farm', a common name throughout Scotland, while *Lamberton* BWK is Lambertun 1095–1100, 'farm of the lambs'. *Paxton* BWK, in Hutton parish is Paxtun 1095 and may well be 'Pacca's farm'. *Swinton* BWK, spelt Suinestun in 1095–1100 is probably 'Swein's farm', since we have it on record that 'Swein son of Ulfkill held Swinton in 1100'. This Scandinavian name is proof of colonisation by Danes in the post Domesday period in SE Scotland. Names like Swanston, Ormiston and Ravelstone in Lothian testify to substantial landholdings by men bearing Scandinavian names during this period.

With so many names in -*ton* appearing on the present map, it is worth referring to only a few in this text. Late Middle English and Norman personal names are evident in several of them, and are usually in favourable locations. *Dingleton* ROX was Danyelstona 1343, 'Daniel's farm' (he was prior of Jedburgh in 1139); *Roberton* BWK is Robertstun 1228; *Samieston* BWK 'Samuel's farm' is on record as Semanstoun 1452 and Simalstoun 1471; *Rowelstane* BWK, in Eccles parish, is Rollandston in 1390, and is named from the Norman French personal name of *Roland*.

The distribution of names in -*ton* is nevertheless very uneven in the Borders. Some areas, such as the upland parts of Selkirkshire and Roxburghshire contain relatively few such names, while in other areas they are plentiful. An important cluster lies north of Peebles, where we find *Kidston, Wormiston, Milkieston, Eddleston, Winkston* and Upper and Nether *Stewarton*, most of which have personal names from the early medieval period as specifics.

As the Anglian settlement developed and prospered, so it became necessary, or fashionable, to use different generics for the coinage of farm names. Some of these were terms used across the Border in England, and were on the point of falling into disuse, or being replaced by others. But they sometimes represented specialisations in agriculture, the development of new resources, or the clearance of hitherto untilled lands. The forest cover which was such an important aspect of the landscape was gradually being felled and brought into cultivation.

Enclosed homesteads, or large habitations with surrounding land were in the south commonly found with the generic *word*. It is rare in Northumberland with only eleven examples in total, and only three exist in the Borders. This enclosure term is often compounded with a personal name in England and two of the Scottish examples are in this category. *Cessford* ROX is first recorded as Cesseworthe in 1296, Gesword 1341, and Sesworth 1415, and may be from an OE personal name *Cessa*. There has been a change from -*worth* to *ford* as the meaning of the original term became obscure. *Jedburgh* ROX is on record *c.*1050 as Gedwearde, and in 1177 as Gedwirth. Clearly the specific here is the river-name, Jed, which is probably Celtic. *Polwarth* BWK is the only Scottish example which has retained its original form. Appearing first as Paulewrhe 1182 and Pollerrch *c*.1200, it becomes Poulesworth in 1296, and may well be 'Paul's enclosure'.

OE *wic*, 'dwelling, village, hamlet, farm, dairy-farm' has a much wider range in Scotland, and all seem to be located in the lower parts of valleys, beside large streams. The generic is common in Northumberland, though absent in Cumberland. Most of the places involved are substantial farms. *Borthwick* ROX (Bordewich 1165–69) means 'home farm', from OE *bord wic*, and can be taken as the farm which supplied produce to the board or table of the lord of the estate. Such farms are liable to be in choice positions, with the richest land. A similar derivation is found in the many *Bordlands* or *Borelands* which occur throughout eastern Scotland, from Galloway to Moray Firth coastlands, as well as in NW England. *Darnick* Rox seems to be OE *derne wic* 'hidden farm' as it lay in dense woodland. *Fenwick* ROX is 'fen farm', and *Hawick* ROX (Hawic 1165, Hawyc 1264) is OE *haga-wic* 'farm surrounded by a hedge'. This word survives in the word *hawthorn*, which was the tree often used for planting a dense prickly barrier around an enclosure, originally for the protection of livestock from predators.

Fishwick BWK is mentioned as 'Fiswic', a *piscatura*, in a Durham charter of *c*.1135, and means 'fish village'. Located on the Tweed, it was obviously a place where fishing was an important part of the economy. *Berwick-on-Tweed* itself is recorded as Berwic 1095 and Berewic 1130–3. A *berewic* was a granary or grange farm; literally, the name means 'barley farm', and in the Domesday Survey is used as a common noun to denote small settlements dependent on a larger one (Nicolaisen, Gelling and Richards, 1970, 51). Nevertheless, because of its site at the mouth of the Tweed, and its consequent strategic position, Berwick had become an important burgh by 1150, and one of the main ports of Southern Scotland.

Another term which appears in the early Anglian period is *botl* or *bodl* 'dwelling', 'house', but it is rare in Scotland, *Morebattle* ROX being the only well documented example in the Borders. This occurs as Mereboda *c*.1124, Merbotil, 1174–99 and Merbotele 1309, meaning 'dwelling on the lake or mere', alluding to the substantial loch which lay between Morebattle and Linton before it was drained in the nineteenth century. One other possibility for this element is *West Bold* PEB, on the south bank of the Tweed opposite Walkerburn.

Fortified sites in the Borders, which were occupied by pre-Anglian folk usually contain the term *burh*. In OE this is limited to certain known Celtic sites like Coludesburh (see above) and *Scraesburgh* ROX which was a large, circular camp on a hillside and must at one time have been an important centre. Today it lies on the English border, in a dominating position. Some of the names in -*burgh* which are to be found in the Borders date from the period when royal burghs began to be created in Scotland from the twelfth century onwards. This is the case with *Roxburgh* (first recorded as Rokesburge, *c.*1120), and *Jedburgh*, which had its -*worth* ending replaced when the settlement achieved the status of a major settlement. But *Dryburgh* BWK, 'dry fort', first on record as Drisburgh *c.*1150, is not in this category.

It was originally thought that OE *ceaster* 'fort', which is usually found as -*chester*, denoted the presence of Roman forts or earthworks. However, none of the seventeen recorded Borders examples are close to Roman sites, but are all beside pre-Anglian earthworks, and never appear in documents before *c.*1050. Such names include *Belchester* BWK, in Eccles parish, *Highchesters* ROX and *Rowchester* ROX, *Whitechesters* ROX (near Hawick) and *Darnchester* BWK near Coldstream are typical. The element sometimes appears in a simplex form, such as *Chesters* in Fogo BWK, which lies between two Celtic forts.

Several terms from the period 800–1200 describe individual houses or groups of houses, some of which were important residences, and others which were clusters of relatively humble cottages. OE *cot*, 'cottage, house dwelling' is one of these, dating from the ME period in Scotland, and not to the earliest stratum of Anglian occupation. In Rox, we have *Gatehousecote, Hoscote* and *Stobitcote* in Teviot. The latter is probably from OE *stubb*, Scots *stob* denoting a house built of tree-stumps. *Butchercoat* BWK, in Merton, is on record in 1465 as Bouchecoitis, and in 1538 as Buscheourcoit, denoting a personal name, *Bouche* of Norman French origin. A more important site tended to bear generics like OE *stede* 'place, position, site', OE *heall* 'hall, mansion house', or OE *hus*, 'house'. It is frequently difficult to establish the dating of these names, since very few of them appear in the documents before 1300. A name like *Newstead* ROX, 'new farm', for example, is first recorded as late as 1548 and *Middlestead* SLK in 1510. *Templehall* BWK was connected with the nearby Priory of Coldingham, and is on record in 1367, while *Charterhouse* ROX (1454 Chartehou) was in land granted to the Carthusian monastery at Perth; *Bowerhouse* BWK, in Edrom, is first on record as Brunhus 1296 and Burnhous 1479, becoming metathesised by the sixteenth century and thereby cloaking its true derivation.

TOPOGRAPHIC NAMES

The Anglian place-names which we have so far discussed all contain habitative terms – in other words, the generic is a word which alludes to some form of human habitation such as 'house' or 'farm'. Many settlements, however, are simply named after topographic features which form an important visual part of the landscape or which have some significant economic function. This category also includes terms like *field*, *green* and the like which indicate agricultural activity, as well as *park*, *haugh*, and *shiel* which have associations with grazing operations.

As mentioned earlier, woodland cover in the Dark Age and Medieval period was particularly dense in parts of the Borders, especially Jedforest and the great Forest of Ettrick, but also in the Melrose area, where the Tweed is joined by the Ettrick, the Leader and the Gala Water. As is to be expected, names containing the element *wood*, (OE *wudu*) are common in these areas, and we can establish quite early documentary forms for some of them, notably *Legerwood* BWK, which is Ledgardeswde 1127, and is from an OE personal name *Leodgeard*, ME *Ledgard*, *Threepwood* ROX, near Melrose, is Prepwude 1180, Threpuude 1186, and is clearly 'disputed wood', from ME *threpen*, 'debated, disputed'. Many small pieces of land were the subjects of disputes over ownership, and there are many examples of *Threiplands*, *Threepmuirs* and *Threipwoods* in Southern Scotland. *Spottiswood*, *Gladswood* (from Sc. *gled*, 'kite, hawk'), *Stobswood* and *Quixwood* are all examples from BWK, but the earliest recorded is *Swinwood* BWK, in Ayton, which is Swinewde 1100, reminding us that pigs were an important part of the medieval economy and were driven from wood to wood to feed on beech and oak mast. Other *-wood* names include *Hartwoodburn* SLK, 'stag wood', *Oakwood* SLK (Aikwod 1567–8), *Torwoodlee* SLK and *Girnword* ROX which may contain the Modern Sc. *girn* 'snare, gin'.

Another forest term, rare in Scotland, is OE *hyrst* 'wooded knoll' copse, hillock, brushwood'. The only Borders example is, however, an important site, *Ferniehirst Castle* ROX, which is 'ferny-wood', and was the seat of the family of Ker, probably dating from the mid-fifteenth century. This is a good example of a prominent castle taking the name of the nearest topographic feature. The OE *pyrne* 'thorn-bush' occurs in names in *-thorn*, like *Nenthorn* BWK (Nathanthern c.1150, Naythinthern 1150–2), perhaps a Celtic personal name *Naitan* or *Nectan* and *Hawthorn* SLK (Hayrtherne 1455, Hartherme 1468) from *har-thorn* 'boundary thorn', indicating the tree as a boundary landmark.

As woodland was cleared, so new settlements came into being. the OE *leah*, 'clearing in woodland, glade', common in England became used in Scotland also, as well as denoting 'open country, pasture, arable land'. The normal ending is now *-lee* or *-lie*, and is applied to a piece of ground which is free of woodland. Going by documentary evidence, some of these places are of eleventh-century origin or earlier. *Blainslie* ROX is Bleineslei 1178, and may be from a personal name *Bleinus*; *Colmslie* ROX is Cumbesley *c.*1160, from OE *cumb* 'valley'; *Horsleyhill* ROX, in Minto was Horsleye in 1251, and is 'horse pasture', while *Hundalee* ROX, in Jedburgh means 'clearing of the dogs' probably indicating hunting-dogs. *Wolfelee* ROX is 'wolf-clearing' or wolf-wood', while *Oatleycleuch* BWK (in Duns parish) appears on the Blaeu map of 1654 as Outlawcleuch, but may simply be 'oat lee'. *Wedderlee* BWK is 'ram pasture', and is spelt Wederleie in 1250. Selkirkshire has a number of *leah*-names, including *Fairnilee* (Farnyley 1405), 'ferny glade', *Huntly* (Hunteleghe 1296) 'hunting wood', *Singlie* (Senglee 1368), obscure and the lost *Blyndle* (Blindley 1543) in Gala, which refers to a clearing in a concealed site. Another lost name on the Yarrow Water is *Schuittingleyes* last recorded in 1573, where shooting contests were held.

We must also mention a few medieval examples of names in *-field*. Originating in OE *feld*, 'open country, unenclosed land, land free from wood' this term becomes widely used to describe any piece of open land. *Jardinefield* BWK was owned by John Jardin of Applegarth in 1476. *Shielfield* BWK is first on record in 1537 as Scheilfield, 'land with a hut', but the most unusual is *Sorrowlessfield* ROX in Melrose parish, which appears as Sorulesfeld in 1208, and was land held by Willielmus Sorules who gave his name to it. In modern times the popular belief was that this farm was the only one in the Borders which had not lost one of its men at the disastrous Battle of Flodden, and hence earned the soubriquet of 'sorrowless field'.

The genuine topographic terms which occur in Borders place-names display wide variety. Settlements which were located at or near a distinctive topographic feature often adopted the name of the feature itself, or used the generic by which the feature was originally named. OE *denu*, 'valley', for example, became Middle Scots *dean*, and is very common, in names such as *Bowden* ROX (Bothendenam 1119, Bouldene 1204), 'dwelling-house valley', *Oakendean* ROX (Akedene 1204), 'oak-tree valey', *Butterdean* BWK 'butter valley', because of its rich pasturage, *Foulden* BWK, (Fugeldene 1095–1100), 'bird valley' from OE *fugol*, *Lindean* SLK (Lynden 1153), 'waterfall valley', and *Oxendean* BWK, 'valley of the oxen'. OE *slaed* gives Scots *slaid*, 'a hollow between rising grounds, especially one with a stream. *Whitslaid* BWK (Wideslade 1209, Whytslade 1371) is 'white valley', and there are many instances of OE *dael*, which cognate with ON *dalr*, and means 'valley' or 'glen' in Scots. *Teviotdale* ROX, *Riddell* 'rye-dale', ROX, *Lauderdale* BWK and *Galadale* BWK are all self-explanatory. *Wedale* was the name given to the area lying between the Gala and the Leader Waters, and is first recorded as such in 1170. Its derivation is obscure, but it is still remembered in the name 'Stow in Wedale' and roughly corresponds to the modern Stow.

Hill-terms find frequent use in border names; not only is *-hill* common in names like *Bowhill* SLK, but *law* 'rounded hill' (from OE *hlaw*) appears in scores of examples, such as *Cocklaw* ROX, near Hawick, *Lempitlaw* ROX (Lempedlar 1190) 'limpet shaped law', *Greenlaw* BWK (Grenlaw 1170) and *Wooplaw* BWK, perhaps 'wolf hill'. Other terms include OE *dun*, 'hill' as in *Eildon* Rox (Eldune 1143) which may be Celtic in origin, *Hownam* (Hunum 1165–92, Hunedune 1165–74, Hunedoune 1454), which may be 'Huna's hill', a personal name and the well known *Earlston* BWK, for which we have Ercheldon *c.*1143 and Ersildone *c.*1300, thought to originate in a British name. Some of these have endings which have been altered significantly since the earliest recordings, reminding us that modern spelling forms are not always a reliable guide to derivation.

Finally, we can refer briefly to a number of elements which are commonly found in Borders names that derive from topographical features. These include *side*, 'slope of a hill or bank', as in *Commonside* ROX, *Falside* FOX, *Bemersyde* BWK (from the Northumbrian bemere 'trumpeter'), *Chirnside* BWK 'hillside shaped like a churn', and *Caldside* BWK, 'cold side'; *ford* is found in names like *Rutherford* ROX, *Ellemford* BWK, 'elmford', and *Howford* SLK, 'ford in a hollow'; *bank* as in *Elibank* SLK; and *burne* 'stream', as in *Otterburn* BWK and *Cockburn* BWK with scores of others in the area.

THE SCANDINAVIAN ELEMENT

No picture of Borders place-names would be complete without some reference to the role of Scandinavian settlers in the area, and the influence which they had on the name stock. The most common ending for Scandinavian names in Southern Scotland is Old Danish *by*, 'farm, village, hamlet', which occurs in several names in Dumfriesshire, such as Lockerbie, Canobie and Sibbaldbie, that are normally ascribed to the 11th and 12th centuries, when the element had been absorbed into Middle English. There are also several Cumbrian examples which survive. Few, however, are present in our area of study, with the exception of *Corsbie* BWK, in Gordon parish, which is Crossebie 1309 and Corsby 1396. It may be O. Dan. *krossa-by* 'farm of the crosses', although no cross has survived locally. Most of the other names contain topographic terms, such as *Whisgills* in Castleton ROX, which contains the dialect *gill* 'ravine', and *Stanygill Burn* in the same parish; a number of stream-names in *grain* 'fork, branch' in ROX and SLK, including *Haregrain Rig* in Castleton, *Master Grain* and *East Grain* running north into the Ettrick Water, and a few names in *fell* (from On *fjall*, 'fell, hill') such as *Dod Fell* in ROX (Castleton), *Capell Fell* in Ettrick, 'horse hill', and *Pike Fell* in Hobkirk. *Hartsgarth* 'stag cleft', again in Castleton, is a final example of a name which contains Scandinavian elements in an English millieu.

Scandinavian influences in the South East are certainly present, not only with the names quoted above, but with clusters of names containing Scandinavian personal names in various parts of Lothian. As with many aspects of the linguistic history of the area, the picture is far from clear, but it seems most likely that people of Danish descent, bearing Danish names were intermingled with both Anglians and Celts, and that part of the stock of Danish topographic terms which they used were incorporated into the dialectal nomenclature of those areas of Southern Scotland in which these folk settled, particularly in Dumfriesshire and the western parts of the Borders, such as Castleton parish.

CONCLUSION

As with any part of Scotland, where the tide of settlement and conquest ebbed and flowed in the Dark Age period, so the Borders have experienced a number of different types of folk, speaking p-Celtic, Anglian, Scandinavian and Gaelic. The place-name record tells us only part of the story, and has to be viewed as especially valuable evidence, but nonetheless evidence that is not always reliable. It is misleading to read too much into the evidence provided by a single name, no matter how well attested, and even the study of distributions of names sharing a common element frequently tells us only a small part of the story. But place-names invariably give clues to all kinds of patterns in history, and if we bear their limitations in mind, they tell us a great deal about a complex and imperfectly understood world of the past.

Sixteen
Dialect

In 1873 James Murray (later Sir James), a Borders man, born at Denholm and eventually first editor of the *New English Dictionary*, began the Preface to his *Dialect of the Southern Counties of Scotland* with the following words: 'The local dialects are passing away: along with them disappears the light which they are able to shine upon so many points in the history of the national tongue that supersedes them, and the contributions which they, more than the artificially trimmed Literary idioms, are able to make to the Science of Language, whether in regard to the course of phonetic changes or the spontaneous growth of natural grammar'.

So far as the life of his own dialect was concerned, this was unduly pessimistic and Murray immediately conceded that of all dialects, that of the southern counties of Scotland was 'the least altered'. Yet today in the Borders as elsewhere, there is still a widespread concern that local dialects continue to pass away as an unconstrained medium of communication amongst local people who share a common life and, by definition, a particular form of speech. This speech Murray categorised as 'being founded solely upon internal characteristics of pronunciation, grammar and vocabulary'. In none of these is there a necessary conformity with what must be called 'standard' language. So, for example, what is 'bad grammar' in dialect speech, if judged by the criterion of the 'standard' language, Murray simply called 'natural grammar'. Dialect, therefore existed in its own right and had its own conventions. And it had historical authenticity. 'Such expressions as 'the men sits', said Murray, 'are not vulgar corruptions, but strictly grammatical in the Northern dialect. The -s is a true plural inflection as witnessed by the 13th century *sittes*, the Old Northumbrian *sittes* or *sittas*'.

The first claim, therefore, which must be made in the study of the Borders dialect, is that it was the substance out of which a wholly new approach was made by an erudite and percipient scholar (who was also a dialect speaker) into the study of dialect, especially the dialects of Scotland. Murray spoke of a 'science of language'. His successor on the Dictionary, Henry Bradley, claimed that in the *Dialect of the Southern Counties of Scotland*, Murray 'laid the foundations of the scientific study of the local varieties of English speech', and it was the third editor of the

Dictionary, Sir William Craigie, who in an address to the English Association of Dundee in 1907, began the movement towards a *Scottish National Dictionary*. The first editor of this Dictionary, William Grant (1929) acknowledged the use he made of Scotland's 'picturesque and vigorous' dialects. His introduction (accompanied by maps) was a concentrated display of the various types of Scots dialect speech, and these were marked off by phonetic criteria, chiefly by the comparison of vowel sounds in a given word. Thus, for instance, the dialect pronunciation of the word 'water' in both Roxburghshire and Berwickshire is 'waeter' and the word 'who' is 'whae'. And these pronunciations appear to set them together. But in Berwickshire the word 'moon' is 'min' and 'roof' is 'rif', whereas in Roxburghshire the vowel sound is formed with rounded lips with produces 'muin' and 'ruif'. And these appear to set them apart. Furthermore, there is what must be called a sub-dialect area, in the fishing villages of Berwickshire – Burnmouth (with Ross and Cowdrait) and Eyemouth – which have 'meen' and 'reef'. This series of words, exemplified by 'min', 'muin', and 'meen' and 'rif', 'ruif' and 'reef' is bound together as a group by the fact that the words descend from an Old English long ō as in 'mōna' for 'moon' and 'hrōf' for 'roof' and so on. Thus there is no suggestion that these are degenerate or wayward pronunciations. They are simply historic instances of a certain stage of development. They are clear demonstrations, displayed geographically, of Murray's 'course of phonetic changes'.*

There can be no doubt that Murray's perception of the value of dialect study laid the foundation for all subsequent linguistic research in Scotland. The latest piece of systematic investigation, the Linguistic Survey of Scotland (L.S.S.) – established in 1949 within the University of Edinburgh, the university which, in 1874, had honoured Murray with a Doctorate for his *Dialect of the Southern Counties of Scotland* – used precisely those categories which he had laid down, namely pronunciation, vocabulary, and grammar, and all of these were applied with some considerable concentration to the Borders. The intention here is to consider these categories as they were used by the L.S.S. and to quote from the findings; and further, to compare these with the work of Murray and Grant. The *present day* dialect of the Borders still awaits systematic study.

*At this point it must be made clear, that since the appeal of this contribution will be to a largely non-specialist readership, a phonetic script conveying narrow details of pronunciation, will not be used. Ordinary orthography can be used to convey a broad and generally unambiguous outline of what is intended. That intention, in Murray's words (and Murray often used ordinary orthography) is 'to represent to the eye the differences patent to the ear between the Dialect and the Standard English'.

PRONUNCIATION

Murray considered that in 'Lowland Scots' speech there were three main dialect groups in Scotland. These were: North Eastern, Central, and Southern. For the first two there were various sub-groupings, but the 'Southern', he said, 'is represented only by the dialect of the Border Counties'. He further defined the Scottish 'South' by quoting from Sir David Lindsay's 'Dreame' as lying 'Almoist betwix the Mers and the Lowhmabane'. that is, from Berwickshire and into Dumfriessshire.

In fact, Murray acknowledged that, in the South, there was another dialect which was not that of the 'Southern Counties'. This was the dialect of 'Lothian and Fife' which, even in Murray's time was also exerting a considerable influence on Berwickshire. Now, this other 'southern' dialect was a descendant of the 'artificial culture and consequent ascendancy over other dialects', which the Scottish Court had imposed under the Stuarts. Yet the older dialect had once extended 'over the whole of the lower basin of the Tweed south of the Lammer Moors and the Muirfoot Hills', that is to say, right through the Merse and into Dumfriesshire. Nevertheless, even in Murray's day 'its most salient characteristics, especially the diphthongal pronunciation, are now almost confined to Teviotdale, the vales of Ettrick and Yarrow, upper Eskdale and Annandale'. The whole area, defined by its salient characteristics (of which more presently) was thus constricted. Tweedside itself was being absorbed by Lothian pronunciation.

The work of William Grant confirmed all this. He, too, established a 'Southern Scots' (Roxburghshire and Selkirkshire) and a large 'East Mid Scots' area extending from Berwickshire and Lothian over the Forth and into Fife and Perthshire. This large area he divided into two sub-areas – (a) North of the Forth, for example said 'cat' and 'black', but (b) South of the Forth, rounded the lips and said 'cawt' and 'blawk'. North, they said 'ane' for 'one'. South, they had developed a fronted sound which turned it into 'yae'. More important, North of the Forth also had that rounded vowel of 'Southern Scots' as in 'muin' for 'moon'. Only Berwickshire (influenced by Lothian) had not. Yet even here there were traces of a former usage. In 1929 Grant noted that 'in East Lothian and Berwickshire older people may still be heard using the rounded vowel'. However, by 1960, out of seven places in Berwickshire (and four in East Lothian) investigated by the L.S.S., not one yielded any instance of this particular vowel sound. Clearly by that time it had disappeared altogether. On the other hand, the same investigation showed that its use in Roxburghshire was well maintained: Denholm, Roxburgh, Ancrum, Eckford, Oxnam, Hownam, Edgerston, Newcastleton, all gave words like 'boot', 'root', 'shoe', 'floor', 'fool', 'school', as 'buit,' 'ruit', 'shui', 'fluir', 'fuil', 'schuil'.

There was, however, for both Murray and Grant an even more noticeable (and exclusive) marker for 'Southern Scots'. This was the diphthongisation of certain vowel sounds. 'The dialect of the Southern Counties of Scotland', wrote Murray, 'is distinguished by its proneness to develop diphthongs out of vowels which were originally simple in Anglo Saxon, and which remain simple in other Scottish dialects'. Grant, too, observed this and quoted in illustration the Lockerbie couplet:

'Yow an' meyee, an' the bern dor keyee
The sow an' the threyee weyee pigs'

We have here, therefore, the 'dialect of yuw and mey'. It may be that Murray's test sentence is still known in the Borders: 'Yuw an' mey'll gang owre the deyke an' puw a pey' contrasted with Lothian, 'Yoo an' mee'll gyang uwr the duyke an' poo a pee'. (You and I will go over the wall and pull a pea). Murray and Grant are careful to point out that, for both 'yuw' and 'mey' there are two types each with its own history and they are not pronounced the same. So, for example, in correct 'Southern Scots' the words 'ewe' and 'you' do not fall together, although as Murray points out, 'they do so in the other Scottish Dialects'. In 'Southern Scots', 'yowe' a ewe, 'howe' a hollow, 'knowe' a knoll, all have the diphthong pronounced 'ow' which, he says, 'differs but little from the long o in no, road, as pronounced in the south of England, the terminal *oo* being more distinct'.*

On the other hand 'yuw', you, 'cuw' cow, 'duw' dove, 'suw' sow, 'thruw' through, have a diphthong in which the first element is 'the Scottish *u* in dull, and this differs from the English'. 'You' and 'ewe' therefore are distinct.

Similarly there are two types for the 'ey' diphthong in 'mey' for 'me' or 'threy' for 'three'. Berwickshire, in Murray's day, had 'ey' in 'cley' for 'clay', 'hey' for 'hay', 'stey' for 'stay' and so on. The evidence from the L.S.S. is that it still has. But Roxburghshire did not use its 'ey' diphthong in *that* set of words. Rather, says Murray, 'this dialect advances a step'. So that in 'Southern Scots' there is 'claiy' for 'clay' and 'haiy' for 'hay'. This means that the 'ey diphthong is reserved for 'me' and 'he'. Murray is quite explicit about the actual sound value of his 'claiy' and 'haiy' spellings. The pronunciation of the diphthong indicated by these spellings comes, he says, 'very near to the pronunciation of *lay, main,* in the South of England, *la-ee, ma-een,* from which it differs chiefly in the greater distinctness of the second element and abbreviation of the first'. This type of diphthongal pronunciation is rather characteristic of Roxburghshire and something more will be said about it.

---

*It is to be observed here that a diphthongal pronunciation has two elements – a 'first' and a 'terminal'. For example English 'eye' is 'ah-ee'.

Murray, therefore, gives a careful analysis of 'yuw' and 'mey' in the dialect. But he is not very hopeful of their long survival. His general remarks on the construction of the 'Southern Scots' dialect area have already been noticed. Even as early as 1873 he could write that 'yuw and mey' are not now heard in Galashiels, Melrose or Kelso and even in Jedburgh and Hawick they are fast disappearing'. And for this the 'railways, telegraphs and metropolitan fashions are all to blame'. So it is pleasurable to recall that on one occasion (so it was recounted to the L.S.S. from Denholm) he may have found some reassurance when, as Sir James Murray, he was saluted on Denholm Green by a lady who had been at school with him, with: 'Mercy Jimsie! is this yuw?"

What, then, has been the fate of this diphthongisation in this present century? The information gathered by the L.S.S. shows that of all the places investigated in Roxburghshire, with one important exception, words like 'ewe' and 'you' had by the 1950s, fallen together into a uniform 'yow'. So this, at least, survived in this levelled out form. The exception was Newcastleton in Liddesdale. There, the pronunciations were quite distinct. In exactly the way in which Murray said it ought to happen, there was for 'you' that distinct first element in its diphthongal pronunciation, an undoubted 'Scottish u in dull'. Equally clearly, for '-ewe' there was that diphthongal pronunciation which 'differs but little from the long o in no, road, as pronounced in the South of England. So too, for Newcastleton, the other words in the series fitted precisely into the pattern: 'ewe'. 'knowe', 'howe' as against 'you', 'through', 'cow'.

As for Murray's 'claiy' for 'clay' and the quite separate 'mey' for 'me' these by 1960 had levelled into a uniform 'cley' and 'mey' – and uniform with Berwickshire too. But, again, Newcastleton was the exception. There, a distinctive diphthong, continued for 'clay', 'hay', 'swey', which was pronounced 'clay-ee', 'hay-ee', 'sway-ee', while 'he', 'me', 'tea', 'three' were 'hey', 'mey', 'tey', 'threy'. The conformity (in pattern at least) with what Murray had to say about the pronunciation of these words is apparent.

In words like 'clay' and 'hay' the vowel sound is final. No consonant follows. But if, for instance, a voiced consonant (like 'd') or a liquid (like 'l') follows, the same diphthong occurs (or at least it occurred in Murray's time, so he tells us), but the second element is very short although perfectly audible. In the records of the L.S.S. Newcastleton alone seems to have preserved this in pronunciations like 'blee-id' for 'blade', or kee-il' for 'kale'. Other places – Denholm, Hownam, Edgerston – had simply 'blade' and 'kale'. It is worth noticing that A.J. Ellis, a contemporary of Murray, who wrote voluminously on the pronunciation of English and who observed this phenomenon in Liddesdale, considered the diphthong to be 'very closely compressed, so as to feel like a single vowel'.

The exact sound of the Roxburghshire diphthong written 'claiy' etc by Murray differed, he said, from South English 'lay' or 'main' only by the greater 'distinctness of the second element and abbreviation of the first'. Phoneticians know this as a 'rising diphthong' – the voice seems to 'rise' to give 'greater distinctness' to the second element. The most obvious example of this in the dialect of the 'Southern Counties' is in another characteristic diphthong. In a whole series of words with the vowel sound 'oo', and which in Berwickshire end in this simple 'oo' sound, Roxburghshire diphthongises into a *rising* diphthong. And this, the L.S.S. was able to record, was well maintained in the 1950's. So 'new' was 'nee-oo', 'blue' was 'blee-oo', 'dew' was 'dee-oo'. It represents one stage (arrested, as it were, in the southern counties) in the transition from an earlier English pronunciation of 'new' or 'dew' which were 'noo' and 'doo' (and still are in America). It may still be possible to hear of a 'nee-oo, blee-oo, see-oot' for a 'new, blue suit' in Roxburghshire.

So far, only vowels and diphthongs have been considered. They are, undoubtedly, the most effective markers in dialect study. But there are also some interesting consonant phenomena. There is, first of all, a common substitution of 'th' for 'f' in the word 'from'. 'He comes thrae Dunse' – 'He comes from Duns'. (Cockneys do it in reverse where 'f' is substituted for 'th'. 'Just come froo' for 'Just come through'. This substitution also happens in Caithness). Then there is the particular treatment in Roxburghshire of the 'ch' sound (as in general Scots 'loch'). This sound does not (or did not) end in the completely straightforward fashion to which Scots speakers are accustomed as, for instance, in 'loch'. In Roxburghshire it is 'ch' *plus* a further sound. That further sound – called by phoneticians a 'voiceless bi-labial fricative' – is simply a final rounding of the lips and an emission of breath. So, for example, 'the Duke of Buccleuch' has more going for him than simply 'the Duik o'Bucclee-ooch'. He has that added bilabial fricative *after* the final 'ch'.

And there is the treatment of the 'r' consonant in the Town of Berwick upon Tweed. The 'r' as pronounced in Berwick is neither the trilled 'r' of the Borders nor the uvular 'r' (the 'burr') of Northumberland. Murray considered that Berwick did have the uvular 'r', and in 1859 a well known traveller in Northumberland, Walter White, who stayed at the Red Lion Hotel in Berwick said that he was offered 'hawings' for breakfast which might imply a uvular 'r' or no 'r' at all. But the Berwick 'r' is, in very many circumstances, 'vocalised', that is, it is pronounced as a *vowel*. This happens in words like 'beard' which is bee-ad', or 'horse' which is 'ho-as', 'flower', is 'floo-a'. The phrase 'I was staggered' is 'Aa wuz staggad' and 'keep your fingers crossed' is 'keep ya fingas crossed'. The 'r' in 'crossed' is a very light tap on the teeth ridge by the tongue (called by phoneticians a 'one-tap 'r') and it so appears in 'The Parade', 'Church Street', 'Marygate'.

VOCABULARY

Dialect words will be considered here in that aspect known as 'word geography'. There are other aspects. There is collection and simple alphabetical ordering as in George Watson's *Roxburghshire Word Book*. There is the aspect which, according to Murray's first principles (Murray did not formally collect), examines the light they are able to shed on the history of the language. This was also done – to a lesser extent – by Watson. And there is an aesthetic and antiquarian aspect, favoured by many, although A.J. Ellis cautioned against the indulgence of 'collecting country words...as an amusement, not as laying a brick in the temple of science'.

The aim of word geography is not to collect words. It is, rather, to try to discern any particular patterning, area by area (the Borders, for example) for a given word in the same way as appeared to be possible for the distribution of particular speech sounds. We have already looked at some of the evidence for areas like 'East Mid Scots' (with 'Berwickshire'), 'Southern Scots', or 'Liddesdale'. In fact, words cannot be so tightly organised, or yield anything so definitive, area by area, as speech sounds. 'A wandering word', wrote the Swiss dialectologist Louis Gauchet, 'is like a stranger who takes up his abode wherever it suits him, a wandering sound knocks only at the door of relatives'.

In the 1950's the L.S.S.. asked by means of a questionnaire distributed very intensively throughout rural Scotland for local words for a very limited number of things and concepts in what can only be called 'country' situations in country communities. The presumption was that such communities would be linguistically stable. But – such is the nature of wandering words – variables and imponderables were not eliminated. In Roxburghshire, for example, the majority response to the request for 'broken pieces of china, used as playthings' was 'playgins', yet there was one instance of 'brock', one of 'dishies', one of 'boodies', one of 'hoosies' and three of 'chuckies'. Selkirkshire had one 'playgins' and one 'peevers', and the majority response was for no dialect word at all. For Berwickshire, 'playgins' was again in the majority, but there was one instance of 'flinders', one of 'peevers', one of 'pigs' and one of 'plafens'.

The extended lists of the L.S.S. – Peebles, East Lothian, Kirkcudbright, Dumfries – show an amazing number of such singularities. 'Kerseckie' turned up once in Roxburghshire for 'a man's undervest' ('semmit' was the general word) and once in Berwickshire. For a 'haystack' (generally 'stack', 'rick', or 'ruck') there was a 'hummel' in Roxburghshire and a 'rance' in Berwickshire. And so it went on. Were these simply strangers taking up an unpredictable abode? What is certain is that it could not happen with *sounds*. Nothing so random could possibly break into the tight pattern of, say, the vowel system of 'Southern Scots'.

(But what child uses 'playgins' now? What farmer builds a haystack? If he no longer uses draught horses why should he have words like 'hup' and 'hie' as commands to turn 'right' and 'left'? Here, then, is a further approach in the study of words, for here are social and cultural connections of words and things).

For the Borders, in the eventual analysis of these types of dialect word, certain indications emerged. First, there was the use of the same word on both sides of the Border. Second, this was much more common (perhaps 75%) in the east, into Northumberland, than in the west, into Cumberland. Third, there was a noticeable distributional difference (East/West) within the Scottish Borders. A few particular examples of these tendencies can be given.

'Playgins' was found on both sides of the Border, but only in the east. It appeared as the most usual word in both Berwickshire and Roxburghshire, but although also very common in Northumberland, the word 'boodies' was commoner still. ('Boodies' appeared only once in Roxburghshire and nowhere else). In Peeblesshire, Selkirkshire, Dumfriesshire and Kirkcudbrightshire there was only one instance each of 'playgins'. In these counties perhaps the commonest word was 'dishies', but this did not extend over the Solway.

For 'left-handed', 'carr-handed' (or 'carrie-handed') was extremely common in Berwickshire and Roxburghshire and it extended very far west even into Wigtownshire. It also extended over the eastern border into Northumberland, but there often in the form 'carrie-pawed', and this '– pawed' form was also found in many instances in Berwickshire, but only once in Roxburghshire. In fact, in this form there was a clear east/west difference. There were only two instances of 'carrie' in any form in Cumberland. There, 'bang-handed' was the most general word, and there was no instance of this anywhere north of the Solway.

The word 'skirl naked' for 'bare naked' was common to Berwickshire, Roxburghshire and Northumberland. It appeared only once in Dumfriesshire and not at all in Kirkcudbrightshire. In the west, a simple 'bar naked' predominated. The Cumberland word 'stone naked' did not appear in the western side of the Scottish Borders.

One word with a very wide distribution – east and west in the Borders, into Northumberland and Cumberland, and even into Northern Ireland – was the word 'grip' for 'the gutter running through a byre'. The word 'syre' appeared twice in both Berwickshire and Roxburghshire and thrice in Dumfriesshire. It occurred more frequently than 'grip' in Northumberland, but never in Cumberland. Neither did it appear in Kirkcudbrightshire.

For 'soap suds' the word 'graith' was common in Berwickshire, Roxburghshire, Selkirkshire and Peeblesshire. It appeared only twice in

Northumberland where it was swallowed up in a multiplicity of 'lather'. And it did not appear at all in Cumberland which shared 'lather' with Northumberland. All of the Lothians had 'graith' very widely distributed, but there were four instances only in Dumfriesshire ('sapples' was the word there) and one in Kirkcudbrightshire (again 'sapples'). 'Graith', then, showed a usage common to the Eastern Borders and, this time, to Lothian.

A wandering word is like a stranger ...

GRAMMAR

Included in Murray's *Dialect of the Southern Counties* is his *Grammar of the Southern Scottish Dialect*. Here, he exemplified many matters which he insisted were 'strictly grammatical' in the dialect. There was, for example, the use and the historicity of the third person plural in '-s' (this example was given earlier) – 'the men sits'. How has this fared in the middle of this present century? The L.S.S. asked for comment on usage in the sentence: 'These horses pulls weel'. In Berwickshire out of 32 informants, two gave 'pulls'. In Roxburghshire out of 28 there were 7. In Selkirkshire out of 8 only 1. In Peeblesshire no 'pulls' at all. In Dumfriesshire nine 'pulls' with 49 informants. In Kirkcudbrightshire, 2 out of 27. It seems that in the 1950s that form of third person plural was decidedly recessive.

Then there is the particular system of demonstrative pronouns. Murray included this in his *Grammar* – Singular: 'this', 'that', Plural: 'thir', 'thae', 'thon', or 'yon'. For Roxburghshire, in the investigation by the L.S.S., there was the complete system except that Roxburgh returned 'these' for the plural 'thir'. In Berwickshire Burnmouth also gave 'these' for 'thir', but in general the system was maintained. Burnmouth, however, gave 'the' for 'thae'. Farther west – Dumfriesshire and Kirkcudbrightshire the system appeared to be not nearly so well preserved. Two places (Hightae and Canonbie) gave the expected 'thir' for the plural of 'this', but elsewhere the plurals of 'this' and 'that' were levelled under 'thae'. In Kirkcudbrightshire the use of 'thir' seemed to be indeterminate. The word was known but used indiscriminately with 'thae'. The general patterning, therefore, in the use of these pronouns appeared as a gradual recession from east to west.

One grammatical feature which, in the 1950s seemed to be found only in Berwickshire was the use of 'no' in imperative and indicative negative sentences, such as 'no dae that' or 'aa no sing'. Murray knew about this but gave it no particular location. In a full conjugation of the verb 'to sing' he gave 'aa dynna syng'. This seemed to make it remote even in Murray's time, but it is, and probably to this day, a characteristic Berwickshire locution.

From the investigation by the L.S.S. one further Berwickshire dialect characteristic appeared to be the use of 'we' rather than 'us' in such sentences as 'she tellt *we* aboot it'. (This also extends over the Border into Northumberland). The Berwickshire form is, rather, 'oo' – 'she tellt oo', 'did ye see thou fellay aback o' oo'? Burnmouth had this form and so had Coldstream. Auchencrow had 'us' and Cockburn had 'huz'. There were one or two examples in Roxburghshire. Eckford and Ancrum both had 'oo', and Roxburgh gave both 'oo' and 'us'. But generally the Roxburghshire form was 'huz'. Farther west in the Borders the 'we' or 'oo' form did not appear at all.

And finally: what has been written here is a very limited and compressed account of abundant linguistic material. But, in any case, how is it all to be *described*? One dialectologist, Ernst Pulgram, put it thus: 'What the linguist has to be is to state his purpose, to explain why he expects benefits from it, and what those benefits will be, and then select and delimit his material accordingly'. The purpose here has been to be comparative. And if the local dialects continue to pass away, can we still know how far and how fast, in what ways and in what places?

For example, how many words in George Watson's carefully garnered *Word Book* are actually used (or even known?) And how will it be in the future? So, too, for pronunciation and grammar. These matters will certainly require further comparable material and further detailed investigation. And in the end, doubtless, another Borders Book.

SEVENTEEN

THE SINGING COUNTRY:
THE BALLADS OF THE BORDERS

A ballad, simply defined, is a folk-song that tells a story. Although ballads were sung for centuries in most parts of the British Isles, Scotland, and especially the Border region, has always enjoyed a particularly rich and varied singing tradition. Indeed John Ruskin once claimed that:

> The Border district of Scotland was...of all districts of the inhabited world, pre-eminently the singing country - that which most naturally expressed its noble thoughts and passions in song.[1]

This may appear now to be somewhat exaggerated, but it is certainly the case that when the early nineteenth century ballad collectors – Robert Riddell, Sir Walter Scott, Thomas Wilkie, William Motherwell and others – began to preserve these traditional verse narratives, the Borders proved to be a fertile source of material.

James Hogg, the Etrrick Shepherd (see Chapter 18), whose mother provided Scott with several ballad texts for his *Minstrelsy of the Scottish Border*, guessed at both the antiquity of the ballad-singing tradition and its essentially oral nature. He wrote to Scott in 1801:

> Till this present age, the poor illiterate people in these glens, knew of no other entertainment, in the long winter nights, that repeating, and listening to, the feats of their ancestors, recorded in songs, which I believe to be handed down, from father to son, for many generations.[2]

Hogg might equally well have said 'from mother to daughter' for, as we shall see, the field collectors of the nineteenth century obtained many of their ballad texts from female singers, women like Agnes Lyle of Kilbarchan, Mary Barr of Lesmahagow, and Nancy Brockie of Bemersyde. It is interesting to discover that the illustration on the title page of William Motherwell's *Minstrelsy Ancient and Modern* (published in Paisley in 1827) depicts a woman spinning flax with two children, a boy and a girl, seated at her feet.[3] I like to imagine that she is singing to them while she works and that they are learning their first ballads – *Tam Lin* or *Thomas Rymer*.

Hogg was right in supposing that the singers of the 'auld sangs' in the Border glens operated as dynastic and familial agents. If we go back two centuries, we find John Leslie, Bishop of Ross, in his *Historie of Scotland*

(1578) noticing the Border folk's love of music and singing and their desire to commemorate the deeds of their ancestors. Leslie writes:

> Thay delyt mekle in thair awne musick and Harmonie in singing, quhilke of the actes of thair foirbearis thay have leired, or quhat thame selfes have invented of ane ingenious policie to dryve a pray.[4]

Driving, taking or fetching a 'prey' is a favourite subject of those Border Ballads that have survived (and many must have been lost over the years). These ballads, narrating the exploits of the 'reivers', or cattle-thieves, men with extravagantly sounding names like Red Rowan, the Gay Galliard and Watty wi the Wudspurs (mad spurs), who would steal anything with four hooves, are the ballads most of us associate with the Borders. What is probably one of the oldest of them *The Battle of Otterburn*, has the characteristic seasonal opening of the 'Riding' ballads:

> It fell about the Lammas tide,
> When the muir-men win their hay,
> The doughty Douglas bound him to ride
> Into England to drive a prey.
>
> (Child 161C, Scott's *Minstrelsy* version)[5]

Similarly, Jamie Telfer of the Fair Dodhead begins:

> It fell about the Martinmas tyde,
> Whan our Border steeds get corn and hay,
> The Captain of Bewcastle hath bound him to ryde,
> And he's ower to Tividale to drive a prey.
>
> (Child 190, Scott's *Minstrelsy* version)

When Father James Dalrymple translated Bishop Leslie's original Latin *Historie* into Scots, he rendered Leslie's 'Rhythmicis suis cantionibus' as 'Harmonie in singing'. This might be more accurately translated as 'composed in verse or rhyme', for this is exactly what we find the Border Ballads to be – songs composed usually in four-line, rhymed verses, with a pronounced 4 : 3 : 4 : 3 beat. Tunes to *The Battle of Otterburn* have survived (which is not, unfortunately, the case with all the Border Ballads) and I have heard it sung in recent years by folk-singers Terry Conway and Rod Paterson.

Often the ballads would have an 'ower-word' (over-word) 'over-turn', or chorus. The ballad singer would take the verses while the listeners would join in on the chorus, giving the singer time to compose, or recall from memory, the next verse of a long ballad that might stretch to 40 or 50 verses (the longest text of *The Battle of Otterburn* has 70). A ballad performance was thus a shared, communal activity. As Willa Muir, who grew up in a ballad singing community on the north east coast of Scotland explains:

The audience for oral poetry is not passive...there is a flow of sympathy between the listeners and the singer; the quality of this sympathetic rapport may lead the ballad singer, almost unconsciously, to shift an emphasis here or change a phrase there to fit the mood of his audience. Oral poetry lives while it is being performed, and with every ballad performance the singer creates it anew, with possible variations in the tune or the stanzas.[6]

One can imagine the 'flow of sympathy', the electric charge almost, between the descendants of Harry Hotspur or James, the second Earl of Douglas, who clashed at Otterburn, and their ballad singers as they relived in verse that moonlit August night in 1388 when

> The stonderdes stode styll on eke a syde,
> Wyth many a grevous grone;
> Ther the fowght the day and all the nyght,
> And many a dowghty man was slayne.

> (Child 161A, the Cotton MS version of 1550)

It seems reasonable to suppose that ballads about Otterburn were circulating on both sides of the Border soon after the battle of 1388. But the ballad does not appear in manuscript until about 1550 and was not printed until 1776 when David Herd included it in his *Ancient and Modern Scottish Songs*. We therefore have a transmission gap of over 170 years in the case of Child's A text and of near 400 years in the case of Child B. This makes the exact dating of the Border Ballads a virtually impossible task.

Still, if Bishop Leslie and the Ettrick Shepherd are to be believed, the Borderers' memories were tenacious where the deeds of their ancestors were concerned. Robert Louis Stevenson was of this opinion, too:

This is the mark of the Scot of all classes; that he stands in an attitude towards the past unthinkable to Englishmen, and remembers and cherishes the memory of his forebears, good and bad; and there burns alive in him a sense of identity with the dead even to the twentieth generation.[7]

This may be one reason why the Border Ballads were still being recited, centuries after the last reiver was hanged. That, and the fact that a certain glamour has always been attached to them, an aura of romance that Scott did everything to encourage in his *Minstrelsy of the Scottish Border*. In his long introductory essay to the 1830 edition, Scott takes an obvious delight in recounting amusing anecdotes about the Border freebooters, men like Sir Walter Scott of Harden who, after a night's reiving, saw a large haystack and thinking it would provide excellent fodder for his newly acquired stock remarked: 'By my soul, had ye but four feet, ye should not stand long there'.[8]

The same Scott of Harden, we are told, used to

ride with a numerous band of followers. The spoil which they carried off from England, or from their neighbours, was concealed in a deep and impervious glen, on the brink of which the old tower of Harden is situated. From thence the cattle were brought out, one by one, as they were wanted, to supply the rude and plentiful table of the laird. When the last bullock was killed and devoured, it was the lady's custom to place on the table a dish, which, on being uncovered, was found to contain a pair of clean spurs, a hint to the riders that they must shift for their next meal.[9]

The motto of the Scotts of Harden was 'Phoebe reparabit cornua' – 'moonlight will replenish the bowl' (literally 'the horn'). A sketch entitled *The Dish of Spurs* by Sir Walter Scott's friend, Charles Kirkpatrick Sharpe, can be seen at Abbotsford, Scott's home on the Tweed (Plate 24).

Bishop Leslie, devout cleric that he no doubt was, also seems to find amusing the customs of the Border reivers. In his *Historie of Scotland* he notes:

> The policie of dryving a pray thay think be sa leivesum (lovesome or pleasant) and lawful to thame that nevir sa fervertlie they say their prayeris, and pray their Beides (beads), quhilkes rosarie we cal, nor with sick solicitude and kair, as oft quhen they have XL or L myles to drive a pray.[10]

Leslie may be playing here on the words 'pray' and 'prey' – a pun which is even more noticeable in the Bishop's original Latin.

The Border Ballads themselves (and not just the texts Scott chose for his *Minstrelsy* collection) often reflect this kind of rough frontier humour. One thinks of Hobie Noble's teasing of Jock o' the Side whom he has rescued from Newcastle jail and who, because his ankles are still manacled, has to ride side-saddle as they escape across the Border into Liddesdale:

> 'O Jock, sae winsomely's ye ride,
> Wi baith your feet upo ae side!
> Sae weel's ye're harnessed and sae trig! (neat, trim)
> In troth ye sit like ony bride.'

(*Jock o the Side*, Child 187B, the version preserved by the Shortreeds of Jedburgh).

In the ballad *Dick o the Cow* (Child 185) the joke is directed in the opening verse at the Armstrong ponies which have grown dull and overweight for lack of good reiving exercise:

> Now Liddesdale has lain long in,
>   Fa la
> There is no rideing there a ta;
>   Fa la
> Their horse is growing so lidder (lazy) and fatt
>   That are lazie in the sta.
>   Fa la didle.

The ballad tells the story of Dickie, a poor Cumberland farmer, whose three kye are stolen by the Armstrongs. Dickie follows the 'Hot Trod' as far as Puddingburn, the Armstrongs' pele, in Liddesdale. He marches bravely into the hall where he complains to the laird's Jock. But instead of restoring to Dickie his stolen cattle,

> Then up bespake the good Laird's Jock,
> The best falla in the companie:
> 'Fitt thy way down a little while, Dickie,
> And a piece of thine own cow's hough I'll
>   give to thee'.

This is 'Dish of Spurs' comedy, to be enjoyed by the whole company sitting round the ingle-cheek on a winter's evening, or at the kirn at the end of the harvest. The humour 'casts a glamourie' over these ballad mosstroopers (Plate 28) just as surely as the elaborate description of the outlaw Johnie Armstrong's costume does in a ballad probably dating back to the 1530s:

> John wore a girdle about his midle,
> Imbroidered owre with burning gold,
> Bespangled with the same mettle,
> Maist beautiful was to behold.

> There hang nine targats (tassels) at Johnys hat,
> And ilk an worth three hundred pound...

(*Johnie Armstrong*, Child 169C, Allan Ramsay's version printed in *The Ever Green*, 1724.)[11]

Despite Scott's assertion in his *Minstrelsy* that

> The common people of the high parts of Teviotdale, Liddesdale and the country adjacent, hold the memory of Johnie Armstrong in very high respect.[12]

it should be remembered that he was a notorious blackmailer, 'a great theiff and oppressour' according to the historian Patrick Anderson.[13] The ravages the Armstrong clan perpetrated on their own side of the Border seem to have been appalling. In 1528, only 2 years before Johnie Armstrong was hanged by James V at Carlenrig, Sim the Laird boasted that

> in the realme of Scotland he wold nevir looke to have justice kepit, seying, that hymself and hys adherentes have endway laid waiste in the said realme lx myles, and laid downe xxxto parisshe churches.[14]

The situation was no better farther west in Annandale where the ballad *The Lads of Wamphray* (Child 184) comes from. This time the 'unbrydlit' men were Johnstones. In July 1593, they descended on

> the lands and territoreis pertening to the Lord Sanquhar...whare, attoure (over and above) the great reaf and spulye that they tuik away with violent hand, they slew and mutilat a great nomber of men wha stude for defence of thair awin geir and to reskew the same from the hands of sik vicious revers.[15]

In the ballad, the justification for the raid is the Johnstones' determination to avenge the death of William Johnstone of Wamphray, 'the Galiard', whom the Crichtons have 'hanged high upon a tree'.

> O but these lads were wondrous rude
> When the Biddes-burn ran three days blood!

'I think, my lads, we've done a noble deed;
We have revenged the Galiard's blood'.

'For every finger of the Galiard's hand,
I vow this day I've killed a man'.

The ballad clearly functions as a male bonding device, a propagandist piece to strengthen clan loyalty at a time of feud. The skirmish of 1593, Scott tells us, led to the revival of the ancient Johnstone-Maxwell feud on this part of the Border.[16] I have never heard the ballad sung, but the short rhyming couplets of Child's printed text (and the 80 continuous lines of Robert Riddell's original handwritten copy in the 1791 Glenriddell manuscript) turn the ballad into a kind of tribal chant. It concludes:

'For where eer I gang, or eer I ride,
The lads o Wamphay's on my side'.

'For of a' the lads that I do ken,
The lads o Wamphay's king o men'.

This spirit of male camaraderie, a marked feature of the Border-raid ballads, can also be found in rescue ballads like *Archie o Cawfield* (Child 188), though the chauvinism is less strident. Two brothers learn that a third is a prisoner in Dumfries, condemned to die because he 'brake a spear i the warden's breast' whilst defending his master's lands. They smash down the Tolbooth door and manage to get Archie on horseback despite the 'fifteen stone of Spanish iron' that 'lyes fast' to him 'with lock and key'. They swim across the flooded river Annan ('and it was running like a sea'), daring the Lord Lieutenant to follow them, and eventually reach home. The ballad must have been sung at a swift pace, lines like the following, which are repeated five times, underlining key episodes and driving the narrative forward from one stage to the next:

And there was horsing, horsing of haste,
And cracking of whips out oer the lee.

This refrain, or 'ower-word', occurs in Miss Fisher of Carlisle's 1780 version of the ballad (Child 188A). But Miss Fisher slows the narrative to a moving and quiet coda in the final verses as Jock the Laird regrets the night's action:

O up bespoke then Jock the Laird,
'This has been a dearsome night to me;
For yesternight the Cawfield was my ain
Landsman again I neer sall be'.

He is immediately rebuked:

'Now wae light o thee and thy lands baith, Jock,
And even so baith the land and thee!
For gear will come and gear will gang,
But three brothers again we never were to be'.

Land, kye, clothes and other material possessions (summed up for the reiver in the one word 'gear') are not all; brotherly love cannot be measured and will endure. Mary Barr, of Lesmahagow, expresses similar sentiments in her rendering of *Lord Thomas and Fair Annet* (Child 73B):

'For gear will come and gear will gang,
And gear's ae but a lend (loan),
And monie a ane for warld's gear
A silly brown bride brings hame'.

Verses like these seem to reveal the woman's touch. Perhaps it would not be too far-fetched to suggest that it was the Border women who, during the long, dark years of the Border 'Troubles' in the fifteenth and sixteenth centuries, began to challenge the old Border code of raid and counter-raid, of blood feud and violence. Perhaps they were not all like auld Wat of Harden's wife. Many of them must have suffered terribly, losing husbands and sons, fathers and brothers during centuries of bloodshed.

We can hear the cries of these Border women as far back as 1388, when they came to pick up the corpses after the battle of Otterburn:

Then on the morne they mayde them beerys (biers)
Of byrch and haysell graye;
Many a wydowe, wyth wepying teyres (tears)
Ther makes (mates) they fette (fetch) awaye.

The sombre mood is evoked perfectly in this verse by the single word 'graye'; the heraldic colours of Percy and Douglas (the stars, white lions, silver crescents and luces argent of their banners) are dimmed.

If not death in Border warfare, death by murder. How many ballads, one wonders, provided an outlet for the grief of women like the lady in *The Slaughter of the Laird of Mellerstain* (Child 239)?

And she staggerd and she stood...

'How can I keep in my wits,
When I look on my husband's blood?'

'Had we been men as we are women'
And been at his back when he was slain,
It should a been tauld for mony a lang year,
The Slaughter o the laird of Mellerstain.

The ballad has only survived as a fragment, but it is eloquent and moving. The point of view is quite different from that offered by the belligerent couplets of *The Lads of Wamphray*. The last verse conveys the sense of frustration and powerlessness which many Border women must have felt, young or old, of high estate or low. Their vulnerability, especially when the fencible men were away (as was the case after the Rising in the North in 1569) is poignantly expressed in a verse from *Rookhope Ryde* (Child 179), a ballad from Weardale on the English side of the Border. The English raiders brag:

> 'Ther we shal get gear enough,
> For there is none but women at hame;
> The sorrowful fend (defence) that they can make
> Is loudly cries as they were slain'.

Yet if they could not wield swords, perhaps they discovered through the ballads the power of words, especially of words allied to a good tune. Though the tunes were not often written down by the early collectors, they sometimes mention them. Thomas Wilkie, for example, took down the words of *Geordie* (Child 209D) from Janet Scott of Bowden, Near Melrose, 'who sung it to a beautiful, plaintive old air'.[17]

It may have been women singers who brought to the ballads that 'nucleus of strong feeling', as Willa Muir calls it, from which the best ballad stories seem to spring.[18] The nucleus of strong feeling in *Rookhope Ryde* is the sense of outrage that 'limmer thieves' should dare to attack a defenceless village 'as if the world had been all their own'. 'Limmer' means 'hound-like' and the ballad depicts the English marauders as an evil and diabolic force, disrupting the natural peace and harmony of the dale:

> Rookhope stands in a pleasant place,
> If the false thieves wad let it be;
> But away they steal our goods apace,
> And ever an ill death may they die!
>
> Lord God! is not this a pitiful case,
> That men may not drive their goods to t'fell,
> But limmer thieves drives them away
> That fears neither heaven nor hell?

Although the ballad ends, conventionally enough, with the entreaty to 'pray for the singer of this song' who 'sings to make blithe your cheer', it may have functioned, as I suspect other Border Ballads did, as more than simple entertainment.

In the period before James VI's 'pacification' of the Border, it seems that ordinary men and women on both sides of the Border were finding a voice in the ballads and adding it to the voices of those March Wardens and other officers whose task it was to administer a frontier in chaos. In 1595, the last year of his jurisdiction as Warden of the English Middle March, we find Sir John Forster urging 'all Christian people' to relent of

'the deadly and detestable feuds existing between (among others) the Reedes, loyall and dutyfull subjectes of England, and the Croziers, lawfull and leige subjectes of Scotland'.[19]

If we turn to the Border Ballads we find 'the deadly foed, the word of enmitye on the Borders, implacable without the blood and whole family distroied',[20] called into question as a way of settling disputes. The anguish of an older generation who, like the Montagues and Capulets, have caused, through personal vendetta, the deaths of their offspring, ends the ballad *Bewick and Graham* (Child 211):

> With that bespoke now Robin Bewick:
> 'O man, was I not much to blame?
> I have lost one of the liveliest lads
> That ever was bred unto my name'.
>
> With that bespoke my good lord Grahame:
> 'O man, I have lost the better block (bargain);
> I have lost my comfort and my joy,
> I have lost my key, I have lost my lock.'

Ironically, each of the old men is still arguing that his son is the better (the cause of the feud) and the ballad ends as it began.

> 'If a man were permitted to make all the ballads, he need not care who should make the laws of a nation',

wrote Andrew Fletcher of Saltoun.[21] Once again, there may be an assumption here that it is men who 'make all the ballads', yet by the late eighteenth century, when Fletcher was writing, the majority of ballad texts were being collected from the recitations of women. They may on occasions be dismissed by the transcribers as 'weak-minded', like Sarah Rae of Balmaclellan,[22] yet their texts persuade us with their range of feeling and depth of emotion, their humane awareness.

As a final example, let us look at *The Death of Parcy Reed* (Child 193B), sung by Catherine, or Kitty, Hall, 'a native of Northumberland' in the early 1800s. She and her ancestors condemn the Border raid passionately in the opening verse:

> God send the land deliverance
> Frae every reaving, riding Scot...

and when Parcy Reed, the Keeper of Redesdale and upholder of Elizabeth I's Border Laws is butchered by the feuding Croziers, she confronts her listeners with the horrific consequences of the old Border code of vengeance:

> Alake, and wae for Parcy Reed,
> Alake, he was an unarmed man,
> Four weapons pierced him all at one,
> As they assailed him there and than.
>
> They fell upon him all at once,
> They mangled him most cruellie;
> The slightest wound might caused his deid,
> And thae hae gien him thirty three;
> They hacket off his hands and feet,
> And left him lying on the lee.

Was it Kitty Hall, or an earlier singer like her, who introduced the figure of the herdsman into this version of the tale? He is an example of human kindness; coming upon the dying Laird of Troughend 'at the hour of gloaming grey', he runs for the nearest water, and

> He made his bonnet serve a cup,
> And wan the blessing o the dying man.

As Willa Muir and others have pointed out, 'ballads flourish best in a close, small community'[23] and the Borders must have been made up of many such communities when 'the verie hart of the cuntrey' was in such 'ane uncertaintie'.[24] Within these communities there must have been sensitive and aware singers like Kitty Hall, who lamented Parcy Reed's murder, George Collingwood who chanted *Rookhope Ryde* in the 1780s, Nancy Brockie and Marion Miller of Bemersyde who recited *Hughie Grame* (Child 191) – Border folk who used their ballads to articulate the fears and prejudices of their contemporaries. There has always been a temptation to suppose that, because folk like them were illiterate, they were incapable of creativity. As R.A. Houston in his study of literacy in Scotland reminds us:

> We must question the notion of a non-literate society as somehow a culturally sub-standard version of a literate one.[25]

The Border Ballads force us to do this. They are like narrative and dramatic time-capsules, revealing to us the way 'poor Jock upon land' tried to make sense of a world of political and social turmoil. They probe the griefs and examine the tragi-comedy of the 'Border-side'. As John Selden observed:

> More solid things do not show the complexion of the times so well as ballads.[26]

References

1. *The Works of John Ruskin*, ed. E.T. Cook and A. Wedderburn, vol. xxvii, 593–4 (London 1907).

2. Scott, *Minstrelsy*, ed. T.F. Henderson, vol.I, 240 (Edinburgh and London, 1902).

3. The etching is by the Scottish portrait painter Andrew Henderson.

4. *The Historie of Scotland*, translated in Scottish by Father James Dalrymple, ed. E.C. Cody, vol.I, 60. (Scottish Text Society, Edinburgh, 1888–95).

5. All ballad quotations are from *The English and Scottish Popular Ballads*, ed. F.J. Child, 5 volumes (Boston, Mass. 1882–98). I have followed Child's numbering of the ballads. He assigns letters alphabetically to each individual version of a ballad.

6. *Living with Ballads*, 35 (London 1965).

7. *Weir of Hermiston*, 54 (London 1924).

8. Scott, *Minstrelsy*, vol.I. 154.

9. Ibid, vol.I, 154.

10. Leslie, *Historie*, vol.I, 101–2.

11. 'Copied from a gentleman's mouth of the name of Armstrang, who is the 6th generation from this John'. Ramsay, op.cit. vol.II, 190.

12. Scott, *Minstrelsy*, vol.I, 342.

13. Anderson, M.S. History, cited R.B. Armstrong, *The History of Liddesdale*, 274-5 (Edinburgh, 1883).

14. *Letters and Papers of the Reign of Henry VIII*, ed. J.S. Brewer, vol.IV, 2205 (London 1862).

15. *The Historie and Life of King James the Sext*, author unknown, ed. Thomas Thomson, 297 (Bannatyne Club, Edinburgh, 1825).

16. Scott, *Minstrelsy*, vol.II, 186.

17. Wilkie M.S., cited Child, *Ballads*, vol.IV, 130.

18. Muir, op.cit., 86.

19. *The Calendar of Border Papers*, ed. Joseph Bain, vol.II, 111 (Edinburgh 1896).

20. *The Calendar of Border Papers*, vol.II, 163.

21. *Political Works*, 265 (Glasgow, 1774).

22. These are the words of the Rev. George Murray who took down her version of *The Lochmaben Harper* (Child 192D) in 1886. See Child, *Ballads*, vol.IV, 20.

23. Muir, op.cit., 35.

24. George Macdonald Fraser, *The Steel Bonnets, The Story of the Anglo-Scottish Border Reivers*, 315 (London, 1971) Fraser is quoting King James VI.

25. Houston, *Scottish Literacy and the Scottish Identity*, 194 (Cambridge 1985).

26. Selden, *Table Talk*, ed. S.H. Reynolds, 105 (London 1892).

EIGHTEEN

BORDER TRADITIONS: FOLKLORE AND JAMES HOGG

There are really two different kinds of tradition in the Borders: one type is to be found in the living traditions of the towns, enshrined in the annual Common Ridings and other festivals that take place throughout the summer months in the Borders. These celebrations have no exact counterpart in any other area of Scotland let alone Britain, and each one of them, though having common elements, also has its own very individual rituals. The traditions of the Border Common Ridings deserve a chapter on their own account, (see Chapter 19).

Then there are what might be described as the traditions of the countryside, the folkloric tales and legends which in former years were handed down by word of mouth but which have now been captured in print. They are the yarn from which the ballads were spun, and have been the inspiration for poetry, prose, music and the visual arts.

Between them, Sir Walter Scott (see Chapter 13) and James Hogg are an almost complete source for the great folkloric traditions of the Borders. The former came to them as a seeker, realising that he lived on the cusp of the survival of the Border ballads by word of mouth, and that if he did not search for them, and write them down, they and much of the legend enveloping them would be lost to future generations. Though Scott's main claim to deserved fame is as a novelist and an original poet, as well as one of Scotland's great national figures, what he did to preserve the traditions of the Borders through his collection and publication of the *Minstrelsy of the Scottish Borders* should never be overlooked. It is fashionable nowadays to deride Scott and to lay the blame for the 'shortbread tin' image of Scotland beloved of much of the tourist trade – indeed he can be identified as the father of that important part of Scotland's economy, through the romanticism of the Waverley novels. But he did care, passionately, and in the very best sense, about Scotland's heritage: and he acted on his feelings.

Nor should Scott's debt to James Hogg be overlooked. The latter was a natural inheritor, not an acquisitor of the tradition, which he gave willingly to Scott when they were both relatively young men. It was the lore that he had learned, not through books, but at his mother's knee, and it informed much of his own writing.

For Hogg's education was not one of book-learning. Born in late 1770 (he believed, until his latter years, that he had been born on 25th January, 1772, thus sharing a birthday with Burns). Even after consultation with the parish registers revealed to him that he had been baptised in the early days of 1771, he still kept that date as a joint natal celebration. He grew up in a community and a household where ballad singing and storytelling were an integral part of life.

Ettrick, sixteen miles from Selkirk up a road impassable for much of the year by wheeled vehicles, was a remote, self-contained community, hemmed in by hills. Hogg's father was the descendant of the Hoggs of Fauldshope, only four miles from Selkirk; but the family had fallen on hard times and removed to the smaller and more distant farm of Ettrickhall. When this farm failed in turn, Hogg's education at the village school, which had lasted for all of six months, came to an abrupt end.

Hogg's mother, Margaret Laidlaw, was a renowned ballad singer and it was in search of her store of ballads that Hogg and Scott first met. Hogg by this time was himself earning a local reputation as a poet, and Scott encouraged him.

But neither Margaret Laidlaw nor her son thought much of the publication of the *Minstrelsy of the Scottish Border*. Mrs. Hogg's comment became famous: 'The sangs were made for singing, no' for prenting and now they'll never be sung again: and furthermore, Shirra, they're no setten doun richt nor prentit richt'.

James Hogg (Plate 29) was critical of some of Scott's forewords and footnotes, which clashed with the version of history he had been told by his mother and his uncle. And when the third volume was published, with much of its contents under Scott's own hand, Hogg felt he could do as well himself. The result was his first major collection, *The Mountain Bard*, which drew heavily on local traditions, as did much of his later work.

These traditions can be arranged loosely into three headings: adventure (including warfare), love, and the supernatural, though there is some crossover between them, especially between the latter two. Legends of love occur in every folk tradition, and the majority are variations of the Romeo and Juliet theme. But those of the supernatural and of adventure are more specific to place, both in terms of history and geography. I propose therefore to deal with these strands.

Principal amongst the adventuring are the legends of the reivers, described in Chapter 7. Many of the reiving exploits described in the ballads have a foundation in fact, and versions are to be found in the contemporary records: the rescue of Kinmont Willie from Carlisle Castle, or the hanging of Johnnie Armstrong by King James V.

But there are legends of the reivers, also, where known historical fact does not march step by step with the stories that have come down through the generations. Many of them concern the great reiver Wat Scott of Harden, whose chronicled exploits are impressive enough. But we are here concerned less with those of fact than those of folklore. Foremost amongst them is the tradition that his wife would hand him a dish of spurs when the larder was empty, to signify that it was time to take to horse in pursuit of English cattle. To his sons, also, legends are attached, which have given birth to ballads and other interpretations.

The best known is that which concerns the marriage of the eldest son, William Scott. The story is that, frustrated by the peace between Scotland and England which had stopped cross-border reiving, he set out for a raid on the cattle of Sir Gideon Murray of Elibank Castle on the Tweed. Captured by Murray, Scott was given the choice between a hanging, or marriage to the plainest of the Murray daughters, Meg. After three days he chose the latter fate, and they lived in marital harmony thereafter, numbering Sir Walter Scott amongst their descendants. The facts are less than supportive: the marriage contract of William Scott to Agnes, not Margaret, Murray, appears to indicate that the nuptials were set up well in advance, not at the gallows-tree, and the bridegroom's career as sheriff and member of parliament would seem to belie a propensity for reiving. And yet, the essence of the tradition must have some foundation.

A further tradition of Wat of Harden is that on a raid to Northumberland, he mistakenly brought home a child, wrapped up in hangings wrenched from the walls of the tower. Alternative consequences follow: one is that the child was swept from his arms when crossing the Ettrick below Wat's tower of Kirkhope, and that as a self-imposed penance he built a bridge, the coat of arms from which is incorporated in the present one at Ettrickbridge. The other version is that the child was brought up with the blood sons of the reiver, but that his temperament, artistic and peace loving, was at odds with his foster brothers. A further twist to this scenario is that the child was the maker of many of the ballads that are set in Ettrick and Yarrow.

The tale of Will Scott and 'Muckle-Mou'd Meg' has passed into literature through the pens of many writers, but Hogg's comic ballad *The Fray of Elibank* is probably the most successful. He uses a version of the incident of the reived foundling in the novel *The Three Perils of Man*, in which he attempted to draw together many of the threads of the folklore that had been handed down to him.

Such incidents are part of the tapestry of inherited oral stories in a region once dominated by warfare, both international and localised.

The tales of the reivers date mainly from the sixteenth century, which was their heyday; the supernatural stories and indeed the romances tend to be of greater antiquity.

In the field of the supernatural, one category of tales is what might be described as domesticated – for example, the Brownies, the little folk who might help or hinder work in the farms depending on their treatment at the hands of those who lived there. The custom – identical to that described by Hans Andersen in one of his lesser-known *eventyr* – was that the farmer or his wife should set out a bowl of porridge and milk nightly for the Brownie. Thus propitiated, he would attend to such matters as the harvest, herding the sheep, or the making of the butter or cheese. But if in any way insulted, he (in all such tales, there is only one Brownie attached to each farm) would undo his work – scatter the sheaves or the sheep, or curdle the cream and separate the butter.

Variations of the Brownie existed for both castle and cottage, and it is significant that the spirit associated with the former in folktales was malignant, in the latter benign. Both were small squat creatures with grizzled lock, but the castle's 'redcap sly' had eyes that were blood shot and staring, and on his head a red cap into which he poured the blood of his victims. The 'Wag o' the Wa' of the cottage hearth on the other hand had gentle saucer like eyes and a tail that helped him to balance on the swee that suspended the family cooking pot over the fireplace. While the former would assist such necromantic figures as the evil Lord Soulis of Hermitage in his practice of the Black Art, the latter would join in the cottagers' family circle at night, and was regarded as totally benign.

Such were the everyday supernatural beings, the belief in whose existence the country people grew up with, and by whom they felt not disturbed, but were as comfortable as with established religion – perhaps more so. The ease with which James Hogg writes of them is testament to their integration in people's beliefs. When Hogg writes about his grandfather the 'far famed Will o' Phaup' and the latter's conversation with the fairies, there is no condescension, no incredulity. His acceptance is as total as belief in the inexplicable elements in Christian mythology.

Hogg introduces the brownie legends into his covenanting novel, *The Brownie of Bodsbeck*, and his excellent short stories are a treasure trove of such beliefs. Even his great lyrical ballad, *Kilmeny*, derives from a local story, and when the young girl of the title is transported to fairyland, the description rings true.

Hogg's fairies are benign, and indeed sexless, but in two of the greatest of the supernatural Border ballads, the Queen of Elfland is a figure of great potency, both sexual and otherwise. In *True Thomas* she transports Thomas the Rhymer to Elfland for seven years, and there is no doubt that she uses him to serve her own sexual appetites. The ballad *Tamlane* also has the theme of thralldom to the same figure, and again the magic period of seven years occurs. In the cases of *Kilmeny* and *True Thomas*, the main protagonists disappear for that period, and return unable to speak other than the truth, a habit which disconcerts their contemporaries. (Thomas, indeed, protests that it will harm his market transactions). In *Tamlane*, the hero has been a plaything of the Queen of Elfland for a more indeterminate time: the seven year period is that at which she must 'pay a teind to hell'. It is a period which occurs over and over again in legend – as it does also in the Old Testament, in the story of Joseph and his brothers.

In True Thomas, or Thomas the Rhymer, we find one of those figures in Border folklore where fact and legend blur. According to legend and ballad, he was spirited away by the Queen of Elfland in the lee of the Eildon Hills, themselves a natural phenomena calling forth stories of differing kinds. The sharp-sided triple peak, topping the undulating countryside round about, was bound to be such a focus – coupled perhaps with the belief that the most prolific 'magic mushrooms' in the Borders today (and presumably also in past times) grow in the glen from whence True Thomas was abducted.

The existence of Thomas Learmont of Ercildoune (Earlston) is documented in thirteenth century records, and his reputed writings include the romance of *Sir Tristan* (believed by Sir Walter Scott to be the oldest extant example of Scots' poetry) – and his prophecies.

These were mainly to do with the future history of Scotland – the death of Alexander III and the crucial battles of Bannockburn and Flodden. There were also more local prophecies, such as:

> Betide, betide, whate'er betide,
> There will aye be Haigs in Bemersyde

and

> The hare shall kittle on my hearthstane
> and there will never be a laird Learmont again

both of which came to pass, but perhaps the most famous is the one where he foresaw that:

> When Tweed and Powsail meet at Merlin's grave
> Scotland and England shall one monarch have.

This prophecy also came true, the Tweed overflowing its banks in the upper Tweed region at its confluence with Powsail Burn, on the day of James VI's coronation as King James I of England.

The mention of Merlin's grave leads us on naturally to another area of legend in the Borders: the Arthurian legends. Though the southwest of England, and Wales, have their better known claims to be the site of Arthurian activity, yet here too there are legends of that semi-mystic figure. They are three fold.

One relates to the area round Stow on Gala Water, known as Wedale.

The name is said to be a corruption of 'Vale of Woe', and to have been given to the area after Arthur's eighth victorious battle against the indigenous pagans. An ancient chapel nearby at Torsonce was reputed to have been built on a piece of the true cross brought back by Arthur from the Holy Land.

The strongest of the Arthurian traditions in the Borders, however, is that referred to in Thomas the Rhymer's prophecy – that Merlin lived out the last of his days in the area and was buried in the upper Tweed at Drummelzier. The site of his grave may be pointed out today, and the surrounding area is called Merlindale. Professor Veitch, writing in the nineteenth century, subscribed to the theory that there were two Merlins – that of Snowdon, and the Merlin Sylvestris or Merlin Caledonius of the Border hills, and that the two were later confused in medieval romance. The Border Merlin was a prophet and poet – and, according to Savourna Stevenson, the gifted clarsach player and composer who now lives in that countryside, a harpist. He was the last of the pagan Cymri tribe, overcome in a sixth century battle at Arthuret, a little to the north of Carlisle, whence he fled via Liddesdale and Ettrick Forest to the upper reaches of the Tweed.

This myth and others have been explored by the contemporary historian Nicholas Tolstoy, who comes down in favour of the authenticity of Merlin's last days being spent in this area. And again, we find James Hogg introducing it into his writings – in this case, his little known play, *The Profligate Princes*, into which an anachronistic Merlin strays and expires.

The third area of Arthurian legend in the Borders would not stand such critical scholarship as Tolstoy's. It takes us back to the Eildons, under which, it is said, Arthur and his knights sleep together in a cavern. There is a story told, that a horse couper from Cumberland was returning from St. Boswell's Fair, where he had sold all his animals except one stallion, for which he demanded an outrageous price. He met an old man, who offered him any sum he chose – but the couper must meet him at midnight by the Tweed. At their meeting, the old men led the horse dealer to the cavern, where the knights all lay asleep, their horses by their side. A horn was inscribed with the words 'When thy land is in peril, blow on me, but woe to him that blows without need'. Overcome by curiosity, the couper blew the horn. The knights came to life, an earthquake shook the cavern, and he found himself standing by the Eildons with only withered leaves in his pocket.

The old man of this tale was Michael Scott, the wizard, the most potent of all the figures of magic that inhabit the folklore of the Borders. To quote from Sir Walter Scott, in his footnotes to *The Lay of the Last Minstrel*, 'in the south of Scotland, any work of great labour or antiquity is ascribed, either to the agency of *Auld Michael*, or Sir William Wallace, or of the devil'. This is a slight exaggeration, but at any rate he is attributed with the splitting of the Eildon Hills (previously a single peak) into three through the agency of a devilish spirit for whom he had to find constant employment. Another task was to 'bridle the Tweed with a curb of stone', which resulted in the cauld at Kelso. Each of these alterations to the geography of the Borders was accomplished in one night; but the final and unending task which freed Michael Scott from the demon's attentions was to set him to weave ropes of sand at Berwick.

The prototype of the wizard Michael Scott was the scholarly figure who straddled the twelfth and thirteenth centuries, and who left his native Scotland for Oxford, and thence to Paris and Bologna where he studied a variety of disciplines – mathematics, theology and law. Proceeding south to Palermo, he became tutor to the future Holy Roman Emperor Frederick II, for whom he wrote books on astronomy and physiognomy, amongst others.

A spell at the new school of translation at Toledo saw this remarkable man translating texts by Aristotle from Arabic to Latin; he then returned to Palermo as Frederick's physician and astrologer. Legend says that towards the end of his life he came back to his native Borders and, dying there, was buried in Melrose Abbey along with his book of 'spells'.

He was a potent figure not just in the Borders; Dante, in his *Inferno* describes Michael Scott's presence in the fourth chasm of the eighth circle of Hell, with other sorcerers and enchanters, and there are many European legends of him as well as those that have been handed down through the generations in the Borders.

The dead Michael Scott features in Walter Scott's first great imaginative work, *The Lay of the Last Minstrel*, and in live and overpowering form in Hogg's *The Three Perils of Man*. These three perils were war, women and witchcraft.

Literacy, rationality and scholarship have eroded the kind of belief in such traditions that were held by the rural population up until Hogg's time. With his death in 1835, their age could be declared gone for ever. Yet still they cast their spell: today's writers weave them into contemporary texts of drama, poetry, opera and novel. In his semi-fictional novel about Sir Walter Scott, (*The Ragged Lion*, published 1994) the highly rational novelist Allan Massie introduces a sequence and indeed a ballad of his own composing that contrives a meeting between the Two Scotts, Michael and Walter:

> Sae, poet, tak dead Michael's hand,
> And feel the bones of death;
> Sae, poet, touch dead Michael's lips
> And taste his icy breath.

Perhaps, after all, their age has not passed.

NINETEEN
BORDER TRADITIONS: THE COMMON RIDINGS

In his chapter on the establishment of the Border burghs (Chapter 14) Walter Elliot describes the conditions laid down in the founding, or affirming, charters. These included the obligation of the burgesses to inspect, annually, the marches (boundaries) of their common grazing lands to ensure that no adjacent lairs had encroached on them. Initially this duty was carried out by the provost and senior burgesses: Provost Muthag of Selkirk died, in 1541, in a fight caused by their infringement. What has evolved over the centuries is a fusion of this custom with others to become that most individual and spectacular of all Border traditions: the annual Common Ridings.

Properly speaking, only four towns boast true Common Ridings: Selkirk, Hawick, Langholm and Lauder. The last-named of these has a tradition which was broken and then revived; Langholm's in its present form dates from 1759, though the riding of the marches on horseback was not carried out until 1819; but those of Selkirk and Hawick boast an ancestry that stretches back unbroken to the early sixteenth century.

The other towns of the Borders have their celebrations too – Peebles' Beltane Festival; Galashiels' Braw Lads Gathering; Jedburgh's Callants' Festival; Duns' Reiver's Week; The Melrose Festival, the Civic weeks in Kelso and Coldstream. Even smaller communities such as West Linton in the north of Tweeddale and Innerleithen in the south have their Whipman Play and the St. Ronan's Border Games. And there is the Eyemouth Herring Festival, which has its own very different traditions as befits a community whose living is not in the land but in the seas.

The origins of most of the festivals referred to in the foregoing paragraph date from times between the nineteenth century and the immediate post-second World War period, and though they borrow much from the old Common Ridings, they have also evolved their own individual characteristics.

The common features are: the choice of a young man to spearhead the year's festivities; the bearing by him, on horseback and at the head of a mounted cavalcade, of the town's flag, over a set route (in the case of the old Common Ridings, that route is around the marches of the old common lands) – a ride of several miles which almost always includes at least one spectacular and potentially dangerous gallop, and often the fording of the

Tweed or the tributary on which the town lies; and the 'bussing' of the flag: the adornment of it with ribbons, attached by a woman (who may or may not be of the young man's choice) who subsequently pronounces the traditional blessing of 'Safe oot, Safe In'.

Around the day which marks the focus of these rituals, is woven a week of festivities. They may be dinners, balls, a spate of informal dances, sports and gymkhanas, horse races, fancy dress parades and concerts. There may be subsidiary rituals or rides, or the solemnity of Kirking. There is much music and song, much emotion – and liberal quantities of alcohol.

There is little clashing of weeks between the towns – the Common Riding calendar is strictly laid down. Hawick Common Riding takes place first, on the Friday after the first Monday in June, then Selkirk, and all the others take their appointed times until finally Lauder Common Riding winds everything up on the first Saturday of August.

The high points, the week and above all the day of the Common Riding or its equivalent draws 'exiles' back to their town: for them as for the current inhabitants it is an affirmation of identity and community.

The public preparations begin in April or May, when the young man who will be his town's principal for the year is chosen. Throughout these months the announcements are made: even at this stage the individual customs become apparent, as does the nomenclature. Hawick, Langholm, Lauder and Peebles appoint Cornets; Selkirk its Standard Bearer (as does Innerleithen), while other towns give names linked to the festival's name: the Duns Reiver, the Coldstreamer, the Jethart Callant, the Kelso Laddie. Only in Galashiels is there any real equality for women, for the Braw Lad and Lass are both chosen by the governing body, and share equally in the duties and ceremonial.

There is generally a committee of interested personnel to make this choice, and the approaches and selection of candidates may move in mysterious ways. In Selkirk, however, the successor to the Town Council for this historic purpose is a Trust composed of the regional and district Councillors for the town and the surrounding valleys. Here, at least, the qualifications for Standard Bearer are clear: an advertisement in the local press seeks applications, and the successful applicant must be a 'souter' (a Selkirk native); He must be unmarried, and have served an apprenticeship as attendant to a previous standard bearer on at least two occasions. There is, currently a ten year waiting list of time-served attendants: no other Border town has such a reservoir of enthusiasm waiting in the wings.

In Selkirk the appointment is made in the old Town Hall; in Hawick the ex-Cornets journey to the house of their chosen man and summon him forth. In Langholm, more democratically, the selection is made at the public meeting of the town's inhabitants, and if there is more than one candidate, a ballot is held.

All of these young men now begin a summer of activity and duties. For the Hawick Cornet, these include twice-weekly rides throughout May to villages or settlements surrounding the town: the most strenuous is to Mosspaul, on the Dumfriesshire border, a round journey over rough territory of nearly thirty miles. Those who complete it become members of the Ancient Order of Mosstroopers, an organisation which commemorates the outlawed men of the Teviotdale and Liddesdale.

Women are specifically barred from riding in the wake of the Hawick Cornet. The Common Riding there is one of the last bastions of male exclusivity in twentieth century Britain. Only the Cornet's 'male equestrian supporters' are invited to follow him, and women are excluded from most of the dinners and social gatherings: only at one ceremony do they move centre stage. That is at the colour bussing ceremony 'The Nicht Afore the Morn', when the Cornet's Lass ties ribbons on to the flag in a ceremony which is totally evocative of the days of chivalry. Of all these ceremonies, the Hawick one is the most complicated in its ritual, and the prettiest: the Lass (the Cornet's own choice) is accompanied by a retinue of maids, all of them attired in long dresses and wide-brimmed hats. The gallery is filled with rows of men, singing the large repertoire of Hawick songs: then the Cornet and his right and left hand men (his predecessors), in their traditional dress of top hats, green frock coats, breeches and boots, enter to the strains of the Hawick Song, *Teribus*, played by flute and drum. The moment when his Lass attaches the ribbons to his town's flag is one of high emotion for the Cornet, and his audience.

Other customs relating specifically to Hawick Common Riding include the ride by the Cornet, early in the week, to St.Leonard's farm, where he orders curds and cream. These are consumed on Common Riding morning. Earlier, there is the taking of snuff; and the 'chases' on horseback up the stretch of road called the Nipknowes also form part of the morning's ritual. For the chases, the equestrian procession divides into two: the Cornet's Chase of unmarried men, led by the Cornet, and the married men's chase, led by his 'acting father'.

The status of the unmarried men, or the Callants, in Hawick Common Riding, is an important one. Much of the tradition surrounds an incident in the town's history which does not appear in the written records of the time. The story is this: in the year 1514, which succeeded that of the disastrous battle of Flodden, Hawick was guarded only by the callants – the youths who had been too young to be called up to serve in James IV's army. A section of the English army was advancing on the town: it was defeated at Hornshole, a spot a mile or so beyond its boundaries, by Hawick's young men.

Hence the line, *Sons of heroes slain at Flodden*, which occurs in the chorus of the town's song, *Teribus y teriodin*, words whose antiquity defy definitive derivation. Song plays a central part in Hawick Common Riding: over 50 songs have been written in praise of the 'Queen of All the Border'', and the central core of above half that number are lively, tuneful outpourings of civic love.

As the Cornet's Ball (at which the Cornet's Reel, danced at midnight, is executed by all past Cornets present at the event as well as the current year's incumbent) and the second day of races on Hawick Moor round off the week's events, a different pattern of festivities and ceremonies is beginning in Selkirk.

Here, the Common Riding, which claims to be the oldest of all, and which certainly attracts the largest mounted gathering (over 600 rode in the year 1985, and the normal number is around 450) is even more closely bound up with the events of Flodden. The men of Ettrick Forest held their lands directly from the king, and were the men at arms who made their stand with him when he met his heroic, useless death. It is said that eighty men rode out from the small border town of Selkirk to follow King James; only one of their number returned, a man by the name – or perhaps the trade – of Fletcher. He carried with him a captured English flag, but was too distressed to speak of the tragedy to his fellow-townsman. In mute despair, he cast the flag around his head, and hurled it to the cobbles.

Such is the tradition. Its place in the Common Riding is the Casting of the Colours, that emotional and beautiful finale to the week's ceremonial.

Song is central to the traditions here as well. *The Liltin*, that immortal lament for 'the Flowers of the Forest'. that is played at battlefields and gravesides world wide, was inspired by the losses of the men of Ettrick Forest at Flodden. The music has its honoured place in the ceremonies of Selkirk Common Riding; so too does the antique-tuned ballad

> It's up wi' the souters o' Selkirk,
> That sew the single soled shoon.
> It's up w' the men o' the Forest
> And Doun wi' the Earl o' Home.

One of the most interesting features of Selkirk is the survival of the medieval crafts guilds, as described in Chapter 14. Those that remain are the Hammermen's Incorporation (principally the building trades; though it now includes such diverse modern trades as printers); the Weavers and the Fleshers (butchers). The Selkirk Merchant Company, over 300 years old, is the only one of its kind that exists from those days except for Edinburgh. The guilds of the Tailors and the Souters – the great traditional trade of Selkirk – feel into desuetude some time ago, but their flags still exist.

All of these surviving organisations – together with the British Legion and the Selkirk Colonial Society (representing 'exiled' souters world wide) also elect their standard bearers for the Common Riding. These flags are carried on foot in procession, and each organisation holds a dinner or concert during the week, when the flag is duly bussed. ('Well and truly bussed', as the lady busser declares after carrying out the ceremony). The spreading and sharing of elements of the Common Riding tradition into so many areas of the fabric of the community, as well as its antiquity, is what gives it such comprehensive support and strength.

For a week, Selkirk floats on a sea of events and of euphoria. The weather is watched with suspense: will the Friday, in the words of the song, by a 'smiling morn?'. On the Thursday evening, the ancient ceremony of 'crying the burley' takes place, as the names of those appointed to ride the marches – the Standard bearer, his attendants, and his four immediate predecessors (the 'burleymen') are read out at various points of the town centre.

The last of the bussing concerts is held; the ex-standard bearers pay homage at the statue of Fletcher, the Flodden survivor. All is in place for the morning.

The Burgh Standard Bearer receives the town's flag from the titular provost at 7 a.m. on the morning of the Common Riding ' at the sound of the second drum'. The streets are crowded: bands – flute band, silver band and pipe band – have been playing from 4 a.m. around the streets as the procession of townspeople following the craft flags and the bands, grows. Each song, played and sung over and over, has its defined place and time in the morning's timetable.

Now, the solemn, elated figure of the Burgh Standard Bearer joins the procession as he and his mounted cavalcade follow it through the town and down to the ford over the Ettrick. The riders cross the water and begin the hard and heady twelve mile ride around the marches. There are two stops: at the grave of the 1790 Selkirk suicide, Tibbie Tamson (a memorial to the worst excesses of small-town unkindness), and at the triple cairns called the Three Brethern that mark the contiguity of the Selkirk Burgh lands with those of the neighbouring lairds.

In the town, the procession reforms and makes its way towards the old toll on the A7, on the northern boundary. Crowds take up their position along the pavements and strain their gaze towards the hills for the first sight of the horseman bearing the flag. Once off the hill, and across the Ettrick again, he leads his followers in at a cracking pace on the A7's tarmac, the flag held high and cheers ringing in his ears.

The cheers continue for every batch of riders that follow him until the very last. Then the crowds make their way to the Market Place for the casting of the colours (Plate 34).

It is no exaggeration to say that of all moments throughout the whole

summer, this is the most emotive. The pattern made with the flags is taught
to the standard bearer by his predecessors during the weeks between his
appointment and the ceremony itself: it has its own technical terms. The
Burgh Standard Bearer is followed by those who have carried those of the
other organisations on foot during the morning, and at the close the band
plays the old lament:

> I've heard them lilting at ilka ewe-milking,
> Lassies a-lilting before the dawn of day:
> Now there's a moaning on ilka green loaning,
> The flowers of the Forest are a' wede awae.

The crowds disperse: there is the rest of the day, the night and the next
day for merrymaking, but the ceremonial, the intense emotion that is an
intrinsic part of Selkirk Common Riding is over until next year.

Meantime, the towns of Peebles and Melrose begin their festivals. Here,
the Peebles Cornet and the Melrosian share the focus of attention with the
children of the primary schools. In each town a girl is chosen as queen, and
a court appointed. In Melrose, her coronation takes place in the ruins of
the graceful Abbey: her court is small, limited to those who, like her, have
excelled themselves in their class. In Peebles, however, the Beltane court
seems to include every school child in the town, and a wondrous
procession of courtiers, archers, soldiers, sailors, cowboys and Indians,
spacemen, flower fairies and characters from other lands and from nursery
books marches along the street to take its place on the steps of the parish
church for the queen's arrival, with her maids of honour, in horse drawn
carriages. (And the mice – oh, do not overlook the army of grey mice, each
with its tail clasped in its hand).

The Melrose Festival dates from a few years before the Second World
War. The Peebles Beltane Festival is considerably older, since it was
founded as part of the celebrations for Queen Victoria's Jubilee in 1897.
And even then it had roots in the more distant past. The initiative, by the
Town Council, first took the form of the resuscitation of the Riding of the
Marches; then, two years later, the first Beltane Queen was appointed.
Beltane itself was a festival, held throughout southern Scotland, of the
greatest antiquity. It is said to date back to pagan times. John Buchan,
whose family came from Peebles, describes terrifyingly in his novel
Witchwood how such festivals came to be debased and corrupted in the
seventeenth century: but he wrote it, fortunately, some years after the
Peebles Beltane Festival was firmly established.

It was an appropriate enough festival for the Town Council to revive.
Peebles was granted the right to hold the Beltane fair by James VI, in 1621, and
a declaration of the original fair proclamation forms part of the ceremonies.

And the song that is sung at Peebles is older still, for it is derived from one written by Scotland's poet-king, James I:

> At Beltane, when ilk bodie bounds
> To Peblis to the play,
> To hear the singing and the sounds
> Their solace, soothe to say;

Both Melrose and Peebles have their ceremonial rides (and in Peebles, unlike other towns, the Cornet may be a married man), but much of the concentration of the week is on the Queen and her court.

As has already been written, equality between the sexes exists to a greater extent in the Braw Lads Gathering in Galashiels than in most towns. It takes place in the week after the festivals of Melrose and Peebles. Dreamed up in 1930, it weaves incidents from the town's history into its pageantry: the prettiest is the ceremony of the mixing of the roses, red and white, at the old Market Cross. The name comes from the lovely song collected by Robert Burns, which is sung at the gathering. Unfortunately, it does not really adapt to community singing, but as a solo song, to music by Hayden, it is amongst the finest to be heard in the newer festivals:

> Braw, braw lads on Yarrow braes,
> Ye wander through the blooming heather;
> But Yarrow braes nor Ettrick shaws
> Can match the lads of Gala Water,
>   Braw, braw lads.

Originally, each of the five electoral wards in Galashiels elected a male and a female candidate for the positions of Braw Lad and Braw Lass, and a role was found for each of them. This number was reduced to six, and in recent years there has been real difficulty in finding three young men to fill each position. No young man who undertakes the duties ever seems to regret it, or to look on the summer as the high point of his youth; but it is a huge commitment, one in which the town's spotlight is never switched off – and one which entails considerable expense. Still, the older the tradition, the more firmly grounded it seems to be.

Throughout July it is the turn of the newer festivals: Jedburgh, Duns, Kelso; the village of Yetholm, deep in the Cheviot hills, pays tribute to its past as the home of the gypsies. Innerleithen's St. Ronan's Games owes its origin to James Hogg, who, with Professor John Wilson ('Christopher North' editor of *Blackwood's Magazine*) and Glassford Bell, founded them in 1827. In the following year, Sir Walter Scott added his lustre to their activities: his novel, *St. Ronan's Well* is set in the small town. The legend is that the sixth-century saint of that name caught the devil ('Cleeked' him) with his crozier, and then immersed him in the well formed by the spring that rises above the town. This act was said to have imparted to the water its distinctive, sulphurous flavour.

During the week of the St. Ronan's Games, it is the boys rather than the girls of the primary school who take centre stage, representing St. Ronan and his monks in a ceremony where not only the burgh's flag, but eleven crosiers are bussed. The Innerleithen Standard Bearer does not put his leg across a horse's back during the week of the St. Ronan's Games; but he receives a drink from the spring from the hands of the young St. Ronan. The Games themselves are not part of a professional circuit, and no longer include the spectacular contests so much enjoyed by Hogg, such as archery, rifle shooting and Cumberland wrestling.

Two features of the St. Ronan's Games week are very individual, and somewhat disconcerting: there is a torch light procession of Masons, in full regalia, to the churchyard, where the boy St. Ronan stands in the circle they form, and he releases two doves which they present to him. Innerleithen's other very distinctive ritual takes place on the Saturday night: on the top of the hill, overlooking the town, an effigy of the devil is burned.

Langholm's Common Riding takes place on the last Friday of July. Though properly not in the Borders region (it lies over the Dumfriesshire Border), in this as in rugby it stands with the other Border towns rather than those in its own local authority. Its origins are in a case heard before the Court of Session in 1759 over land boundaries between three proprietors of land on the outskirts of Langholm. In its judgement, the Court opined that part of the lands in dispute belonged in fact to the burgesses of Langholm.

As a result of this judgement, the burgesses paid greater attention to their right over the lands, placing beacons and cairns and pits at strategic points. A man was appointed annually to inspect the marks, make any necessary repairs, and report any encroachments.

The first man who performed this duty, Archibald Beattie, did so for fifty years. He also proclaimed the Langholm Fair to his fellow townsmen on his return from inspecting the marches, which he did on foot. It was his successor who initiated the Riding of the Marches; in the same year horse racing became an integral part of the day's activities, and in the following year saw the first selection of Cornet.

The day of Langholm Common Riding begins, as it does in Selkirk, with the Flute Band perambulating the town to wake such of its inhabitants as have been to bed. (While the railway still existed, it was the custom for the band to meet the last train to arrive on' the nicht afore the morn', full of Langholm exiles. Indeed, though no train has stopped at Langholm for over two decades, the band still makes the Thursday night visit to the station).

Langholm has its own very distinctive features. First, at 6.30 a.m. is the hound trail: a race between especially bred and trained foxhounds over a ten-mile circuit. Two hours later, at the Town Hall, the Cornet is presented with the town's standard. After the horsemen have proceeded around the town, they return behind the Cornet to the Market Place, and the fair is cried. It is unlike anything that happens anywhere else, where proclamations are made in legal phrasing read from a scroll. Not so in Langholm: a man climbs onto the rump of a horse and, steadying himself on the shoulders of the rider, proclaims:

> Now, Gentlemen, we're gan' frae the Toun',
> An' first of a' the Kil-Green we gan' roun';
> It is an ancient place where clay is got,
> And it belangs tae us by Right and Lot;
> And then frae the Lang-Wood we gan' throu;
> Where every ane may breckons cut an' pu';
> And last of a' we to the Moss do steer,
> To see gif a' oor Marches they be clear;
> And when unto the Castle Craigs we come,
> I'll cry the Langholm Fair and then we'll beat the drum.

Then the Cornet and his supporters set off in pursuance of the fair-crier's instructions: as they leave the Market Place they gallop, full tilt, up the narrow vennel that takes them to the hill above the town. When they return – it is a short ride compared with many others – they join the procession which has formed in the town behind the town band, and in which distinctive emblems are carried. First come the Barley Bannock and the Salted Herring, fixed to a wooden platter by a 'twal-penny nail' and brandished aloft on a pole: they represent rights of the neighbouring baron in grain and in fisheries. Next to be borne aloft is the Spade, the very essence of Langholm Common Riding, used as it is for cutting sods on the Common. Third comes a gigantic thistle (here is a competition for the privilege of providing it). Its place in the ritual is obscure: possibly its prickles are a warning to anyone tempted to cause trouble, or perhaps it is just there because of its significance as Scotland's national emblem. Lastly, comes a floral crown, which again defies exact explanation, though the official handbook opines that it may be a symbol of loyalty to the sovereign.

In Langholm's Common Riding procession, the children are given a special place, carrying besoms (brooms) of heather, some of them lavishly decorated. One child, asked to explain why she carried one, replied, 'I dinnae ken – we just do'; which is as good and appropriate a description as any of much that happens at Border Common Ridings.

The return to Langholm's wonderfully hemmed-in Market Place by Cornet, riders and procession gives the Fair Crier the opportunity to deliver the second Fair Crying, which contains the following splendid admonition:

...a' land-loupers, and dub-scoupers, and gae-by-the gate swingers, that come here to breed hurdums or durdums, huliments or buliments, hagglements or bragglements, or to molest this fair, they shall be ta'en by the order of the Bailie and the Toun Council, and their lugs be nailed to the Tron wi' a twalpenny nail.'

Again, in Langholm, one sees the small things that make each Common Riding so special to its own place. There is dress: just as the Hawick Cornet wears the distinctive, early nineteenth century green frock-coat, Langholm's Cornet is shod in old-fashioned brown gaiters. Every other town has its own permanent colours: Hawick's and Lauder's are yellow-and-blue; Selkirk's and Jedburgh's scarlet-and-blue, Peebles red-and-black, and so on. Through each Common Riding week, the town is hung with bunting in the appropriate colours, and people sport rosettes. (In Selkirk, the Standard Bearer also chooses his own personal colours, in which additional rosettes will be made and worn). In Langholm, however, there are no permanent town colours: they change year by year, and dictated not by any local event or taste, but by the colours that are worn by the winning jockey at the Epsom Derby!

As August unfolds, the Border Common Riding season draws to a close. On the first Thursday of the month, during Coldstream Civic Week, the riders cross the border into Northumberland (Plate 30) and make their way to Flodden field. Here, on the calm hillside that saw so much slaughter, so much waste, that has haunted Scotland and in particular the Borders down the centuries, homage is paid to all the fallen, in all wars – but above all to those 'Flowers of the Forest' who followed James IV in his great misadventure:

> From Liddel and Esk and Cheviot, from Teviot Tweed and Jed,
> They were gallant hearts who followed, and a king himself who led,
> From Carter Fell and Cheviot, to lone St. Mary's Lake
> They failed not at the summons, who knew the black mistake.

But at the last of the Common Ridings, there is no hint of sadness. Lauder's ceremonies on the first Saturday of the month are very simple: there is almost nothing that is not found elsewhere, but at Lauder it is somehow distilled. The essence of all that makes up a Border Common Riding is there. The cornet receives the flag; it is bussed, and he is charged to carry it round the marches and return it 'unsullied and untarnished'. Then he sets off at the head of his cavalcade, along the High Street, through the back streets of the medieval burgh, and out of the town till he sets off, at the gallop, along the side of the golf course and up into the hills. Underfoot, the heather is in bloom and Lauder's Common Riding has a scent as well as sounds and sights that are its own. One of the latter is the accompanying of the riders by the huntsman and hounds of the Lauderdale hunt.

At the boundary between Berwickshire and Midlothian, there is a stop, while horses and riders rest, and the Cornet and ex-cornets sing the Lauder song. Even that has a particular charm; it is neither related to battle, nor a paen of praise to the burgh or its inhabitants: it is simply a fresh and charming love song.

And, later, on the return journey, up on the heather clad hills, you will hear it again, sung not as part of an ordained ritual, but simply out of pure enjoyment, in the saddle, and into the August air.

'At the heart of the Common Riding', said a speaker at one of the many, many dinners at one of the many Common Ridings last year, 'are horses, and song'. There is much else as well. But as Lauder Common Riding ends, the great pageantry that has permeated each Border town over the summer months goes into hibernation – until the next year.

TWENTY

THE KING'S OWN SCOTTISH BORDERERS

On the morning of Saturday the 3rd of April, 1993 a most remarkable parade took place on the streets of Galashiels. What seemed like the entire population of the town and countless other Borderers both military and civilian, turned out on the streets to see their local Regiment, The King's Own Scottish Borderers, exercise their right to the Freedom of Ettrick and Lauderdale District 'with bayonets fixed and Colours flying'.

This was no ordinary Freedom march for it was in thanksgiving for the reprieve granted to the KOSB from the threatened amalgamation with The Royal Scots which had been proposed by the Government as part of the so-called Peace Dividend, marking the end of the Cold War (1945–1989).

What was the cause of this spontaneous support for the local Regiment? Bear in mind that no fewer than 8211 Borderers had paid the supreme sacrifice in two World Wars and the memory of these grievous losses lived on in nearly every family throughout the Borderland. Nevertheless, when the absorption of The Regiment's identity was threatened the whole Border – in the case of the KOSB this means the whole six counties from Berwick to Stranraer – erupted in an outraged public campaign to retain the Regiment. The campaign, coupled with the undoubted 'overstretch' on the Infantry as a whole, convinced the Ministry of Defence 'tae think again'. They had good cause, for The King's Own Scottish Borderers had served the Crown for no less than 304 years and is one of only five British Line Regiments[1]. of that seniority to have remained unchanged and unamalgamated since its formation (Plate 31).

The Regiment was raised on the 19th of March 1689. The scene: Edinburgh in turmoil with the Jacobites in control of the Castle and the Royalists cowering in the Parliament Hall halfway down the Royal Mile. David Leslie, the 3rd Earl of Leven, was immediately empowered to raise a Regiment in defence of the city. This he did in the space of two hours. Within days John Graham of Claverhouse, or 'Bonnie Dundee', the Jacobite leader and hero, had withdrawn from the city to rally the clans up north. This was surely a turning point in British history. Only the abortive uprisings in 1715 and 1745 remained before the Jacobite flame flickered and died.

1. Royal Scots (1), Green Howards (19), Cheshires (22), Royal Welch Fusiliers (23) KOSB (25)

In these days Regiments were named after their Colonel so the KOSB started s Leven's or The Edinburgh Regiment. It was later number '25' and so it has remained all these years – always a lucky number for Borderers at Bingo!... It was not long before the Regiment saw its first action at the Pass of Killiecrankie. This proved to be a victory for the Highland clans who held the high ground, and the Royalist army withdrew to Stirling in disorder. General Mackay, their commander, reported that Leven's Regiment 'behaved themselves with extraordinary Bravery and Resolution; maintaining their ground to the last; and keeping the field after the rebels had drawn off to the hills'. In the melee, Claverhouse was struck by a stray bullet and died soon afterwards.

On returning to Edinburgh, Leven's Regiment was granted the historic privilege of beating up for recruits in the City of Edinburgh without seeking permission of the Lord Provost (as sanctioned by the City Magistrates) – a privilege which they exercise from time to time by marching down world-famous Princes Street.

For the next 200 years the Regiment traversed the world on the King's business. They had no fixed home but always fiercely retained their Scottish traditions. They recruited where they could and the records show that, although many of the soldiers came from Edinburgh and The Borders, there were also English, Irish and foreigners in the ranks. Life was hard, discipline was savage and enlistment was for life; the only way out was for desertion, disablement or death. All for tuppence a day! (By 1797 it had become a shilling a day. In Kipling's time, a hundred years later, it was still a shilling. By the time the author joined up in 1940 it had risen to the princely sum of two shillings. They knew how to control inflation then!)

It is not possible in this short account to record all the battles fought by the Regiment in the 18th and 19th centuries. There were plenty of them.[2] One is remembered with particular pride by the KOSB – the battle of Minden on the 1st of August 1759. On this occasion Britain was allied with Hanoverians and Hessians in the Seven Years' War against the French and Austrians. On a blasted heath near the River Weser Gap, the Battle of Minden was fought, resulting in the rout of the French Cavalry by six Regiments of British Infantry.[3] The KOSB casualties of 19 killed and 126 wounded seem modest by the 20th century standards, but many were in hand to hand combat. This was the first battle in which rifles were aimed at the enemy by looking along the muzzle. Previously, they had been fired from the hip. In typical British fashion 'aiming' was considered rather unsporting! After the battle Prince Ferdinand and the Allied Commander

2. For further reading: *All the Blue Bonnets* by Robert Woollcombe from KOSB Museum, Berwick-upon-Tweed, £9.95.

said: 'It was here that the British Infantry won immortal glory'. Moving up to the battlefield, the men of the 25th plucked roses (or more likely sprigs of heather) and stuck them in their headgear. As a result all ranks of The King's Own Scottish Borderers wear a red rose on Minden Day (each year on the 1st day of August) and celebrate a Regimental holiday (Plate 32).

A glance at some of the names of the Colonels of the Regiment, who succeeded the Earl of Leven, leaves no doubt that the 25th were held in high esteem within the Scottish establishment:

John, Earl of Rothes
Hew, Lord Semphill
John, Earl of Crawford
William, Earl of Panmure
William, Earl of Home
Sir Henry Erskine Bt
Lord George Gordon Lennox

It was probably due to the influence of Lord Gordon Lennox in court circles – he was Colonel for a record 43 years – that the Regiment was granted 'Royal' status in 1805 – as The King's Own Borderers – no 'Scottish' at this stage, but they were gradually 'coming home'. The Buccleuch family have always been strong supporters of the Regiment both in the East and West Border. The 3rd Duke commanded the Regiment when it was stationed in Edinburgh in 1780–82. When they were in camp in Dunbar he presented them with a silver headed cane, formerly used by his footman when he ran before his carriage. It was for use by the Drum Major. This story has a sad ending as 'The Drummie' – wretched man – left it behind 'by neglect' on the Isle of Wight in 1799.

As the 19th century progressed Scotland's profile within Great Britain was accentuated for a number of reasons – their sturdy attitude to the threat of invasion in Napoleon's time, the popularity of Sir Walter Scott, the fame of the Scottish Regiments in policing the Empire (the 'pax Britannica'), the visit of King George IV to Edinburgh and Queen Victoria's obsession with all things Scottish. Coupled with these factors was a realisation – at last – that 'Tommy this and Tommy that', in Kipling's words,

3. The Minden Regiments.

In 1759	*Now*
12th (Napier's)	The Suffolk Regt. (part of the Royal Anglian Regt)
20th (Kingsley's)	The Lancashire Fusiliers (part of the Royal Regt. of Fusiliers)
23rd (Hulke's)	The Royal Welch Fusiliers
25th (Howe's)	The King's Own Scottish Borderers
37th (Stuart's)	The Hampshire Regiment (part of The Princess of Wales's Regt. – Queen's and Royal Hampshires)
51st (Brundenell's)	The King's Own Yorkshire Light Infantry (part of the Light Infantry)

had had a raw deal, and that the Army was due for considerable modernisation.

Enter the two C's – Messrs. Cardwell and Childers, Ministers of War in 1873 and 1881. It was Cardwell's Localisation of the Forces Act which finally brought the Regiment home to its natural location on the Scottish Borders – but not without a struggle. The Powers-That-Be, not for the first time, said that Scotland was 'over-Regimented' and, anyway, there were no barracks on the Borders and no militia and Volunteers with whom the two regular battalions could be affiliated. They even tried to locate the Regiment in York! Fortunately, common sense prevailed and the Regiment moved to Ravensdowne Barracks in Berwick-upon-Tweed – in England but indubitably on the Borders – and there they have been ever since. The militia and Volunteers problem was easily solved by affiliation to the admirable Scottish Borderers Militia with Volunteers units spread between Berwickshire and Galloway. The icing on the cake was the conferment (in 1887) of the proud title King's Own *Scottish* Borderers.

From their new home at Berwick the Scottish Borderers played a notable part in many wars and armed engagements in 'furrin' pairts' – The Sudan, Burma, the 2nd Afghan war, the Relief of Chitral and the Tirah campaign of 1897. Then the 1st Battalion, the 3rd (Militia) Battalion and other Border Volunteers were heavily involved in the South African or Boer War from 1900–1902. In the Orange Free State at Bottaville Lieutenant B.H.B. Coulson then serving as Adjutant with the 7th Mounted Infantry won The Regiment's first Victoria Cross for rescuing a dismounted NCO under heavy fire. Sadly, it was posthumous.

The year 1908 marked a significant development in the link between the KOSB and its native Borderland. Under Secretary of State for War Haldane (an Edinburgh Academical from Gleneagles) the various volunteer units were merged into the Territorial Force (or Territorial Army as we know it today) which was to serve the country so well in the 20th century.

In the Eastern Borders was created the 4th (Border) Battalion KOSB (with its second line in war the 6th (Border) Battalion) with its Headquarters in Paton Street, Galashiels, and detachments in all the main centres of population:

Berwickshire: Duns[4], Coldstream[4], Chirnside, Ayton, Greenlaw, Gordon and Earlston.

Selkirkshire: Galashiels and Selkirk[4].

Roxburghshire: Hawick[4], Jedburgh[4], Kelso[4] and Melrose[4].

4. These Royal Burghs and Burghs have all granted their Freedom of entry to the King's Own Scottish Borderers. So have Berwick-upon-Tweed, and the Districts of Ettrick and Lauderdale and Annandale.

In the West the 5th (Dumfries and Galloway) Battalion KOSB (with its second line in war the 7th [Dumfries and Galloway] Battalion) with HQ at Nunfield House, Dumfries and detachments in:

Dumfriesshire: Dumfries[4], Annan[4], Langholm, Lockerbie, Moffat, Thornhill, Sanquar[4] and Kirkconnel.

The Stewartry of Kirkcudbright: Castle Douglas, Kirkcudbright[4], Dalbeattie and Gatehouse of Fleet.

Wigtownshire: (at one time Royal Scots Fusilier territory) Wigtown[4], Whithorn, Newton Stewart[4] and Stranraer. [4]

The appalling tragedies of the two World Wars are well known to most readers.[5] The following table may appear to be a rather callous way of describing such epic events but it does demonstrate the immense support which Borderers, East and West, gave to their Local Regiment in the dominant events of this century:

	1914–1918	1939–1945	Remarks
Population – 6 Counties	261,615	249,671	251,043(1991)
Battalions of KOSB: Active Service	8	6	
Home defence and drafting	6	2	+ Home Guard 13 Battalions
Borderers killed in action	6859	1352	
Wounded	20,577	4056	

For a population of 250,000 to have suffered 33,844 casualties (1 in 7 of the population) in Two World Wars is a full reflection of the remarkable loyalty and spirit of the Borders.

It must be remembered, too, that in addition to these KOSB-badged Borderers, many other Borderers served in the Royal Navy, in Highland Regiments and other corps in both wars, particularly in the Royal Air Force during World War II. The contribution of the Borders to the war effort was therefore all embracing.

In terms of gallantry, their record was equally impressive – four Victoria Crosses in the First War: Company Sergeant Skinner from Glasgow, Company Quartermaster Sergeant Grimbaldestone from Blackburn in Lancashire, Sergeant McGuffie from Wigtown and the legendary Piper Laidlaw from Norham, 'the piper of Loos' who rallied the 7th Battalion by playing his pipes on the parapet – and continued to do so until he fell, wounded.

After the Second World War, in so-called peace time, the 1st Battalion KOSB continued its world-wide operations – in Egypt, Palestine, Hong Kong (twice), Korea (another V.C. – Private Bill Speakman), Northern Ireland (many times), Malaya and Singapore, Berlin (three times), Aden

5. For further reading: *1914–1918 The KOSB in the Great War* by Captain Stair Gillon. *1939–1945 Borderers in Battle* by Captain Hugh Gunning.

(twice) Sarawak, Germany (twice) with occasional tours of duty in Scotland (in Edinburgh or Fort George) and England.

The Territorial Battalions continued to give yeoman service during the Cold War, training the admirable National Service element until 1961 when compulsory service ended (and more's the pity!). In 1967, the TA was, very sadly, reduced to two companies, one on each side of the Border. Following the tragic disbandment of the Cameronians (Scottish Rifles) in 1969 the county of Lanark was incorporated into the KOSB recruiting area.

What of the future? No account of the Regimental story would be complete without a salute to the Army Cadet Force, a youth organisation with a military flavour for young men and women. Founded in 1915 and nurtured by a succession of dedicated KOSB officers there are now 200 KOSB-badged cadets on the Borders carrying the flag for the Regiment in 15 of the main centres of population. Many of them subsequently decide on a military career.

As this books goes to print the regular Battalion of the Regiment is back in Edinburgh where it was raised 306 years ago, ready to keep the peace anywhere in this troubled world.

'ONCE A BORDERER, ALWAYS A BORDERER.'

Battle Honours
The King's Own Scottish Borderers

Namur 1695, Minden, Egmont-op-Zee, Martinique 1809, Afghanistan 1878–80, Chitral, Tirah, Paardedberg, South Africa 1900–02.

The Great War – Mons, Le Cateau, Retreat from Mons, Marne 1914, 18, Aisne 1914, La Bassee 1914, Messines 1914, Ypres 1914, 15, 17, 18, Nonne Bosschen, Hill 60, Gravenstafel, St. Julien, Frezenberg, Bellewaarde, Loos, Somme 1916, 18, Albert 1916, 18, Bazentin, Delville Wood, Pozieres, Guillemont, Flers-Courcelette, Morval, Le Transloy, Ancre Heights, Arras 1917, 18, Vimy 1917, Scarpe 1917, 18, Arleux, Pilckem, Langemarck 1917, Menin Road, Polygon Wood, Broodseinde, Poelcapelle, Passchendaele, Cambrai 1917, 18, St. Quentin, Lys, Estaires, Hazebrouck, Kemmel, Soissonnais-Ourcq, Bapaume 1918, Drocourt-Queant, Hindenburgh Line, Epehy, Canal du Nord, Courtrai, Selle, Sambre, France and Flanders 1914–18, Italy 1917–18, Helles, Landing at Helles, Krithia, Suvla, Scimitar Hill, Gallipoli 1915–16, Rumani, Egypt 1916, Gaza, El Mughar, Nebi Samwil, Jaffa, Palestine 1917–18.

The Second World War – Dunkirk, 1940, Cambes, Odon, Cheux, Defence of Rauray, Caen, Esquay, Troarn, Mont Pincon, Estry, Aart, Nederrijn, Arnhem 1944, Best, Scheldt, Flushing, Venraij, Meijel, Venlo Pocket, Roer, Rhineland, Reichswald, Cleve, Goch, Rhine, Ibbenburen, Lingen, Dreirwalde, Uelzen, Bremen, Artlenberg, North-West Europe 1940, 44–45, North Arakan, Buthidaung, Ngakyedauk Pass, Imphal, Kanglatongbi, Ukhrul, Meiktila, Irrawaddy, Kama, Burma 1943–45.

Kowang-San, Maryang-San, Korea 1951–52.

The Gulf, 1990.

TWENTY-ONE
RUGBY FOOTBALL

I was parking my car at Mansfield Park before the Hawick Centenary Sevens in 1994 when I suddenly noticed that the yellow-coated car park attendant waving me to my place was none other than the well-kent smiling figure of Hughie McLeod, (40 caps for Scotland), one of my rugby heroes. A similar courtesy had once before been accorded to me at the Melrose Sevens by Davie Chisholm (14 caps for Scotland) – unaccompanied for once by his half-section, Eck Hastie (13 caps). No doubt Eck was doing a similar duty in another part of the ground 1and their respective wives would be preparing mountains of hot pies and cauldrons of tea in the clubhouse.

Why should these Rugby heroes be performing menial chores on the day of their club's 'Sports' instead of sitting in the best seats in the stand which was surely their due? The answer can only be loyalty – to the club, the burgh and the Borders, an old-fashioned attribute which must have shown through in every chapter of this book. The club is at the core of Rugby organisation and from it stems the fierce rivalries, coupled with enduring friendships, which are the hallmarks of this universally popular sport on the Scottish Borders. As a teenager in Melrose I can still remember the thrill of running down the street in response to the cry: 'The teams for Saturday are up!'

From returns recently received from club secretaries, I estimate that one person in ten in the Borders is actively engaged as player, official, or spectator of Rugby Football. Every week 167 teams take the field so that over 2000 young men (and now women too) are enjoying what the great Jimmy Ireland (11 caps) called the three F's – Fitness, Fun and Friendship. Their sport is organised by an army of officials, referees and coaches numbering 472 and their supporters are listed as approximately 10,000 people.

IN THE BEGINNING

It all started a long time ago – long before the famous, or infamous, William Webb Ellis in 1823 picked up the ball at Rugby School. I am inclined to go along with the theory that the love of football on the Borders, including the handling game, goes right back to Roman times when the soldiers are known to have played a game called Harpastum. Surely it is not just a coincidence that within sight (and a long drop goal?) of the Roman fort at Trimontium there are no fewer than four Rugby clubs, Earlston, Gala, Melrose and St. Boswells? What is certainly not in doubt is the custom of Handba' which has been recorded on the Borders for centuries either between the Uppies and the Doonies or other districts of the burgh or in the form of a Marriage Ba' when the youth would (and still do) battle all day long – to the grave peril of shopkeepers and the populace in general.

It was said to be the fertile brain of Sir Walter Scott which thought up the well-recorded Ba-game at Carterhaugh on the Duke of Buccleuch's Estate at Bowhill, Selkirk, in 1825, with support from his rival the Earl of Home. To all effects it was a mock battle between the shepherds and the townspeople from the whole Border – ... about 750 players took part before a great crowd including noblemen and gentry. The ball was small, leather-skinned and packed with wool so the game was more hand ball than foot ball. The Carterhaugh game has recently been re-enacted to the great relish of today's players who no doubt revelled in the absence of laws – and a referee! About the same time there is evidence that some form of handling game was being played in the High School of Edinburgh where, since 1696, a half-day off had been permitted for sport (in a 6-day week).

EARLY DAYS

In England, no doubt due to the Pax Britannica and emerging affluence, public schools were devoting more time to leisure and the formal adoption of Rugby Football in Scotland was undoubtedly due to public school boys from England coming North to earn their living in textiles.

If a Border schoolboy were to be asked where the game started in the South of Scotland he would probably answer: 'Hawick, Sir'. Wrong! It was none other than their arch rivals, Langholm, over Mosspaul, who were first established as a club on the Borders. Their club history (by Walter Bell) makes fascinating reading and their record could undoubtedly be taken as typical of the other clubs. 'It was Old Year's Day in 1871 when three young men, William Scott, Alfred Moses and William Lightbody, all sons of local tweed makers, who had been educated in England, invited the young men of Langholm to join them in this 'new-fangled' game of Foot Ball as it was called'. Such was the throng that turned up that Scott had to walk through the middle of the crowd to pick the sides. Although this was but a basic introduction to the game it was decided to form a club. William Scott emerged as the natural leader and was captain, president, secretary and treasurer all rolled into one.

Next, the Hawick club (1873) emerged from the existing Cricket Club.

The first practices were played on the full cricket pitch which was good for fitness but very exhausting. The first proper match was played against 'The Muckle Toon' (Langholm) and resulted in a draw.

Gala (1875) and Melrose (1877) were founded shortly after and, as might be expected from these doughty rivals only 3½ miles apart, their birth pangs were painful. 'The Galashiels Football Club' was formed as a conjoined venture between both Melrose and Gala with a joint committee, the key man being W.H.Hudson of Melrose who held the influential appointments of Hon. Secretary, Hon. Treasurer and Chairman of the Selection Committee! Matches were to be played alternately at Mossilee (the Gala cricket ground) and The Greenyards, Melrose. Significantly, the colours were black and yellow, those presently worn by Melrose. It was clearly not a happy amalgamation, 'differences arose' and the split came on 8th October, 1877. Melrose went off with the minute book and, it is alleged in Galashiels, with the jointly-owned goalposts. Melrose must have accepted the accusation for they generously presented Gala with a replica set of silver goalposts in the Gala R.F.C. centenary year of 1975.

The Earlston club was founded 'sometime in the 1870's' and there followed Jed-Forest and Walkerburn in 1884 and Kelso in 1886.

The game expanded rapidly. Fixture lists were drawn up against all the existing Border clubs and the newly established railway route, 'The Waverley Line', enabled them to travel to the cities – no doubt quite an adventure for players of that time. There was no shortage of problems, notably with the rules or laws as they are now known. For some time 20-a-side was the rule, hacking was permitted and there was no referee, the captains being left to adjudicate. Rough play, then as now, was a constant problem. This is an account of an early game: 'Players were flailing their arms at each other on the ground...about 15 minutes from the close the referee stopped the game on account of rough play and squabbling'. The spectators who had paid good money to see the game could not have been pleased.

Considering the thrawn nature of the Scottish character it was really a remarkable achievement that the Scottish Rugby Union was formed in 1873. Fairly quickly, agreement was achieved on a form of laws. As governing body of the game – not popular but largely respected – their jurisdiction has remained unchallenged, although the laws are now co-ordinated by the International Rugby Football Board which was formed in 1886.

INNOVATIONS

The Border clubs have shown astonishing initiative in developing and publicising the game. The Hawick club achieved an amazing first by organising a game under floodlights at Mansfield on 24th February 1879. The lights were merely dynamos providing candlepower and barely sufficed to illuminate the players who kept falling over each other and passing the ball to a shadow. The crowd – an incredible 5000 – loved it. The takes were only £63 because only one person was on duty at 'the seat of custom' and he was literally swamped by the crowd.

Soon followed the unique invention of Rugby Football: Seven-a-sides. In 1883, as a fundraising venture, Ned Haig of the Melrose club (formerly a butcher in Jedburgh) thought up the idea of a knock-out competition which would take place alongside the usual athletic events associated with a sports meeting. This was wildly popular and Sevens have now spread over the globe. The Melrose Sevens (Plate 33) on the famous Greenyards are still the doyen and the reward, a simple medal, is the trophy every player yearns to win. Long may it continue.

A NEW CENTURY

The early years of the 20th century saw the arrival of the Selkirk club (1907). Rugby had been played in Selkirk before that and they actually had a team in the first Melrose Sevens, but soccer had also taken a hold in the town. There was plenty of room for both, and the club was destined to play a notable part in the world of Rugby Football, adding many illustrious names to its roll of honour.

Even earlier, another startling innovation took place in season 1901/02. The Big Seven – Langholm, Hawick, Gala, Melrose, Jed-Forest, Kelso and, later, Selkirk – decided that the run-of-the-mill once or twice a season fixtures against each other and against city sides were no match for the red-blooded competition of a League. And so was formed, in the back room of the King's Arms, Melrose, the Border League, the oldest rugby league in the world. It was startling in more ways than one as the Scottish Rugby Union did not approve. The word league had connotations with the Northern League in England which had broken away from the (English) Rugby Union in 1896 over the payment of broken time for players who lost wages as a result of playing Rugby. The S.R.U's disapproval lasted for 72 years until 1973 when, with a red face, they started their own leagues. To win the Border League is just as important to a Border club as the winning of the present First Division of the S.R.U. Championship.

The powers that be were slow to recognise the merits of the Border players, who were renowned more for their robustness than their tactical skill (a facet of play which was to change). The first Rugby International was played between Scotland and England at Raeburn Place, Edinburgh in 1871. From that date to the outbreak of war in 1914, one hundred and eighteen internationals were played and yet only 11 players from Border clubs were selected in those 43 years. Undoubtedly, the Old School Tie still held sway. The most capped players in that period came from Hawick and Gala, the largest towns. They were A. Dalgleish (Gala) and M. Elliott, W.T. Forrest, W.E. Kyle, and W.R. Sutherland (Hawick).

The devastating interruption of the First World War brought rugby to a standstill. Many, many players paid the supreme sacrifice including the aforementioned internationalists Wattie Forrest and Walter Sutherland ('Wattie Suddie'), both of Hawick, and from all accounts two of nature's gentlemen.

THE GOLDEN YEARS

More than one club history refers to the inter-war period of the 1920's and 1930's as 'The Golden Years'. Firstly, there was the relief and elation of peace after such a horrific war, then the great expansion of the game to junior and semi-junior clubs, but most of all in my opinion because the game was then truly amateur with none of the stresses and pressures which are placed on players today. The material rewards were meagre – a jersey (if you played for the right club), a second-class rail ticket and pocket money of nine old pence (3½ p!) which came with the admonition: 'Now mind ye spend it on yer tea!' Alas, 'twas not always so. Changing was usually in a cafe or hotel and only the fleet of foot arrived in time for the hot water. People didn't rush home to watch television after the match. They mingled with their hosts, had a few beers in the pub, then tried their hand with the lassies at the jiggin' – and went home boasting of their prowess and singing raunchy songs!

Some junior rugby had been played during the war. In Hawick this resulted in the formation of Hawick's well-known second tier clubs, the Trades, the Harlequins, Linden, P.S.A. and Y.M. which have provided such a strong nursery for the parent club. In Gala the same role is played by Gala Red Triangle, Star, Wanderers and Y.M. Higher up the Tweed, Walkerburn had long been established.

In addition to the Border League there was also established as long ago as 1885 an Unofficial Scottish Club Championship – 'unofficial' because, once again, the S.R.U. did not approve of its existence. It was wholly administered by the newspapers, who decided on a rough and ready system of qualification. The title of Unofficial Scottish Champions was much sought after and many a Border Clubhouse proudly displays photographs of championship teams. In the 20's and 30's the title came to the Borders 3 times, Hawick in 1927 and 1933 and Gala in 1932.

In the international sphere Border clubs were beginning to make their mark, The following names still bring a ring of pride to the older Rugby generation today:

Gala: T.G. Aitchison, T.F. Dorward, J. Ferguson, G.L. Gray, A.H. Polson, G.D. Shaw, A. Wemyss, G.R. Wood.

Hawick: J.A. Beattie, D.S. Davies, R.A. Foster, W.B. Welsh, R.W. Barrie.

Kelso: J. Graham, R.M. Grieve, R.T. Smith

Melrose: J.W. Allan, J.D.H. Hastie.

Selkirk: W.E. Bryce, J.A. Waters.

Jed-Forest: W. Purdie, G. Douglas.

Langholm: J. Goodfellow.

Most of them were, of course, known by their christian names, but these were never used in official records until comparatively recently.

HITLER'S WAR

In 1939 the world was again engulfed in war and, once more, the grim reaper took its toll of Border Rugby players, notably 'Yid' Crozier of Hawick and Tommy Dorward of Gala along with his club-mate Jock Dun. (Tommy's younger brother, Arthur, featured prominently for Gala and Scotland, post-war). Fortunately, Rugby continued to be played, mainly in the Services and many players made their mark in Service matches and internationals which were to lead them to recognition internationally after the war.

'DEARER YET THE BROTHERHOOD'

Once again the youth of the Borders, robbed of five years of rugby, returned to the game with relish. The spirit of the late 40s and 50s was undoubtedly encapsulated in one player – the swashbuckling Charlie Drummond of Melrose who in his speeches both as player and later administrator used to quote with passion the lines from Newbolt's poem, Clifton Chapel:

'To love the game beyond the prize
dearer yet the brotherhood
That binds the brave of all the earth'.

All the Border sides had their never-to-be-forgotten seasons but Charlie Drummond's Melrose XV of 1951–52 was 'something special'. How many winners of the Unofficial Championship (and their own Sevens) have a Reunion every year for 40 years, joining again in the rousing songs written by their late captain and his charming wife, Kathy? Every man was a hero but the names which are most remembered are those of Jimmy Johnston, Derek Brown, Alastair Frater, Tommy Hook, Leslie Allan, Ivor Hogg and Jack Dun. Later, Frank Laidlaw was to prove a world-class hooker for the club, country and the British Lions.

The Gala club surely reached their zenith in 1971 when on two successive Saturdays in March no fewer than seven of their players represented Scotland against England – and won on both occasions. They were Arthur Brown ('Hovis'), John Frame, Jock Turner, Dunc Paterson, Peter Brown (he of the corkscrew place kick), Nairn McEwan and Ken Oliver. Writing about Hawick's rugby would take a whole chapter to itself. They have always been The Tops – or gey near it. Hawick teams are always the ones everyone wants to beat; and they don't often do it! In the period of which we speak their top players were – Jackie Wright, Stewart Coltman, Robin Charters, Jack Hegarty, Hughie McLeod, Adam Robson, Wattie Scott and George Stevenson ('Stevie'). Selkirk's 'annus mirabilis' was the season 1952/53 when they won both the Scottish and Border championships under the captaincy of George Downie, supported by 'Basher' Inglis, Jock King and the Cowan brothers. At Kelso the names to conjure with at that period were Roger Baird (senr), Ian Hastie, Arthur Hastie, Ken Smith and Charlie Stewart. Jed-Forest's greatest hour was still to come but the 1956/57 side, although light on international players, walked off with the Border League and were joint winners in the Unofficial Championship. Down at Langholm, Donald Scott, Billy Steele and Jimmy Maxwell were the local heroes.

In Scottish Rugby's Hall of Fame (the list of ex-internationalists) one of the most prestigious names is that of Elliott – and it appears more often than any other. The doyen was undoubtedly Douglas Elliot (W.I.D.). Although he played for Edinburgh Accies he was a Border farmer. For eight seasons he dominated the Scottish scene and scared the daylights out of opposing fly-halves. Others of the clan were the redoubtable Tom from Gala and Christy and T.G. from Langholm.

From the start of the official Leagues in 1971, with few exceptions, Border sides swept the board – Hawick, Gala, Kelso and Melrose, who are currently leading the field – an interesting reversal of the early days. This era saw the arrival of a new and exciting generation of players who were to do wonders for Scottish Rugby, culminating in the Grand Slam triumphs of 1984 and 1990. From Gala Jim Aitken, Peter Dods and Derek White; from Hawick Norman Suddon, Ian Barnes, Alastair Cranston, Norman Pender, 'Twinkletoes' Jim Renwick, Colin Telfer, Colin Deans, Alan Tomes and Derek Turnbull; From Kelso Roger Baird (jnr), Gary Callander, John Jeffrey, Andrew Ker and that richly entertaining Sevens player 'Pakki', Eric Paxton: from Melrose the effervescent Keith Robertson and from Selkirk that world-class No. 8 Iain Paxton and stand-off John Rutherford who enjoyed such a long and fruitful partnership with Roy Laidlaw of Jed Forest. I had the privilege of touring with many of them in Japan in 1977.

All these gladiators count themselves fortunate to have trod the hallowed turf of Murrayfield. There is a small select band of Borderers who for one reason or other didn't quite make it and one's heart goes out to them: Johnny Gray of Gala, Derek Brown and Alastair Frater of Melrose,

Wattie Scott, Graham Lyall and Wat Davies of Hawick, Roger Baird (senr.) of Kelso and Hector Monro of Langholm.

Administratively, too, the South District has done the Scottish Rugby Union proud – 13 Presidents since the war, international referees in Sandy Dickie and the Burrell Bros – 'Dod' and Bob – of Gala, and Jake Short, Eric Grierson, Barrie Laidlaw and Ken McCartney of Hawick, plus a string of outstanding coaches now headed by the Director of Scottish Rugby, Jim Telfer, who has served the Melrose Club and Scotland so magnificently over the years. The Borders have also provided the Voice of Rugby – Bill McLaren – a modest, couthy, Teri who has popularised the game world-wide.

In the 90s the game is more popular than ever. At the top level it is now 'big business' and, like other amateur sports, is threatened by professionalism. The point to remember is that for every star player who may be benefiting financially from permitted 'off the field' activities there are 99 others who are just enjoying a healthy afternoon's sport. The administrators would be wise to take note of the reaction of that second magnificent Jed Forest scrum-half, Gary Armstrong. The best scrum-half in the world, he took a season off, saying: 'Sorry, too much hassle; I'm more interested in my family and my work'.

The other day, travelling by train to Inverness, I witnessed the crowds of golfing enthusiasts disembarking at Gleneagles for the Bells Scottish Open Championship. Most travelled standard class. Not so the Scottish Rugby squad. They emerged from the 1st class compartments, courtesy of their sponsors no doubt.

And good luck to them!

As we go to print in 1995, Gavin Hastings' Scottish XV, bristling with Borderers, has just returned from South Africa, having played the most attractive rugby in the World Cup – only one minute separated them from glory. The future is bright.

TWENTY-TWO

BORDER ARCHIVES AND LOCAL HISTORY

GENERAL

The Borders Region Archive and Local History Centre was established in 1984. Based in St.Mary's Mill, on the North Riverside Industrial Area, Selkirk, the Centre for archives of Border interest grew from a policy to provide essential sources for the study of local history under one roof. Housed within the Borders Regional Library Headquarters, the Centre was begun with MSC staffing. The first full-time permanent Archivist was appointed in 1988 and with the last MSC Supervisor forms the Centre's two members of staff.

The Centre has a research room at St. Mary's Mill which seats six people around one large table, and four microfiche readers, a microfilm reader and a microform reader printer. It is the job of the Archivist to collect copies of written and printed items connected with the Borders, to organise and catalogue them and to make them available to people who wish to consult them. Most of the items in the collection are for reference only although we do loan books to other libraries, both within and outwith the Borders.

The archives are stored in an air-conditioned strongroom, an expensive facility resulting in the centralisation of records in Selkirk. The documents are stored in acid-free boxes and are consulted under supervised conditions. All visitors must sign the visitors book as a security measure and for statistical purposes. We insist that pencils are used for note taking as pens can leak and ink is almost impossible to remove. If the documents are lost or damaged or altered they would be impossible to replace as most are unique. The information they contain will not be held anywhere else and so they have to be carefully looked after to ensure their long term survival. All items are produced by the staff on request as it is a closed access collection. Researchers can discuss their line of enquiry with staff, look through the lists and catalogues and fill in a form for each item they require. Then staff will extract the requested item out of the strong room.

So what kind of material do we keep? The main part of the collection is books on every aspect of life in the Borders. We try to obtain a copy of any book written about the area, or by a local author, or set in the Borders. We buy books as they are published, both from big mainstream publishers and small local presses, which may only produce a few copies of a slim pamphlet. We have books which are over two hundred years old and extremely rare and valuable, as well as books which cost less than one pound and are on sale in any local newsagents. The aim is to gather information which will illustrate the way of life in the Borders. This includes how people lived, the architecture of their houses, their work, recreations, and culture including poetry and ballads. Of course, not every subject has been conveniently written into a book. Some aspects of everyday life are very poorly documented whilst there may be several different works on others. For instance, it is much easier to find information on the history of a town such as Kelso or Selkirk than a small settlement in Berwickshire. There is more published on the architecture of Melrose Abbey than on a shepherd's bothy.

A large part of the printed book collection covers local authors. The Borders is rich in talented people writing novels and poetry and we try to obtain copies of works produced by authors living and working in the Borders, and also works based in the Borders or inspired by the life or scenery, printed and published here or illustrated by a local artist. Perhaps the most famous local author is Sir Walter Scott. In addition to collecting copies of authors' works (in different editions for an author such as James Hogg) we collect biographies and critical works which help the researcher to put their work into context. Some authors just happen to live locally and write on a totally unrelated subject, a Mills and Boon author for instance. In this case we would aim for a 'representative sample' of their work.

It can be extremely difficult to track down copies of local publications. Those published by major publishers appear in bibliographies such as *British Books in Print* and we may receive advance notification from the library supplier. Staff read all the local newspapers to see whether any pamphlets or books are being promoted. The local branch librarians throughout the Region keep their ears to the ground and notify the Archivist if they hear about a local publication, however small. Sometimes authors will let us know directly either by sending a sample copy of their books or a dust jacket. We are always pleased to accept copies of local titles for the collection, plus manuscript notes and background research which is added to the archive collection. For instance, we hold the manuscript notes and correspondence of author Jane Oliver. Some publications, inevitably, we miss and may not obtain until many years later. We purchase out of print titles from antiquarian book dealers who often give us first refusal on particularly rare and interesting books.

We subscribe to the journals of local learned societies eg, The Berwickshire Naturalists' Club and The Hawick Archaeological Society.

These proceedings are bound in volumes to help preserve them and ensure that particular sections are kept together. We hold a complete run of the *History of the Berwickshire Naturalists' Club* dating back to 1831. The Borders Region Archive and Local History Centre has a fund for binding and conservation and sends both old decaying volumes to be repaired and new books to be given a sturdy reference cover to extend their life. Although many copies of any one title will be published at a time, we aim to preserve at least one copy for use by enquirers both now and in the future.

The collection also includes ephemera such as local telephone directories, rugby programmes and posters. It is part of our job to collect and preserve items to form the local history of tomorrow. Last year's telephone book may not be of interest to anyone at the moment, but in a hundred years time a researcher will find the information it contains fascinating. We look at items which were usefully preserved from previous centuries and try and keep equivalent items now. With modern technology this leads us to keep records, cassettes and compact discs with local songs and ballads or performances by local artistes. We have videos which were commercially produced eg, 'Jim Clark: Profile of a Legend' and copies of television programmes provided by Border TV: for instance a programme on the Eyemouth Herring Queen Festival and one on Selkirk Common Riding. We purchase amateur videos covering the local festivals and sometimes receive copies as donations. We have been given ciné film but send this to the Scottish Film Archive in Glasgow who have the proper facilities for storage and showing of films. They do, however, provide us with a video copy. We are happy to accept information on computer disk and hold the Border Country Life Association collection in this format.

THE ARCHIVES

Apart from printed and published material we hold the archives proper. The main part of the archive collection comprises the records of the pre 1975 County Councils of Roxburghshire, Berwickshire, Peeblesshire and Selkirkshire, the predecessor authorities of the Borders Regional Council. Within each county the records are divided into the departments which created them eg, the County Clerk's Department contains the minutes of the meetings of the County Council; The Highway Authorities, County Treasurer's Department and Education Department include minutes of the Turnpike Trusts, abstracts of accounts and school log books. We also hold Parish records (the department which in many respects was the forerunner of the social work department) including registers of the poor. We do not have a complete set of all records produced by the four County Councils. Records are still coming to light and being handed in for the archives collection. We hold log books for most of the schools in the Borders which have now closed, as well as many of the early volumes for schools still in existence. The school log book gives a day by day account of events in the school, and often incidental information such as severe weather conditions and epidemics. Pupils' names are rarely given. We hold many of the pre 1919 school board minute books which discuss such matters as the appointment of teachers and repairs to the school building. We do have a few admission registers which list pupils with dates of birth and date of leaving school, often with an address for the parent.

The parish records give details of individual paupers, their circumstances, family situation and amount of relief granted. The relief included cash, food, clothing and coals. Some of these records make distressing reading.

The County Council records include information on public health, particularly in Roxburghshire, mainly Kelso, and throw light on the social improvements which have taken place over the last one hundred and fifty years. The highway authority records reveal the amount spent on building and maintaining roads in the Borders and the decision making process involved. These records also show that little changes, as there were problems then in enforcing locally a central government edict and ensuring that the work was done to standard, on time and within budget.

The valuation rolls in the County Council collection give the names of the owner, occupier and tenant and the rateable value of each property.

The archives also contain a great many collections of records which have been given to the Borders Region Archive and Local History Centre by local firms, organisations and individuals. We have the records of the Melrose Literary Society, one of the oldest in Scotland, the Oxton Bovial Society, the Selkirk Merchant Company and the Border Union Agricultural Society, which still organises the annual Border Union Show. The benefits of the archives holding an organisation's records are that we can store them in the air conditioned strong room and make them available to researchers under proper conditions that ensure their long term survival. There are lists of the items in each collection which researchers may consult. We hold many firms' records which include minute books and financial records eg, James McCaig and Sons, Wool Merchants, Galashiels, and Aimers McLean and Co., machinery manufacturers who equipped textile mills world-wide. There are collections of family papers, church records and details of burials, first drafts of novels and even an essay on the use of divining in identifying archaeological sites in the Borders.

The best approach to historical research is to read what has already been published on a subject before moving onto the archives. These are the original records and are arranged in the order the original creator found most useful. They can be very time consuming and intensive to read through just to find one small piece of information. Most of the archives are unique and irreplaceable. We do everything possible to ensure their long term survival for future generations, and to keep archives being created today to form the history of tomorrow.

FAMILY HISTORY

A large part of the enquiries received at the Borders Region Archive and Local History Centre involve family history. We receive visitors from all over the world, particularly during the summer months, in addition to letters and telephone calls from people interested in tracing their Border roots. The vast majority of our enquirers are Borderers, many of whom are tracing their ancestry. We hold many sources of interest to genealogists. Many of these are on microfilm and microfiche. Microfilm is very space-saving and convenient but does require a reader which is expensive and bulky. Two readers are available, one of which will print out from microfilm and microfiche so that copies can be provided subject to copyright restrictions. The main records on microfilm are the census returns 1841 – 1891, every ten years, for the counties of Selkirkshire, Roxburghshire, Peeblesshire and Berwickshire, plus Stow, Heriot, Fala, Soutra and Temple for the 1891 census. The latter were originally in the county of Midlothian but are now included within the Borders Region. The census is an excellent source as it lists families by household and includes everyone who was present on census night;: babies, servants and visitors. Apart from the names and family relationships, the age, occupation and place of birth are given from 1851 onwards, making it possible for the researcher to study the social makeup of just a few neighbouring houses. The number of rooms with windows is included in later census returns which gives a clear indication of housing conditions from the number of inhabitants listed. The enumerator went from house to house so that the people are not listed in alphabetical order.

Another useful source on microfilm is the Old Parish Records, held for the counties of Roxburghshire, Selkirkshire, Berwickshire and Peebles-shire. These records, like the census returns, were purchased from the Registrar General for Scotland, who keeps these records and the statutory registers of birth, marriages and deaths post 1855 for the whole country. The census records are closed for one hundred years before they may be consulted. The Borders Region Archive purchased the 1891 census in 1992. The Old Parish Records held at the Borders Region Archive cover births, marriages and deaths before 1855. The early ones in particular, and some date back to the 1600s, can be very difficult to decipher. The order in which the records are kept is approximately chronological but the different ministers kept them in varying degrees of order and legibility. It must also be remembered that before 1855 it was not compulsory to register births, marriages or deaths and many will not be included in these records. The fullest information is usually given for the births/baptisms, with marriages often giving only the names of the two parties involved and deaths being simply a list of payments.

We do hold an index on microfiche to births/christenings and marriages given in the Old Parish Records for each county in Scotland. This index was produced by the Church of Jesus Christ of Latter Day Saints. The indexed names are arranged in alphabetical order making it very easy to use. The Centre also has the International Genealogical Index (1992 edition) produced by the Mormons. It gives births and marriages, listed alphabetically within each county, for the whole world. The IGI is not complete as it is an ongoing project by the Church of Latter Day Saints to locate and extract information. However, it is a useful starting point for researchers. All the births and marriages included took place at least one hundred years ago; deaths are not included.

NEWSPAPERS

The Centre has a microfilming programme to obtain copies of Border newspapers. There were and are large numbers of local Border newspapers produced. Because of the fragile nature of newsprint the best conservation is to obtain microfilm copies for use. The original papers can then be stored safely and preserved from damage by handling and light. We have been purchasing microfilm copies from the British Library in London which has excellent collections of Scottish newspapers and an established microfilming unit. Some of the newspapers in the Borders Region Archive and Local History Centre are unique. We now have a complete run of the *Kelso Chronicle*, a very good Border-wide newspaper, which ran from 1832 to 1983. Additionally, there is a standing order for current copies of the *Southern Reporter, Berwickshire News, Border Telegraph, Peeblesshire News* and *Hawick News* which means that we receive a microfilm copy at the end of each year. These newspapers are useful now and will be preserved for the future.

The Borders Region Archive and Local History Centre has a few photographs and a large collection of postcards. These were obtained by donation and also by purchase from dealers. Most of the early ones were photographic images and show pictures of even the smallest village and church.

Our collection contains some maps, mainly early Ordnance Survey ones from late last century and early twentieth century. The large-scale maps in particular are interesting to historians, often showing detail such as the layout of gardens and railway lines, and marking churches, schools and sites of antiquity.

The numbers of visitors to the Borders Region Archive and Local History Centre increases every year and we receive more and more enquiries by telephone and letter. There were three times the number of visitors in 1993 compared to 1988, and more than four times the number of letters. It is usually essential to book a microfilm reader before visiting and an appointment is always appreciated. With the growth of interest in local and family history and peoples' increasing awareness of their heritage we can only expect this growth to continue. Local Government reorganisation in 1996 may bring more changes and it should be remembered that the burgh records are still with the District Councils as their successor authorities. In 1996, of course, there will be one authority as the successor to all the previous Border councils. These will be interesting times indeed; although as history teaches us, the more things change the more they remain the same!

BIBLIOGRAPHY

Anson, P.F. 1950. *Scots Fisherfolk*, Saltire Society

Armstrong, R.B. 1983. *The History of Liddesdale*, Edinburgh.

Bain, J. (Ed.) 1896. *The Calendar of Border Papers. Vol.II,III*, Edinburgh.

Baldwin, J.R. 1985. *Exploring Scotland's Heritage: Lothian and the Borders*, HMSO.

Barrow,G.W.S. 1965. *Robert the Bruce and the Community of the Realm of Scotland*, Eyre & Spottiswoode.

Barrow, G.W.S. 1973. *The Kingdom of the Scots*, E. Arnold, London.

Beattie, J. 1778. *Essays: on Poetry and Music*, Edinburgh.

Breeze, D. 1979. *Roman Scotland: a guide to the visible remains*, Newcastle Upon Tyne.

Brewer, J.S. (Ed.) 1862. *Letters and Papers of the Reign of Henry VIII, Vol.IV*, London.

Brown, R.L. (Ed.) 1972. *Robert Burns's Tour of the Borders*, London.

Camden, W. 1695. *A Second Edition of Camden's Description of Scotland*, London.

Child, F.J. 1882-98. *The English and Scottish Popular Ballads, 5 vols*, Boston, Mass.

Clapperton, C. (Ed.) 1983. *Scotland: A New Study*, David & Charles.

Clark, A.M. 1969. *Sir Walter Scott: The Formative Years*, Edinburgh and London.

Cody, E.C. (Ed.) 1888-95. *The Historie of Scotland*, translated in Scottish by Father James Dalrymple, *Vol.I*, Scottish Text Society, Edinburgh.

Cole, G.D.H. (Ed.) 1927. Daniel Defoe *A Tour Thro' the Whole Island of Great Britain*, London 1724–27, London.

Cook, E.T. & Wedderburn A. (Eds.) 1907. *The Works of John Ruskin, Vol. XXVII*

Cowan, I.B. 1960. *The Scottish Reformation*, The Saltire Society.

Craig-Brown T. 1886. *The History of Selkirkshire*, David Douglas, Edinburgh.

Crawford, B. 1987. *Scandinavian Scotland*, Leicester.

Cruden, S. 1960. *Scottish Abbeys*, Edinburgh.

Cruden, S. 1960. *The Scottish Castle*, Edinburgh.

Daiches, D. 1977. *Scotland and the Union*, Book Club Associates.

Donaldson, G. 1960. *The Scottish Reformation*, Cambridge Press.

Dunbar, J.G. 1978. *The Architecture of Scotland*, London.

Duncan, A.A.M. 1979. *The Making of a Kingdom*, Oliver & Boyd.

Exchequer Rolls of Scotland 1878–1908. Edinburgh.

Fawcett, R. 1985. *Scottish Medieval Churches*, Edinburgh.

Feachem, R. 1977. *Guide to Prehistoric Scotland*, 2nd Edition, London.

Fenton, A. 1976. *Scottish Country Life*, Edinburgh.

Fenton, A. & Walker B. 1981. *The Rural Architecture of Scotland*, Edinburgh.

Fenton, A. & Stell, G. 1984. *Loads and Roads in Scotland and Beyond*, John Donald Publishers Ltd.

Fraser, A. 1974. *King James*, Book Club Associates, London.

Fraser, G.M. 1971. *The Steel Bonnets*, Barrie & Jenkins.

Gelling, M. Nicolaisen, W.F.H, & Richards, M. 1970. *The Names of Towns and Cities in Britain*, London.

Gifford, J. McWilliam, C. & Walker, D. 1984. *The Buildings of Scotland: Edinburgh*, London.

Gilbert, J.M. 1979. *Hunting and Hunting Reserves in Medieval Scotland*, Edinburgh.

Gilbert, J.M. (Ed.) 1985. *The Flower of the Forest*, The Selkirk Common Good Fund.

Gray, M. 1978. *The Fishing Industries of Scotland 1790–1914*, OUP

Grierson, H.J.C.(Ed.) 1932-37. Letter to Bernard Barton, 4 October 1824 in *The Letters of Sir Walter Scott* 12 vols, *Letters 1823–1825*.

Grierson, H.J.C. (Ed.) 1932–37. Letter to the Earl of Dalkeith, 23 November 1806. *The Letters of Sir Walter Scott. Letters 1787–1807*.

Haldane, A.R.B. 1952. *The Drove Roads of Scotland*, Edinburgh.

Hardie, R.P. *The Roads of Medieval Lauderdale*.

Henderson, T.F. (Ed.) 1902. Scott, *Minstrelsy Vol.I*, Edinburgh and London.

Holloway, J. & Errington, L. 1978. *The Discovery of Scotland: The Appreciation of Scottish Scenery through Two Centuries of Painting*, National Gallery of Scotland, Edinburgh.

Houston, 1985. *Scottish Literacy and the Scottish Identity*, Cambridge.

Hume, J.R. 1976. *The Industrial Archaeology of Scotland: 1 The Lowlands and the Borders*, London.

Imrie, J. (Ed.) 1960 and 1969. *The Burgh Court Book of Selkirk*, The Scottish Record Society, Edinburgh.

Jeffrey, A. 1838. *The History and Antiquities of Roxburghshire*, Menzies.

Lang, J. & J. n.d. *Stories of the Border Marches*, Nelson.

Lenman, B. 1975. *From Tweed to Esk*, Blackie.

Leslie, Bishop J. 1830. *The History of Scotland*, The Bannatyne Club, Edinburgh.

Liber S. Marie De Calchou, 1846, The Bannatyne Club.

Liber S. Marie De Dryburgh, 1847, The Bannatyne Club.

Liber S. Marie De Melros, 1837, The Bannatyne Club.

Lochhead, M. 1968. *Portrait of the Scott Country*, London.

Lockhart, J.G. 1837–8. *Memoirs of the Life of Sir Walter Scott, Bart.* 7 vols., Edinburgh & London.

Lynch, M. 1991. *Scotland: A New History*, Century Ltd.

Macleod, D. 1983. *Land of Tweed*, Edinburgh.

MacKie, E.W. 1975. *Scotland: an Archaeological Guide*, London.

Maley, T. & Elliot, W. 1993. *The Selkirk Protocol Books*, The Stair Society and Walter Mason Trust.

Maley, T. & Elliot W. Forthcoming, *The Protocol Book of Sir Ninian Brydin 1536–1564*.

McAdam, A.D., Clarkson, E.N.K, & Stone, P. 1993. *Scottish Borders Geology: An Excursion Guide*, Edinburgh Geological Society/Scottish Academic Press.

McKean, C. 1983. *Edinburgh: an illustrated Architectural Guide*, Edinburgh.

McNeill, P. & Nicholson, R. (eds.) 1975. *An Historical Atlas of Scotland, c400–c1600*, St. Andrews.

Millman, R.N. 1975. *The Making of the Scottish Landscape*, London.

Morton, R.S. 1976. *Traditional Farm Architecture in Scotland*, Edinburgh.

Naismith, R. 1985. *Buildings of the Scottish Countryside*, London.

New Statistical Account of Scotland, Vol III, 1845. Blackwood.

Nicholson, N. 1955. *The Lakers: The First Tourists*, London .

Nicholson, N. 1984. *The Discovery of the Lake District*, Catalogue of an exhibition at the Victoria and Albert Museum, London.

Nicolaisen, W.F.H. 1976. *Scottish Place-Names*, London.

Ogilvie, A.G. et.al. (Eds.) 1951. *Scientific Survey of South-East Scotland*, Brit. Ass.

Old Statistical Account of Scotland, 1791–9, Vol. III. 1979, EP.

Oliver, J.R. 1887. *Upper Teviotdale and the Scotts of Buccleuch*, J. & W. Kennedy, Hawick.

Parkinson, D. (Ed.) 1987. *The Eildon Hills*, Scottish Wildlife Trust.

Parry, M.L. & Slater, T.R. (Eds.) 1980. *The Making of the Scottish Countryside*, Croom Helm.

Pennant, T. 1774. *A Tour in Scotland, and Voyage to the Hebrides: MDCCLXXII*, Chester.

Pennant, T. 1776. *A Tour in Scotland, MDCCLXXII, Part II*, London.

Percy, T. 1765. *Reliques of Ancient English Poetry*, London. (Quoted from the edition of 1812).

Pitcairn, R. 1833. *Criminal Trials in Scotland 1488–1624*, Wm. Tait, Edinburgh.

Ramm, H.G., McDowall, R.W., Mercer, E. 1970. *Shieling and Bastles*, HMSO.

RCAHMS 1909 & 1915. *Berwickshire*.

RCAHMS 1956. *Roxburghshire* (2 vols.)

RCAHMS 1957. *Selkirkshire*.

RCAHMS 1967. *Peebleshire* (2 vols.)

Register of the Great Seal. 1984. Various Editors.

Renwick, R. 1903. *Peebles in Early History*, Peebles.

Reynolds, S.H. (Ed.) 1892. *Table Talk*, London.

Ritchie, G. & A. 1972. *Edinburgh and South-East Scotland*, London.

Ritchie, G. & A. 1981. *Scotland: Archaeology and Early History*, London.

Ritchie, R.L.G. 1954. *The Normans in Scotland*, Edinburgh.

Robertson, J.L. (Ed.) 1904. *Marmion, Introduction to Canto 3. Walter Scott, Poetical Works.*

Robertson, J.L. (Ed.) 1904. *Marmion, Introduction to Canto 2. Walter Scott, Poetical Works.*

Roy, W. 1793. *The Military Antiquities of the Romans in Britain*, London.

Scottish Archaeological Review, Vol. 8: The Archaeology of Industrial Scotland, 1977, EUP.

Scott, W. *The Black Dwarf*, Garside, P.D. (Ed.) 1993. *The Edinburgh Edition of the Waverley Novels*, Edinburgh.

Scrope, W. 1975. *Days and Nights of Salmon Fishing in the Tweed (1843)*, J. Thin.

Shaw, J. 1984. *Water Power in Scotland 1550–1870*. J. Donald.

Simpson, A.T. & Stevenson, S. 1980. *Historic Selkirk*, Scottish Burgh Survey.

Simpson, A.T. & Stevenson, S. 1980. *Historic Lauder*, Scottish Burgh Society.

Simpson, A.T. & Stevenson, S. 1981. *Historic Duns*, Scottish Burgh Society.

Sissons, J.B. 1976. *The Geomorphology of the British Isles: Scotland*, Methuen.

Smout, T.C. 1969. *A History of the Scottish People, 1560–1830*, London.

Spence, A. 1992. *Discovering the Borders I*, John Donald.

Spence, A. 1994. *Discovering the Borders II*, John Donald.

Stewart, B.H.I.H.1967. *The Scottish Coinage*, Spink & Son.

The Agriculture of South-East Scotland, 1976. ESCA Bulletin No. 15.

The Oxford English Dictionary. 2nd ed., 1989, Oxford.

The Third Statistical, Account of Scotland, Bulloch, J.P.B. (Ed.) 1964. *The County of Peebles*, Collins, Glasgow.

The Third Statistical Account of Scotland, Urquhart, J.M. (Ed.) 1964. *The County of Selkirk*, Collins, Glasgow.

The Third Statistical Account of Scotland, Herdman, J.(Ed.) 1992. *The County of Berwick*, Scottish Academic Press.

The Third Statistical Account of Scotland, Herdman, J.(Ed.) 1992. *The County of Roxburgh*, Scottish Academic Press.

Thomas J. 1981. *Forgotten Railways: Scotland*, David & Charles.

Thomas, J.& Paterson, A.J.S. 1984. *A Regional History of the Railways of Great Britain, Vol.6: Scotland, The Lowlands and the Borders*, David & Charles.

Thomson, T. (Ed.) 1825. *The Historie and Life of King James the Sext*. Bannatyne Club, Edinburgh.

Tovey, D. 1890. *Gray and his Friends*, London.

Tranter, N. 1962–70. *The Fortified House in Scotland*, Edinburgh.

Tranter, N. 1978. *Portrait of the Border Country*, Hale.

Watson, W.J. 1926. *The History of the Celtic Place-Names of Scotland*, Edinburgh.

White, J.T. 1973. *The Scottish Border and Northumberland*, London.

Whittow, J. 1992. *Geology and Scenery in Britain*, Chapman & Hall.

Whyte, I. 1990. *Edinburgh and The Borders: Landscape and Heritage*, David & Charles.

Williamson, M. 1943. *The Non-Celtic Place-Names of the Scottish Border Counties*, Unpublished Thesis, University of Edinburgh.

Index